Praise f

T0090111

"Choosing Truth is what I want to do every day of my life! Harriette Cole helped me to understand that I am not alone on the journey to pursue it."

—Alicia Keys

"Choices, choices, choices—we all have them, but the ability to identify them and then choose wisely is the key. *Choosing Truth* provides tools for making wise choices."

—Tavis Smiley, host of *The Tavis Smiley Show* on NPR

"Harriette Cole has given us a practical and useful guide to the art of successful living, made rich by her own experience."

—Phylicia Rashad

"Cole does a terrific job of highlighting simple yet profound ways that people can actively choose truth in their everyday lives. . . . *Choosing Truth* is rich in content, and Cole manages to condense a lifetime of experiences into a small but effective package. She goes beyond the typical self-help formula to give readers an engaging and enlightening look at what it means to 'live an authentic life.'"

—*Black Issues Book Review*

"Cole imparts wisdom without self-righteousness. . . . In an intelligent, confessional writing style, she . . . presents her information, which covers an extensive range. . . . The strength and wisdom of her message . . . make it through."

—*Publishers Weekly*

"Thoughtful advice on how individuals can reach deeper levels of understanding and use that self-revelation to change their relationships."

—*Booklist*

ALSO BY HARRIETTE COLE

How to Be: A Guide to Contemporary Living for African Americans

Jumping the Broom: The African-American Wedding Planner

Jumping the Broom Wedding Workbook

Choosing
TRUTH

*An Inspiring Prescription
for Living an Authentic Life*

HARRIETTE COLE

SIMON & SCHUSTER
New York   London   Toronto   Sydney

SIMON & SCHUSTER
Rockefeller Center
1230 Avenue of the Americas
New York, NY 10020

Copyright © 2003 by *profundities, inc.*
All rights reserved,
including the right of reproduction
in whole or in part in any form.

First Simon & Schuster trade paperback edition 2004

SIMON & SCHUSTER and colophon are registered
trademarks of Simon & Schuster, Inc.

For information about special discounts for bulk purchases,
please contact Simon & Schuster Special Sales:
1-800-456-6798 or business@simonandschuster.com

Designed by Bonni Leon-Berman

Manufactured in the United States of America

1   3   5   7   9   10   8   6   4   2

The Library of Congress has cataloged the hardcover edition as follows:
Cole, Harriette.
Choosing truth : living an authentic life / Harriette Cole.
p.   cm.
Includes bibliographical references and index.
1. Self-actualization (Psychology)   I. Title.
BF637.S4 C652 2003
158.1—dc21   2002036679

ISBN 0-684-87311-7
0-684-87312-5 (Pbk)

Acknowledgments

SO MANY PEOPLE have contributed to the creation of this book. Many are apparent to me, and even more have touched my life in one way or another often though neither they nor I recognized the significance of our encounters in the moment. I want to thank my family for their endless and unconditional love and support, my neighbors in Baltimore who showed me what a loving neighborhood can be, my friends from around the country and around the world for being there for me when I have needed them. Specifically for this book, I want to single out a few friends who worked through many tough issues with me and helped to illuminate some profound Truths: LaJerne Cornish, Jonell Nash, Cheryl Riley, Courtney Sloane, Swami Akhandananda, Swami Anantananda, Peg Galbraith, Dianne McIntyre, Sheela Hewitt, Jocelyn Cooper, Sharon Pendana, Sheila Bridges, DeLora Jones, Rashid Silvera, and Dwight Carter. I also sincerely thank Richard Pounds for the consistent, objective, healing support he has offered.

I have discovered that there is a lesson in each encounter. Even the most challenging of situations can yield tremendous fruit when you are able to see it. This is why I thank even those people whom I once considered enemies. Now, instead of anger or fear, I send them love and blessings.

I am grateful to my literary agent, Madeleine Morel, who has stood with me from the beginning as I have brought book ideas to print, offering her honest guidance and unwavering support.

DeLora Jones deserves great props for coming to my rescue again and again, for finding time in the midst of her tremendously busy schedule to read and edit this book as she has my others.

I thank the conscientious team over at Simon & Schuster. My editor, Sydny Miner, spotted this book idea out of a list and believed from the start that this was the next project I should write. I am so grateful that she saw fit to encourage me this way. Laura Holmes, Sydny's assistant, has kept things on track. Loretta Denner, the angel in Copy Editing, was here once again to provide her resources of information and support. Beverly H. Miller, the copy editor, read this manuscript with such care. Jackie Seow, the art director, worked hard to assemble the book so that readers would be able to easily engage it.

ACKNOWLEDGMENTS

I thank Uma Hayes for reading my manuscript so carefully and for offering her keen insight.

I want to thank all of the people who shared their lives so openly and honestly with me, through focus groups, one-on-one interviews, e-mails, and telephone conversations. I offer a special thank-you to the 2001 senior options class of Scarsdale High School.

I am forever grateful to my staff, who work countless hours with me, ensuring that I can be my best and, in turn, offer wisdom to others: Jamiyl Young, for his ironic and astute observations, Nadia Symister, for her honest and precise input, and Marsha Ganthier, for her gentle wisdom.

Kervin Simms, Esquire, my friend and attorney, has been with me since the early days, when Truth sometimes seemed like a faraway notion. I appreciate his standing by me through it all.

I want to thank my husband, George Chinsee, for capturing me at my best on the cover of this book and for supporting me through every up and down along the way. Without his commitment and love, I would not be where I am today. It is my great blessing to travel through life with him.

Finally, I offer gratitude to myself. It took a tremendous amount of courage to write this book. I am grateful that I put forth that effort, and I trust that it will inspire you to do the same.

*I DEDICATE THIS BOOK TO THOSE
WHO HAVE TOUCHED MY LIFE THE MOST:*

My maternal grandmother, Carrie Elizabeth Alsup
Freeland, showed me that you can live in love
every moment of your life.

Without my parents, Doris Freeland Cole and the
late Harry Augustus Cole, I would not be here as
the woman I am today. For their eternal love,
strength, and guidance, I am forever grateful.

To my sisters, Susan Cole Hill and Stephanie Cole Hill,
I offer my gratitude for loving me as me,
no matter what, and always.

From my husband, George Chinsee, I have been
given a precious gift- -the beauty and consistency
of unconditional love that extends beyond the
ties of blood in partnership.

The most auspicious moment of your life is when you make the commitment to know the Truth, a commitment so firm there is no turning back.

—GURUMAYI CHIDVILASANANDA,
MY LORD LOVES A PURE HEART

Contents

Introduction

CHOOSING TRUTH is a book devoted to supporting the search for the deepest understanding of Truth that we can find: The answer to the age-old question, *Who am I?* It is a subject that I have held close to my heart for my entire life, even when I wasn't sure what my search really was. Because this is so, this book has come to be filled with more of my own stories than I ever imagined I would dare reveal. I also share numerous examples of other people's stories about their personal transformation as they have faced challenges, triumphs, and defeats. I do so because if I and others have the courage and willingness to shed light on our lives as they are, then, perhaps you will be willing to do the same. The only way to live a full and dynamic life is to be willing to examine it as it is right now, without adornment. God knows us and sees us through and through—as we are. In moments of insight, we also see ourselves and each other for who we really are. This is true no matter how artfully we may have sculpted ourselves into appropriate packages.

The genesis of this book came long before September 11, 2001, but the events of that day made me reassess whether I was still headed in the right direction. This disaster was an unprecedented, unthinkable attack. Safety had to be redefined. Freedom needed to find a new face, an honest face. The "Whys?" begged to be answered so that the errors of the past would not be repeated. Perhaps for the first time in contemporary culture, more Americans and others around the world began to think a little harder and a lot more seriously about their own lives, about their mortality: What really matters? Am I living the life that my heart tells me to live? What do I need to do to improve my way of being? How do I protect myself when the world around me doesn't feel safe?

My intention in writing this book is to support all of us in our quest for the answers to life's fundamental questions. This project came to be as I was sitting in meditation at the ashram that is my spiritual home in upstate New York. I had just finished my book *How to Be,* and I wanted to know what I was supposed to work on next. The question I had in my mind as I slipped into meditation was: *What is my purpose now? What am I to do?* In the stillness of a deep meditation, out of a serene space of silence came a voice: *Choose the Truth.* What did it mean? As

I racked my brain, there came an Aha! moment. "Is this supposed to be a book?" And so I began to contemplate what a book about Truth would be. I polled a few people to learn their ideas on the subject. Members of my spiritual community were accustomed to grappling with this topic. Others gave their take as if they were contemplating it for the first time. Some had different definitions, depending on the circumstances at hand. "The Truth is relative to the situation, isn't it?" one woman asked.

Armed immediately with a breadth of inspiration and opinion, I sat still in order to gather my thoughts. To consider choice and Truth together was powerful. How would I do that and really serve people's needs? My initial idea was to look at the different relationships that we find ourselves in—marriage, parent-child, friends, lovers, coworkers, employees, neighbors, and enemies—and with this plan in mind, I began interviewing people of all ages and backgrounds all over the country. I wanted to know whether people chose to be honest with their coworkers and parents, as well as how often they intentionally lied to their lovers and creditors. What was the balance of Truth as people revealed details of their various relationships?

What I found changed the whole construct of this book. Although people rationalized their degrees of honesty a little more when it came to work situations, the reality is that those who lie were equally likely to do so with lovers, spouses, and children as with employers or employees. Whether I was talking to teenagers or senior citizens, the range of stories was pretty consistent. Some people barely addressed the surface of their feelings; instead, they lived day to day in varying degrees of happiness or discomfort. Others dove deep into the heart of their emotions and experiences. Some people courageously stood up for their beliefs, while others either immediately cowered in the corner or ran to the front of the line to hand over their ideas in order to support someone else's. What was the thread that linked them all together? As I listened and digested story after story, all the while probing my own heart for clues, I discovered that Choosing Truth has less to do with how we behave in relation to others than it does with how we relate to our own Selves. If we dare to stand naked in front of a mirror and examine what we see—on the surface and layer upon layer below—then and only then are we able to choose Truth in our lives.

After more than a year of pursuing one path for this book, my course was redirected. The course I had been on all along in my personal life became the course I was to follow to help others. To protect those who so generously opened up their lives to this pursuit of Truth, I have altered names, occupations, and residences as needed. Through the many examples and principles woven throughout these chapters, my intention is for each of you to seek out your own understanding of what Truth is for you. This book requires your active participation. You will be invited to probe your own heart and mind to discover the voice within that is waiting to guide your steps. You will be encouraged to journal about your discoveries so that you can capture your own wisdom on paper and refer to it again and again. The purpose of this book is to inspire you to continue forward on your path to you.

The process of CHOOSING TRUTH is sometimes difficult. It requires diligence and patience. So often many of us seem to live in a fog, even when we are actively walking on a spiritual path. I know in my own life I have frequently discovered what's actual about a situation I'm facing long after it first presents itself. Due to some emotion, such as anger, anticipation, fear, or even guilt, I have initially envisioned the scenario in false colors, unknowingly misrepresenting it to myself and, in turn, to others. Although this often happens unintentionally, this distortion of reality has proven to be a deterrent in my own progress. Only after deep contemplation, prayer, and focus do answers usually emerge. Knowledge, like a delicious cup of tea, seems to reveal itself only after steeping.

I go back to that day when the Twin Towers fell. My office borders Greenwich Village and Chelsea in New York City. Standing on the corner of Fifteenth Street and Fifth Avenue, I could see the Towers blazing with fire and puffing out huge clouds of smoke. Hours later, I could see smoke where there had been majestic buildings. How could the Towers be gone? I kept wishing that it hadn't happened. I wanted to be awakened from this bad dream and reclaim life as it had been hours before.

Life is what it is. It is our duty to see that. But just as was true in New York, as rescue workers struggled endlessly to clear away the rubble, we have to exert consistent and focused energy to see clearly. It takes work to cart away the debris clouding our vision and tremendous effort to sort through the many distractions that capture our attention. Only when we put forth this effort can grace do its part and show us what is real.

Although I do not claim to have all the answers, I do have recommendations, gleaned from many years of study, for how we can seek out and choose to live in the space of our own Truth. What is essential is that we recognize and accept that before us in every moment is a matter of choice. We can and must choose our destiny. It is our own steps, our own thoughts, words, and deeds that will either guide us to the revelation of who we really are and what our role in life is, or propel us deeper into a life of smoke and mirrors.

I look at life as a precious gemstone that bears many facets. Depending on how we tend to the needs and subtleties of our gemstone, its facets will either shine brilliantly or lack clarity. This book represents an examination of many of the facets of our lives. I encourage you to use it as a tool to assist you so that your gemstone, your precious life, can become crystal clear and shine as magnificently as is possible.

I offer it to you with all my love,

harriette

I

KEEP A JOURNAL

IT'S IMPORTANT FOR YOU to understand something right away: the process of choosing Truth in your life can be simple, but that certainly does not mean that it will be easy—at least not all the time. Chances are you already know this, at least intellectually. But since we are just starting out, I want to reinforce a point that will resurface again and again throughout this book. *Choosing Truth requires a tremendous and consistent amount of your own personal effort and willingness.* You must be willing to look at all aspects of your life anew. You must have the courage to see what is before you, even if its impact could change the course of your life entirely. In order to stand firmly planted in the space of your own Truth, you must also be willing to let go of all that stands in your way. The good news is that you're not expected to change your whole life right this minute. Instead, the intention for you to hold is that you will make the commitment to approach your life with fresh eyes, be willing to look at what is before you as if it's the first time you ever saw it, listen to and follow your inner wisdom, and live your life with the complete consent of your entire being.

One of the greatest joys you may ever experience is learning how to choose your own Truth. Being able to live in Truth is liberating because there are no preconceived notions, patterns, or biases clouding your vision. Finding yourself living in the space of your own Truth can feel like gliding through the clear blue sky just as a kite does in a brisk summer wind.

To support you on this great adventure, you can adopt the daily practice of journaling. This is an effective and gentle means of identifying your own Truth. Like the Dear Diary books of your youth, your journal can become your best friend and companion. On a daily basis (or as frequently as possible), take a few minutes to write down your experiences and give yourself the gift of personal honesty. You can write about whatever has come up for you that day, and this may lead to threads that link together patterns of thought and behavior in your life. As you write, you will find layer upon layer of your former beliefs and understandings about yourself first become apparent and then fall away. Over time, you may gain the ability to see your true Self emerge, free of the clutter of any false concepts that you may have previously been clutching.

When you are tackling uncomfortable topics, journaling can support you. For instance, if someone has approached you with criticism during the day, take some quiet time and examine that situation when you write. What did the person actually say to you? Is there any Truth in what was said? Can you see what your role was in the situation? How might you rectify it in the future, either by addressing the person or by changing your behavior? What is the lesson that you need to learn? This process works even if you were the one doing the accusing. Even if you feel that you were appropriate in calling someone out for a mistake, ask yourself what your role was in creating the situation. What might you have done to help alleviate the tension? Did you handle the critical moment in a supportive, uplifting way? What can you learn to take with you into the future? Exploring your life on paper is a key way to unlocking the treasures of wisdom and clarity that reside within your own being.

KNOWING YOUR OWN TRUTH

HOW CAN YOU TELL that you are Choosing Truth? Although there are endless sources of support that you can seek and that may be of help, they cannot single-handedly provide the ultimate answers for your life. The answers to your life's puzzle lie within you.

Back in the eighties, when I was going through a rough period, I was fortunate to have a small network of friends who offered me a lot of support. One friend was especially patient and compassionate. Jesse would listen to me drone on and on about my problems. Month after month, without judgment, he was there for me, and yet nothing changed in my situation. One day, he sat me down and very lovingly said, "Harriette, I think we should stop talking about this." I looked at him, crestfallen, and he continued, "I love you, and I want to be here for you, but I think you have to find the answers to these questions on your own." At first I was angry with him. How could he reject me at the very moment when I needed him the most? Was he really my friend, or had I just believed something that wasn't actually true?

After a few days passed, I calmed down. Instead of continuing to pick up the phone and connect to the other sources of support that were part of my spiritual network—which, by the way, was what I was aching to do—I sat still. It was then that I understood that Jesse was right. From that point on, I became more focused on my journals, writing endlessly with the intention of discovering a clear way out of my challenges. I was no longer a burden on my friends, and I created the space so that I could begin to see what the mirror of my life was showing me. I could read it through my own words.

I marveled that although I was unhappy, my life seemed fabulous on the outside. At that time, I was a successful magazine editor with what looked like a picture-perfect life, yet on the inside, things were not so cozy. I wrote about all of it in my journal: my fears, my dreams, my apprehensions, and my triumphs. Nearly every word I wrote was in lowercase letters. (I suppose I fancied myself a modern-day e.e. cummings.) For the most part, I reserved one word for capitalizing: Self. Actually, I wrote this word two ways. I had it in my mind that the small self was the one that I was trapped in at that time. It was telling me that I could not be as great as I envisioned and had me stuck in this pit of loneliness. Even as I felt stuck, I held out for the capital Self. My heart was crying out to assure me that deep within my own being resided a powerful, confident Self who had the capacity to override the feelings of smallness and compromise that were crippling me. I believed that this Self would indeed rise up and take charge. The only question was, "When?" It took a few years before my inner Truth came bursting forth. Yet the flames of that inner awakening were ignited during that time through my own introspection.

I was lucky; my life's transformation had begun. But that's not always the case. Often we receive advice from people that specifically addresses our issues. Sometimes the advice is perfectly on the money, and we are able to accept it. Other times, even the most brilliant advice falls on deaf ears. No matter how sweet the presentation or how perfect the presenter, it doesn't necessarily make it any easier to swallow. Has this ever happened to you? Think about it: Do you remember a time when you asked a friend for advice? Then after you got it, you didn't believe the friend or recognize the Truth through the person's reflection of it to you. How many times has a loved one or even a stranger revealed something to you about your personality or your life, especially when it was regarding an aspect that needed attention or change, and you brushed the person off—possibly with an attitude to boot?

If this has happened to you more than once, don't beat yourself up. It is hard to accept criticism, no matter how well intentioned the person doing the offering happens to be. The knee-jerk response that many of us have is to consider the adviser's words or actions as an attack and to retaliate instinctually, seeking out ways to demean the "attacker." That behavior needs to end. In its place, we have to choose to change the way we respond to what's before us. This can start with how we face that which we see about ourselves. Just as I did, you can turn away from the listeners and naysayers toward yourself.

KEEPING A JOURNAL

EXPLORING YOUR LIFE on paper is a key way to unlocking the treasures of wisdom and clarity that reside within your own being. Following is a prescription for recording and protecting your experiences:

- *Select a time of day when you want to write.* It could be in the morning after your daily meditation or at night before bed. Some people choose to write at lunchtime when they have a quiet pause in the day.

- *Use a beautifully bound book that is both visually appealing and secure,* so that pages will not fall out. Select a book that is small enough for you to carry with you so you can travel with it. Alternatively, you can assign one journal for travel and another for home.

- *Date and describe your point of entry.* I write the time, date, and location of my entry, as well as my overall state of mind before starting. This paints a picture for me of the environment that is supporting my writing and helps me to remember my state when I review my thoughts later.

- *Express yourself in whatever creative ways show themselves.* You may want to draw or sketch images that capture ideas that come to mind. Sometimes I can't find words that convey the essence of what's happening for me. Instead of leaving a blank page, I let my pen follow its own course. Remarkable miniature works of art have emerged in those moments.

- *Dare to tell the full story.* Whatever is going on deserves to be shared in its entirety when you are sharing it with your Self.

- *Be free.* This is your opportunity to pour forth your own inspiration from your soul. Let the words, thoughts, and feelings flow from your core uncensored.

- *Protect your journal.* In order to trust that this can be the repository for your deepest contemplations, you have to take care of your journal. Keep it in a place where no one else will read it. Have a particular location where you store filled journals for later perusal. (I have a provision written in my will for what should be done with my journals and writings.)

• *Carve out time to review your journal entries so that you can track your life's evolution.* I recommend reviewing your journals frequently—once a week at first, so you notice your progress—and quarterly to get an overview.

The most important thing you can do for your personal growth is to be honest with yourself. So often we fear what our honest words will mean to others. What about what those very same words mean to us? I remember my therapist telling me that I had developed the fine art of diplomacy so effectively that I was being too diplomatic with *myself.* He urged me to take a giant leap of faith and step out of my shell so that I could better see what lay before me. At first, this was tough. For starters, I didn't understand what he meant. But, even after I understood, I found it impossible to take the action needed. For me, diplomacy had unknowingly become a shield that didn't allow me to see accurately either my vulnerabilities or strengths. Once I became willing to let my guard down, at least in my journal and in my therapy sessions, I began to see the issues that I was actually facing. After that, with a huge dose of prayer and grace, I was able to push past some old stuff that had kept me stuck for years.

What is your Achilles heel? What is standing in the way of your seeing and living your Truth? Your active practice of self-inquiry will help to answer these questions. This is a primary function of your journal. You will engage in an ongoing dialogue with your highest Self, probing into the deepest regions of your own thinking and feeling. Journaling is a powerful practice for both novices and longtime practitioners. May it bring you the clarity and focus that you deserve.

Your Journal Entry

Dearest Friend,

I am writing to you today to express my love and gratitude to you. I am so happy that you have decided to embark upon this journey of self-exploration with me. My intention is to be vigilant and gentle in my honesty. My goal is to discover the Truth about who I am and how I can live an honest and fulfilling life in the here and now.

I love you,
Me

NOW IS THE TIME to begin your inner exploration. Use your journal as an essential tool for processing the facets of inner learning that will take place:

- *Record your intention for your journal.* What do you intend to accomplish by engaging in the active pursuit of writing about your thoughts, words, and deeds?

- *Use your journal space now to focus on your reasons for embarking on this journey.* Be as clear and specific as you can to sharpen your own understanding of the value of Choosing Truth at this time in your life.

- *Talk to yourself lovingly.* That's why I call myself Dearest Friend. I know that what I want most in life is to be loved and that love starts with what I offer to myself. As I write, I am writing to that gentle, loving spirit who is my very Self.

- *Find your voice.* Discover your Self by writing to that precious one within.

2

CULTIVATE A SPIRITUAL LIFE

WHEN I WAS GROWING UP, my sisters and I were very active in our church. We went to Sunday school every week and learned about Jesus and how to apply his teachings to our lives. We went first to the church where my mother grew up—Sharp Street United Methodist Church in downtown Baltimore, a majestic old church in the heart of the Black community. We later moved to St. Mark's United Methodist Church that was nearer to our home. Every week and often during the week throughout our formative years, we were in church. We sang in the choir, attended Bible study classes, and participated in youth activities. It was our safe haven. Because of my parents' strong beliefs as well as those of my maternal grandmother, we were well versed in the principles of Christianity.

This was very important for me. Core values about how to treat people that my parents had been instilling at home were reinforced each time we walked through our church doors. We learned how to behave with discipline, how to sit still and pay attention (or at least try to!), how to contemplate questions of morality, mortality, and love from our ever-changing growing-up perspectives. Even when significant challenges came, we felt safer dealing with them thanks to the protection of our sanctuary. Reality seemed easier to handle.

SPIRITUAL DISILLUSION

THE DOWNSIDE about being in church so often—as I saw it through my child's eyes, anyway—was that we also discovered discrepancies between philosophy and reality. We witnessed, for example, that not everybody does what the Bible or the minister says—at least not all the time. Some people say one thing and do quite another. Other folks followed the Holy Word on Sundays but not during the rest of the week. Some ministers preach a good sermon while leading glaringly different lives. Some pastors are conscientious, paying attention to the congregation, while others are self-absorbed and unaware of the needs of their flock.

As I grew older, I became disillusioned by the seemingly two-faced nature of religious institutions. Then, during a period when my classmates and I were beginning to enter adolescence and question our faith, a friend in high school hanged herself on her birthday. My perception was that she had lost religion—even though her family had strong religious convictions.

Life continued with its ups and downs. In the midst of great joys, such as good grades, new friendships, vacations, new neighbors, and lots of hobbies came a series of blemishes. Official news and gossip told of one minister after another in our city who had defamed the name of God. Teenagers, including our friends, got pregnant, even though we were taught that having sex out of wedlock was a sin. Parents we knew divorced each other in spite of the vows they took when they married. Boys in church played nasty tricks on girls (myself included) even while under the church roof. Slowly but surely, the notion of religion as the seat of purity stopped making much sense to me.

SPIRITUAL SEPARATION

LIKE MANY OTHER young adults, when I went away to college, to Howard University, my spiritual anchor didn't go with me. Among other things, it wasn't fashionable to be spiritual—or, should I say, religious. Instead, I became a student learning about life. Having been largely sheltered in my suburban Baltimore home and community, I hadn't had much experience with boys. At college, I excelled in school and failed miserably at the dating game and much of social dynamics. All the while I ignored the need to pray. Those years of discipline and learning in the shelter of my church and family arms had largely evaporated.

Naturally, my inner world took a nosedive. It didn't occur to me during the ensuing period that my lack of faith could have provoked such sadness and conflict. Away from my parents and my sisters—the eldest who protected me, the youngest who nurtured me—in a world filled with strangers, I relied on my instinct as well as my intense desire to be liked, loved, and accepted by my peers. I felt as if I was on a roller-coaster, not knowing which way my emotions were going to take me on any given day. I consulted my astrological chart looking for answers as to why I was the way I was. Being a Piscean, it made sense that I would have creative mood swings, first euphorically happy and in the next minute depressingly sad. But learning this about my nature didn't seem to help it go away or make my dramatic emotions cool down.

I entered tentatively into one relationship after another (albeit not that many) without being on sure footing first myself. I swung from good guy to bad guy. The worst bad guy presented himself so skillfully that I trusted him, even as my heart thumped louder and louder that he was not to be trusted. I reached an all-time low when I found myself walking across a playground in Washington, D.C., in the wee hours one morning to confront him about his flagrant indiscretions. I knocked on his door at 3 A.M. only to have his cousin stall me as "my man" climbed out of the window and ran away too ashamed to admit his part in the web of deception that was our relationship. It took physical abuse in the presence of a hallway full of strong men who bore witness without lifting a finger to help before I began to wise up. I had given a man my heart and soul and he abused my gift terribly. Most important, though, is that I should have never given it away.

SELF-ACCEPTANCE

IT WAS MANY YEARS LATER after I was living in New York—after a failed marriage to a good man, though not my life partner, and several years of clandestine alcohol and drug abuse—that I began to come to my senses. Although my parents had no clue as to what was wrong with me, when I was at the worst low of my depression, they knew I needed help. My mother and sister Stephanie used to call me regularly to beg me to pray. I remember my mother saying, "Just pray, Harriette. God will hear your prayers. If you pray, you will get better." I remember telling her one time, "Don't waste your breath. I know prayer won't help me. I don't believe in it." I had shut out all hope. My soul was perishing, and I didn't know how to save it. My mother assured me that although I didn't believe in prayer, she would continue to pray for me.

One morning I woke up groggy after another fitful night's sleep and in the softness of the early morning light realized that I had a choice: I could choose to wallow in a state of depression that would lead to certain death or I could choose to let my spirit live. I remembered my mother's and sister's prayers, and although I didn't understand what they meant, I was grateful for them.

I picked myself up out of my bed, took a long shower, and decided that I could make the decision right then and there to cultivate a life worth living. A whirlwind of thoughts swept through my head. I remembered my dear friend

Jackie who took her life on her sixteenth birthday. Life had lost meaning for her. I thought of Little Grandma, my mother's mother, who professed with her every breath that God would take care of us if we let Him. I remembered bits and pieces of the series of actions that had led me to that moment and was certain that between the good and the bad, there was choice.

I pledged allegiance to my own heart and soul on that morning. I stood in my tiny Harlem bathroom and stared in the mirror as if I were looking at myself for the very first time. I saw the sadness seeping out of my eyes and the devastation in my heart that was painting its way across the terrain of my body. I knew that I had reached an all-time low. I was alone. I was emaciated. I was listless. As this list of negatives began to cloud up my mirror, I stopped myself. "What else is there?" I wanted to know. "Remember the rest, Harriette. Remember."

And so I did. Still transfixed by the stranger in the mirror, I began to tend to her—to me. I brushed my teeth and washed my face. I gently brushed my hair. I slowly began to massage oil into my body. And I did something my mother has always encouraged my sisters and me to do: I began to count my blessings. I had a beautiful apartment. At age twenty-eight, I had a great career that had suffered only marginally during my period of pain. Indeed, I had immersed myself in my work as a way to protect myself and stay on a course to success. I had a solid reputation for being a hard worker, an intelligent thinker, a shining star. My family loved me unconditionally. I had great friends who had stuck by me through thick and thin. I remembered a Nigerian friend from Howard who had listened to me read some of my poetry one evening. In the middle of one piece, Niyi interrupted me: "Why is it that African Americans are always so sad? Don't you realize how great your life is?" I contemplated his question seriously that day, perhaps for the first time. I had already achieved many outstanding accomplishments, and I wasn't thirty yet. Was I to be a shining star or a shooting star? Was I to turn my life around and make a difference—or fizzle out like so much hot champagne?

I chose to pursue what M. Scott Peck calls "the road less traveled." I chose to discover me. Exploring my creativity seemed to be the method to follow. I pursued my writing with great vigor, as I've known since I was twelve years old that this is my greatest gift. I also kept my eyes open for other creative opportunities that would allow me to flourish. In so doing, I met the man who is now my husband, George Chinsee. We met on the phone, working on *Songs of My People,* a photo-documentary book of life in Black America. Having the protection of space and relative anonymity between us—just voices on the phone—we worked together forging a union of concepts. As I was healing at home, I also began to have an ongoing dialogue with George about life and possibility, art and joy. It was refreshing and frightening at once. The happier I got, the more fearful I became. I couldn't imagine truly allowing myself to feel what I was feeling. It was too soon. I was in the middle of a divorce and recovering from a period when I had neglected myself completely. Though I believed I was not fit to be a partner, George saw differently. We had been officially dating for about a month when he sat me down and matter-of-factly told me: "I want to spend the rest of my life with you." I laughed. "Sure," I thought. "That's a good line!" He continued: "I have prepared for you. I am ready for you." Seeing that he was serious, I stopped laughing and looked at him. I said with all the conviction in my heart, "But I'm not ready for you." And I wasn't. No matter how I looked on the outside, my life was a shambles, and I had some serious work to do in order to even consider being in a relationship again. His response: "I'll wait for you. Take all the time you need."

That's exactly what I did. Three years later, we got married. However, five months after we began dating, Thanksgiving 1990, we both found ourselves at a meditation retreat. George had heard about meditating from some friends of his and had learned that there was a special meditation retreat to be held on Thanksgiving weekend in upstate New York. He wanted us to go. I unequivocally said no. It was Thanksgiving, and I always went home for the holidays. But, George was so adamant about this retreat that I began to pay closer attention. Although he and I had been together for only a short time at that point, I believed that we *were* going to spend the rest of our lives together. Ultimately, I decided to go to the retreat to see how his life was going to change after being there. Then I would understand how to be with him.

MY SPIRITUAL AWAKENING

DURING MY FIRST guided meditation, I had a vision of my life, rather like what people describe the flash of one's life to be just before death. The scenes were all intensely painful ones during which I had done something hurtful, or something devastating had been done to me. As I watched this "movie," I did not feel anything. I had become a peaceful observer. It was then that I realized what the spiritual teacher who was leading this retreat, Gurumayi Chidvilasananda, had been telling us. I learned that I was not defined by my experiences. No matter how uncomfortable or intense they have been, they are not who I am. My true nature is pure and divine, and God's light lives within my own being as me.

That the essence of who I am is the Self—with a capital S! My beliefs that I had held onto for so long were acknowledged. I was the Self. I had the potential to soar to the highest heights as I served others with my every step. That day I was transformed.

I had found my spiritual home. Many of the lessons I received that day and that I have been given since reflect the wisdom that my parents and grandparents, and some of my former ministers and teachers, have offered. Yet on that day, coming from Gurumayi, the lessons took on greater meaning. Finally, I had found something that resonated in my heart. Although many of the elements of the path of Siddha Yoga Meditation, which I began to follow, were new to me because they were based on Indian tradition, the fact that this practice was from a different culture did not stand in my way. As an adult, I had found a connection to God that empowered me to be my best. This was what I had always been searching for. That's all I needed to know.

FIND YOUR OWN SPIRITUAL PATH

YOUR LIFE STORY, whether it's filled with joy or sadness, questions or solutions, can become more valuable if you support it through spiritual discipline and practice. Know that there is a power greater than you that lives within you as your own true Self. Recognize that you can benefit from a spiritual practice that will support you in your efforts to live an honorable and fulfilling life. The best way to make the connection to your spiritual center is to find a spiritual home.

I've talked to many people across the country who have experienced an overall strengthening and clarity in their lives as a result of making this connection. Quite often, the moment of commitment comes after a person becomes an adult and is able to make a conscious choice. Perhaps that's why the rite of adult (in contrast to infant) baptism occurs when it does. In some churches, one participates in the sacred rite only when ready. Study is required, as is a verbal and spiritual affirmation of commitment to the practices and principles of Christian life. Baptism symbolizes a person's rebirth in Christ after one believes.

In other traditions, different rites mark initiation or rebirth. In his fascinating book *Of Water and the Spirit*, the scholar Malidoma Some talks of the spiritual life that sustains the members of his people, the Dagara of Burkina Faso, in West Africa. All male members of the community participate in a spiritual initiation that gives them the insight and power to carry on their lives with strength and clarity. In the United States, some families have found African religious philosophy to support their lives including various forms of Khamitic religion, the spiritual practices of ancient Egypt. I met two of the leaders of these groups and talked to them about their philosophy. Although I had met African people from many different countries, I found myself ignorant, and therefore afraid, of their religious ideas. Vowing to break through the stereotypes that were clouding my vision, I sought out the teachers so that I could learn about their beliefs.

What I had learned from Malidoma Some's work, the Khamitic teachers, Hebrew and Hindu scholars, and Christian ministers, as well as many other spiritual teachers, is that when you probe a little deeper, you will find that people all over the world since the beginning of time have been searching for a way to understand the true meaning of their lives. Many have considered the various spiritual and religious traditions that have made their way to their homelands and have often incorporated aspects of them into their traditions. When I visited Bahia, Brazil, for example, I saw the melding of two spiritual traditions at a convent where an order of nuns had blended their Catholic practices with the Candomble rituals of their African ancestors. Although the Catholic church considered these women controversial, the nuns had committed to honoring both sides of their heritage. In this way, they believed that they were paying tribute to the fullness of their spiritual heritage.

You may find that your spiritual life is not defined by a particular religious philosophy. That's fine. I am definitely not arguing that you should become a member of one religion or another. I encourage you to cultivate a spiritual life that includes worship and respect of God as you understand that divine power.

George and I have dear friends who are both from the South. They grew up in the Baptist church as members of large families and still practice many of the rituals of their Baptist upbringing. Over the years, they have also explored other spiritual options. Having had the chance to travel all over the world, they have seen that there are many ways to worship, from Native American rituals to African tribal dances, from Muslim prayer to Yogic asanas or postures. They have adopted a personal, inclusive approach to faith by combining elements of each of the paths that they have crossed into a regular practice that they share. They go to church with some frequency, they practice meditation daily, and they read from the sacred texts of the various peoples they have met along the way. Married for more than twenty years, these two affirm that it is their commitment to loving God as the source of life itself that keeps them focused. The packaging for how to love God is not as important to them as the practice itself.

A CALL TO SPIRITUAL ACTION

WHEN YOU STOP and look around you, can you see that there is a power greater than your individual Self that has made this world manifest? Every spiritual tradition has developed an explanation for the existence and sustenance of the world. Science tackles the topic through its vehicles. Mathematics traverses through its theorems. And in daily life, people experiences flashes of acknowledgment. That Aha! moment occurs when the only thing that can really explain what's happening must be attributed to a power that lives in and beyond us.

Philosophers and spiritual advisers alike commonly maintain that Truth is the ultimate answer to life's questions. And Truth, as I understand it, in its purest form is a reflection of the divine in the world and in us. So, what are some tools that we can use to be able to recognize our own Truth? Following are some suggestions for spiritual actions you can take. Keep in mind that they are not meant to steer you into any specific religious direction. Rather, they are meant to provide a platform for supporting your spiritual exploration. Beyond the entry point into your spiritual path is the commitment to walk on that path.

Invoke Your Inner Spirit

When you are looking for a source of strength, call on God through prayer and meditation to strengthen you from within. When you are feeling uncertain, turn inside. Why is this a good or practical idea? If you think about your body, you have to marvel at its intelligence. It wakes you up and puts you to sleep, and can do so without bells, whistles, stimulants, or depressants, even if you have become accustomed to being supported by such aids. It jumps out of harm's way when it comes too close to fire. It reaches out to protect a child in danger, even if you "think" you don't like children. It repairs itself from within whenever it is injured until it absolutely cannot handle it anymore. The body is the ultimate forgiver. It is willing to carry all of your necessary and superfluous belongings from point A to point B. It responds openly to tenderness and can help you maintain control when you are angry. Best of all, it is yours.

The reason that your body can do all of these amazing things is that God designed the human body as the ultimate machine. Your eternal spirit fueled your creation and entry on this planet, and it is your spirit that is here to show you the way. Your challenge is to nurture your own spirit. To do this, you have to pay attention to your own being. Listen to your body and your spiritual intuition that guides you. Be aware of its messages, such as physical pain or discomfort, which God gave you as warning signs of health problems. And when you are in need, in addition to turning to others, turn to God for direction and to yourself to receive the answer.

Meditate

The way that I have learned to get in touch with myself is by meditating. I read once that praying is talking to God and meditating is listening to God talk to us. Going back to the premise on which I base my understanding—that God dwells within me as my very own Self—I see meditation as the way that I can access that divinity within my own being. It's possible to tap into your own connection to God without going somewhere else to do it. You don't have to wait until you go to church, to temple, to the ashram, to the mosque, to any place other than your own being in order to find that source of love with which you are blessed at birth.

Meditation is not a practice that follows a specific course leading to the same end for everyone. Rather, each person's experience of turning inside is unique. What happens for me when I close my eyes and focus my attention inside is guaranteed to be exclusive for me in that moment, whereas my husband or the person sitting next to me, my best friend, or a stranger may have a completely different experience. Meditation is different from listening to a scriptural reading or a lesson from a spiritual teacher. Its mystery is a gift—the gift of the revelation of the Truth given to us by God within our own heart.

Meditation occurs in almost every religion. Christian mystics regularly practiced meditation, as do nuns and priests today. In churches across the country, more and more Christians are adopting the practice, to the extent that special meditation groups exist in many churches nationwide. In Eastern spiritual philosophies, meditation has been a foundation point for spiritual practitioners for generations.

The fruit of meditation comes from your own regular practice. It emerges from your soul to lead the way to fulfillment of your life's goal. This simple practice is possibly the most beneficial activity that you can adopt.

This has been my experience again and again. As I practice meditation compled with contemplation and prayer, I find that I have the capacity to be more focused and relaxed no matter what I am facing in my day. At different junctures, I am able to let go of beliefs that I have had about myself or my life that previously had been impossible to release. When I have struggled with issues in my mind, I have lost the battle time and again. When I have surrendered the subject to my heart, there has been an about-face, and my heart wins.

YOUR MEDITATION PRACTICE

IN ORDER TO PRACTICE meditation, you don't have to adopt any particular religion. Here are the basic steps to turning inside that I have adopted:

- *Dedicate a space in your home where you can sit for meditation.* Make sure it is clean and quiet.

- *Select a time of day that you would like to devote to spiritual practice.* You may want to meditate in the morning before you start your day or at night before you go to sleep.

- *Create a comfortable space for sitting on the floor or on a chair.* If you sit on the floor, sit in a cross-legged posture, and use a pillow or folded blanket to sit on to put your body at ease. If you sit on a chair, put your feet flat on the floor.

- *Sit down and lengthen your spine naturally.* Put your hands on your knees or thighs, palms down, with your thumb and forefingers touching. Close your eyes.

- *Breathe in deeply,* allowing the breath to fill your entire body from your pelvic floor to the top of your head. Breathe out slowly. Take several long breaths as you invite your mind to quiet.

- *Still your mind so that you can become aware of and embrace God's wisdom as it comes forth from your being.* To still your mind, imagine it as the clear blue sky. With your eyes closed, notice the landscape of the sky and how sparkling and empty it is. As clouds come across the sky, let them pass. Another cloud may come. You can notice that one too, and again let it pass. In the same way that you observe the passing clouds on the terrain of the sky of your mind, you can observe your thoughts. They will come and go. They may be happy thoughts or sad ones, exciting or depressing. Either way, let them pass so you can continue to still your mind.

- *Use your breath to support you.* Watch your breath with your mind as it goes in and out. Breathe in, and focus on your breath. As you continue to breathe naturally, stay focused on the movement of your breath. If thoughts arise, return to your breath as you watch them pass by just like the clouds.

When you first begin meditating, you can sit for ten minutes at a time. As you build up a comfort level, you can extend your period of meditation up to an hour daily. What's most important is to develop the daily discipline of meditating.

You may want to keep a special journal to record your meditation experiences. I find that great inspiration often comes to me during meditation. Once after I had sat for meditation, I got the complete plan for how to reorganize my business so that it could be more financially lucrative. When I sat down to meditate, I didn't have that or anything else as an agenda. I was simply doing my practice, and out of that discipline came great resolve and conviction that helped to support my daily work.

You may find that sometimes your meditation is a bit rocky. Don't give up if that happens to you. Just like any other practice, meditation requires discipline. The reality is that you already have experience at meditating—on your work, your household, your hobbies. Anything that you focus your attention on doing while shutting out other thoughts is, in essence, a meditation. That same intention and commitment to mastering a project that you have learned to devote to other activities you can now offer to the inner journey. This is the key to discovering your own Truth and learning how to choose it in your daily life.

HONOR THE EXAMPLE OF YOUR ANCESTORS

I HAD A VERY intense relationship with my father. Being named for him, I always felt the need to live up to his grand expectations. My father had an incredible historic career, being the first at nearly everything he attempted, including the first Black judge on the Maryland Court of Appeals. I felt enormous pressure to measure up. I also felt angry at him at different points in my life for being particularly harsh and for requiring so much from me. Even after his death, mixed feelings about the nature of our relationship remained. Sometimes I felt locked into a defensive posture in relation to him. But I also had the sense that this defensiveness was holding me back in other parts of my life, and I wanted it to be gone. During a long meditation one afternoon, my father's image kept coming up. At first I thought I wasn't meditating, because I kept seeing my father's face. But after a while I realized that I was being given a gift—an opportunity to look at my relationship with my father with fresh eyes. During the course of this meditation, I experienced a powerful healing. As I recalled different scenarios in our life together, it became undeniable how much my father loved me. There was one example after another of how proud he was of me, though he rarely said it with words. All of the things that I couldn't quite be certain of when we were actually in each other's company became crystal clear as I looked at our life without judgment or emotion. When the meditation was over, I felt completely refreshed and free of many lingering impressions I had had about what our relationship really meant. It was liberating.

TAKE A BREATH

PERHAPS THE MOST commonly ignored and most powerful gift that each of us has is the ability to breathe. The breath is the sustenance that invigorates and enables our bodies to function. It is through the vehicle of the breath that we are able to think, speak, move, and live.

It appears as if the breath happens on its own. Each one of us breathes in and out, in and out, all day long, even as we sleep. Because of the miraculous functioning of the human body, we rarely give a thought to the myriad activities that sustain us, including the physical act of breathing.

Think back to birth. By most accounts, the passing from the womb into the world is a traumatic experience for an infant. For an entire lifetime, nine months, you were completely protected and cared for. You breathed in the liquid sac of love your mother provided. At the point of your entry into the world, you had to make a choice to live. Sure, the doctor or midwife may have given you a jolt of reality, that smack on your bottom that caught your attention. But you had to make the choice to respond. Through your cry, perhaps of outrage at being smacked, came your first breath. And then another. And another.

Come back to today. What does it take for you to remember your breath now? A smack in the face of reality? A sickness? A heartache? A beautiful day? Over the course of several years, I have observed people during moments of tension to see what choices they make to take care of themselves. Amazingly, I have discovered that many people hold their breath when they are angry, afraid, tense, or otherwise living in an extreme emotional state. At the very moment when they need their breath the most, they put it on hold, suspending the life force that gives them the power to move forward.

We see how beneficial the breath can be when we use it for meditation. By consciously engaging the breath, we support our expedition within. What about at other times? Have you ever noticed what you do when you get nervous, frustrated, excited, or otherwise emotional? Watch yourself. What do you do when you feel anxiety? It could be about work, your family, a challenging friendship, a call from a bill collector. If someone brings you bad news, if you are nervous about a promotion or a mistake you made at work, if you get a call in the middle of the day from your child's school, what happens? Do you close your eyes and wish it away? Do you hold your breath and attempt to fast-forward into the next moment? Do you choose to face what's before you? Chances are you stop breathing. What this means is that in the very moment when you most need the support of your own life force, you have rejected it.

Think about a time when this may have happened to you. Depending on how long you held your breath, you may have gone into panic mode thinking, "How can I possibly handle this situation?" Because you gave away your power by cutting off your source of vibrancy and strength, it's only natural that you would begin to panic and fear that you lacked the capability to work through the situation.

A HAIR TALE

IN COUNTLESS SITUATIONS, breath can come to your rescue. Let's say you find yourself in a situation where someone asks you a question that seems to have no good answer. Perhaps a woman who has just come from the hairdresser wants your opinion on her hair, and you don't like it. You want to tell the truth, but you don't want to hurt her feelings. You know that she has just begun to go out again after being confined to her bed for a month recuperating from an illness. Should you tell her that you hate her haircut? This seemingly petty situation could be critical for the woman who is just blossoming into a period of personal rejuvenation. Is it necessary to tell her your opinion about her hair? Is that Truth the greatest point here? Instead of standing there shell-shocked or lying your way out of the moment or growing more and more uncomfortable, breathe. That's right. Take a deep breath in and ask your inner wisdom to guide you. What Truth would be most beneficial to your friend at this time? How can you support her as she turns this new page in her life?

When I have done this exercise, I've gotten creative and uplifting ideas. I could tell my friend I think it's great that she has taken a positive step toward getting her life together. I could ask her how she feels after being pampered at the beauty parlor. I could ask her about her social plans and how she intends to spend her time in the coming days. I might recommend other beauty treatments that have helped me to relax and feel great, such as massage and manicures. In these ways I can support her and help build her confidence without getting into the very subjective nature of her hairstyle.

You may easily face a much tougher situation. What if your son is caught cheating on an exam? What do you say when he comes home from school? You may want to scream and holler, maybe even give him a spanking. But instead of going into a rage, which will definitely *not* help your son, breathe. Ask your inner wisdom how you can support him. What can you say and do in this moment that will benefit him? How can you show him that even in school, he can live by spiritual principles? Engage your breath as you think about the situation. Know that your ability to be in control of yourself and, in turn, be inspired to find a positive solution, will be key to supporting your son.

USE THE BREATH AS THE DOORWAY TO YOUR SOUL

THERE ARE MANY TIMES when you can use the breath to give you insights into your life. I worked with a gifted trainer who focuses on breath work. One of many techniques that Jules Paxton uses is to encourage his clients to "listen with the breath." He says, "The breath is a great teacher of where our mind is. If you watch the breath and listen to it, it will talk back to you. It's just like having a conversation with a friend." As Jules and so many other yoga practitioners teach, only when you control the breath can you control the mind. When you control the mind, you have the capability of bringing your entire being into alignment so that your mind, body, and spirit can serve as one cohesive unit.

A health practitioner I met in Jamaica who has a practice in Miami demonstrated another great use of the breath. Gaia's approach is to relax the body and then invite the patient to follow the movement of the breath as she does what she calls emotional body release work. Through Gaia's probing work, she engages a patient's breath so that it releases whatever emotional issues that person may have been holding inside. Many people have described her work as equal to ten sessions at a therapist's office. One man who participated in a session with Gaia revealed that one of his greatest fears is that he will become fat. He had spent many years as a chubby youth and had been living with the fear of returning to that body for many more. After working with Gaia, Tommy said that he was able to relax. He no longer needed to hold onto memories of the person he used to be—that he was lovable as he is, however that is. That meant that his regular workout schedule could have a different focus. Instead of obsessing over a need to create a slim body, Tommy could shift his awareness to his intention to develop a healthy body that would support him in every way he needed. Again, the point is that when you invoke the power of your own breath, you are able to see inside your soul. You gain access to your own heart. Once you are there, you will learn how to respond in a given situation. You will be able to move forward with your heart's consent.

REMEMBER TO PRAY

EVERY TIME that my family went to church when I was growing up, my mother would get down on her knees in our pew and close her eyes for a few moments. I never quite knew what she was doing or saying at that time, but I watched her. The moment was still. No matter what our age, we knew to be quiet while Mommie did her business at the pew. When she was finished, we all sat down and participated in the church service. Years later, I asked my mother what exactly she does when she takes that silent moment. She told me that that moment is her time for prayer. She asks God to reveal to her whatever lesson she is to learn that day. She asks God to give her the focus to listen and learn. And then, with full faith, she sits down and listens and participates.

Long-Distance Prayer

The spiritual practice of prayer can be powerful and effective. A recent study bore witness to this. There was a group of severely ill people for whom a group of people prayed; the second group of sick people received no such support. All of the test group who received long-distance prayer support survived and healed. The placebo group did not fare nearly as well; several people died, while others barely hung on, and only a couple healed fully. Because it's extremely difficult to prove the power of prayer scientifically, the creators of this study admitted that it can still be shot full of holes. Yet it brings up a point: that the power of prayer, regardless of where the prayer happens, travels or disperses on someone's behalf into the universe. God is everywhere, and His power can help you and heal you.

It makes sense that this can happen. Take the converse: if you call a woman (or man) a bad name to her face or behind her back, she will likely feel the ramifications of your anger. As so many people have pointed out, the world is small. Imagine: Somebody calls you incompetent, and all of a sudden somebody on your job begins to question your ability to get things done. Quickly, more people begin to question your integrity. What if someone prayed for your success and spoke positive words of love and support about you, both to you directly and in others' company? A blanket of positive energy would likely come your way just as the negative arrows came racing to the unknowing victim.

Worthy Prayer

Is it all right to pray to receive a Grammy when you are a recording artist or to win a football game if you are the quarterback? Is it okay to pray for a raise in your salary or for a miracle to help you to take the vacation you've always wanted? Is it okay to pray for whatever you believe you want or need? What constitutes a valid prayer?

These excellent questions come up frequently. Many people do pray for success in their chosen fields, often for selfish reasons, so that their lives will improve. Even more, some people bargain with God, saying, "If you do this for me, I will do that for you." Although I am not here to pass judgment on anyone, I will say that my experience shows that prayer is of greatest benefit when it is offered unselfishly.

What's essential is for you to contemplate carefully what your intention is before you begin to pray. Ask yourself what you *really* want. Is it a promotion—or the wisdom and capability to respect the resources at your disposal? Or would you rather pray for a winning lottery ticket? Is your intention to grow stronger in your ability to practice virtues such as kindness, compassion, or forgiveness—or to find a new mate who is the person God has chosen for you or both? Perhaps you intend to gain greater understanding of your past so that you can create a firm foundation for guiding your life today—rather than to have your parents accept full responsibility for all of the problems in your life. If you are in a depressed state, you may want to seek spiritual guidance to help lift your feelings of negativity—instead of enough money to escape for a vacation. Do you see how creating an overarching intention will help to direct your prayer? In each of these situations, you could have chosen a quick fix that would not have helped you to help yourself. When your intention reaches for the highest, your prayer will too. For example, you can pray for guidance on how to be honest when it's more convenient to lie. Or for how you can be of greater service to your loved ones and neighbors. Or for courage to have discipline as you care for your body so that you can be strong enough to be there for those who need your support. Or you can generously pray on behalf of others—for those in need, for the world community.

Prayer works. I've witnessed it time and again. Those prayer circles and prayer chains that people sign up for in church do support others, as do the telephone vigils that friends and loved ones conduct for those who are in need. In the church of a friend of mine in Iowa, for example, when a prayer request comes in, the deaconesses all call someone; then that person calls someone, and everybody prays for the request. Sometimes they all pray at the exact same hour, like during a surgery. Knowing that the energy that you offer in a prayer reaches beyond you to that power that sustains the universe is powerful knowledge. Your contribution to that circle of support is significant. It also requires faith. Just because you pray for something, even the noblest cause, doesn't mean that your prayer will be answered when or how you have requested. You need to believe that everything is in divine order. When you look at your life in that way, you will be better able to perceive the blessings as they manifest.

How to Pray

Praying is a beautiful practice that can inspire you every day of your life. Although there are many ways to pray, you may consider the following guidelines to get you started:

• Thank God for your blessings and your challenges and problems.

• Ask for forgiveness for your wrongdoings as well as understanding and wisdom so that you will not repeat these mistakes in the future.

• Believe that God will answer your prayer. Know that this doesn't mean you will get what you want each time. It does mean that God will give you what you need. Your faith will sustain your belief.

RAISE YOUR VOICE IN SONG

ONE OF MY FAVORITE THINGS about the Christmas holiday season is the sound of music in the air. From Thanksgiving through New Year's Day when I was growing up, my house was filled with beautiful music. My mother often played the piano, and we would all gather around to sing carols and other songs with her. When we weren't making our own music, our father was filling our home with jazz and other soothing sounds that he filtered through the quadraphonic speakers that enabled sound to waft through every room of our house.

Singing went way beyond the holidays. From the time we were very small, we sang. I'm sure this is because Mommie was filled with joy, and she shared it through song. For many years, she sang in the choir at church, and she brought those beautiful sounds home to us. We sang when we were happy, and we sang when we needed a boost. We sang as we did our chores and before we went to sleep at night. This practice is one that each of us has carried with us into our own homes and our own lives. Stephanie has carried on the tradition directly by offering her angelic voice to her church and for many events. Susan and I reserve our singing for less formal environments—when we are in the background but still giving it all we have. We all draw on its calming power again and again.

Do you like to sing? Even if you think you don't have a perfect voice, go for it. Think of an uplifting song that you have enjoyed in your life. Sing its syllables, whether you start off squeaking or belting the tune right out. When you offer the love in your heart to the syllables, a sweet sound will emerge. I'll never forget an older woman in our church in Baltimore who was committed to supporting the church in every way. That included being a member of the choir. Mrs. Wilcox was exuberant. She sang with the fullness of her heart—and she was almost always off-key. Even so, it was beautiful. I have often thought about Mrs. Wilcox and her singing. What has consistently come to mind is the great understanding she had! God loves us as we are, and when we offer our best, the Lord is truly happy.

So, sing. When you're feeling happy, give your voice to the Lord's music. When you are feeling down, lift yourself up through song. Whenever you feel that you need a friend, give your own voice a chance to be that support. Engage in uplifting song, and watch your spirit soar.

LET GO, LET GOD

A GREAT SPIRITUAL LESSON to contemplate is to allow God to work through us. So often we believe that we have a lot to do. We have to be in control of everything. While it is true that to become spiritually and intellectually strong, we must practice self-restraint, this doesn't mean that we are ultimately at the helm of our lives. I have long thought about this concept with wonder. We have to put forth tremendous personal effort to accomplish our goals and stay on course. At the same time, I have learned that there is a powerful force far greater than myself who is really in charge. So how do you balance these two—putting forth effort and having faith that the Lord will provide? By stepping out on faith, meaning you pray for God to bless your situation, you also have to do all that you can to make it happen. God will do the rest. But you have to help yourself first and believe while doing so. Then God will open doors you never knew existed.

I spoke with the minister who married George and me about his understanding in this area. The Reverend Dr. Eugene Callender has been a pillar in the Christian community of New York for many generations. He has had a stellar career, serving on behalf of the Black community through the New York Urban Coalition and the National Urban League, as well as the Federal Council on Aging under five U.S. presidents. Before talking with him this time, I had considered Dr. Callender's life as a perfect example of what one can become if he chooses to live in the Truth—in the ways of the Lord. I still learned that Dr. Callender has a different way of looking at his life. He explained, "We don't live our lives. Our lives are being lived." This stumped me. Here was this renowned pastor who had been inspiring people for many years to live in the heart of God's love. What did he mean?

He explained, "I don't believe we choose Truth. I believe Truth chooses us. God chooses us. If we are blessed in this lifetime to be a seeker, that for which we are seeking is doing the seeking." Using his own example, Dr. Callender said that there would be no way that he could have envisioned the life that he has led. A "poor Black boy from Massachusetts," he said he could easily have remained in obscurity, leading a simple or even tragic life. Instead, he says that God chose him to do His work. What he had to do was to follow God's lead—to let go of whatever preconceived ideas he had and to trust that his inner intuition would guide him as he addressed the opportunities that came his way. Because he did follow his calling, he has lived an amazing life that has grown richer experience by experience.

Dr. Callender's recommendation to us is that we listen to our hearts. Pay attention to the wisdom that resounds within us, because that is God's wisdom that wants to lead us on our way. Don't let your ego or your busyness get in the way of your being able to connect to the divine within your own being—that alignment with God that allows you to step into oneness with the ultimate Truth. Pay attention to the signposts along the way that show you that God is supporting your every step. Continue to put forth your full effort. Do so with the understanding that God—however you understand this Power—is leading the way.

SURROUND YOURSELF WITH LOVE

THE PROMISE OF SPIRITUAL LIFE is an abundance of love. Every spiritual tradition sees God as love. By nurturing your understanding of your role in the world, you gain greater access to the love in your own heart and in turn are able to share that with others. At every turn joy is to be experienced. Before us in the euphoric moments, as well as the most challenging ones, is a ray of light and love. By engaging in spiritual practices, such as regular worship, prayer and meditation, reading uplifting spiritual literature, and being in the company of others who celebrate their lives, your ability to recognize the beauty of your life will expand. Choose to know God. Choose to love your life. Choose to see the beauty in everything around you. When you choose love, you will be able to embrace happiness.

My Journal Entry

Dearest Friend,

This world is dynamic. That we are able to live on this planet and experience joy and sorrow, defeat, and triumph is a blessing. Let me cultivate a spiritual connection to God, to the creator of the universe who also lives within my own heart. Let me stand strong in my knowledge of that divinity. Show me how to nurture the presence of God in my life.

I love you,

Me

A HUMAN LIFE is sacred. Our role is to recognize the power in ourselves and to let our light shine out over every aspect of our lives. In this way we can honor the gift of human life in our every thought, word, and deed. As you write in your journal for this chapter, do the following:

- *Review and record your spiritual history.* Write down memories of your earliest understanding of God.

- *Pay attention to any conflicts that may have come up along the way.* Has anything ever stood between you and your faith? If so, what happened during that period? How did you heal? What healing is left to be done?

- *What do you do now that fortifies your spirit?* What do you want to do that will make you stronger spiritually?

- *What commitment can you make now to nurture your spiritual life?* You don't have to come up with something big. It can be a simple, specific action that you can manage on a daily basis. One of my first commitments was to count my blessings.

- *How can you incorporate your spiritual understanding into your daily life?* Regular contemplation can be a great support here. You may want to review your journal weekly is to see how you are melding your worldly life into your spiritual foundation.

3

LOVE YOURSELF

BEFORE YOU CAN TRULY love another, you have to love yourself. Before you can significantly help someone else, you have to be able to help yourself. It's the nature of the human experience. And yet this simple fact evades so many of us for so long.

On a cursory level, you could argue that people do all kinds of things for each other without really thinking. Most of us take actions that do end up helping others. It *is* possible to provide a certain level of support without being aware of our own true value. We can give someone a seat on the subway or bus, hold a door open for a person with many packages, send money to relief organizations, and volunteer at retirement homes during the holidays, as well as countless other beneficial activities. All of these efforts do support others, but when they happen without conscious intention, they don't carry nearly the value that is potential in each act.

What happens when we embrace who we are? What does life look like when we dare to love ourselves and bask in the beauty of who we are? If you think about your life, you probably already have some answers. The reason we can even ask these questions is that each of us has experienced flashes of the Truth of who we really are. We have had moments when everything clicks, and it feels as if a power within and beyond us is propelling our actions, like there is a guiding hand directing our steps even as we are making the moves. When you come to recognize that guiding hand as the hand of God within your own being, you are headed down the right road. That person within you who resonates with the light of your true Self is the one you can love.

STEP INTO YOUR LIGHT

DURING THE SIXTIES and seventies, many people in America began to search for the meaning of life by exploring alternative lifestyles. Hippies sought to support the love that they felt inside in ways that were nonviolent and liberating.

Some people attempted to capture a fleeting feeling of brilliance by using psychedelic drugs. Others chose spiritual activities.

The Beatles' George Harrison began to pursue his spiritual life as a young man, just as his musical career was taking off. George discovered Eastern spiritual philosophy in his twenties and was so deeply moved by the music and wisdom of yoga that he incorporated its messages into some of the music that he created with the Beatles.

This is what happens when you come to love God. In turn, you grow to love yourself more and more. You begin to recognize the beauty of your own life and celebrate that through each outlet that you encounter. You walk with the light of God as you discover the gifts he has blessed you with, and that light illuminates your every step.

A Mother's Glow

As a small child, I witnessed the inner light that people carry through my mother, who remains a shining light of love and strength. There has always been something about her that people have gravitated toward. Yes, she has striking physical beauty, but all who have met her concur that this beauty goes far deeper than her appearance. My mother, Doris Freeland Cole, carries a flame of love with her wherever she goes, and her inner brilliance touches those who come into her purview. When I was a college student, this was a source of great frustration for me. I didn't understand much about personal spiritual power at that time. What I did know was that the only time that any significant number of boys expressed interest in me was when my mother came on campus. Then there would be a string of young men following us around, pretending that they wanted to talk to me, while in actuality they were waiting for the moment when my mother would give them a glance or a moment of her precious time. For a while I was jealous. I was mad at those boys and at my mother. She had a husband, *and* she was much older than my college friends. Why weren't they paying attention to *me*?

Rather than acting on envy, I looked for the wisdom in this experience. I did that by observing my mother more closely. Her radiance acts like a magnet. Because it is true through and through, it serves her and everyone around her beautifully. Instead of becoming envious of the attention she was getting, which she hardly noticed anyway, I determined that I would continue to embrace all of the lessons that she was sharing with me, including those that I gleaned being in her company. My mother had fully committed herself to her children when we were born. She has made it her mission to teach us how to love and take care of ourselves. Living in my own light and nurturing the goodness that allows it to grow was the lesson I learned from this experience. I didn't need to be Mommie. I needed to be me. My own light is what attracts the right people and possibilities to me.

From Caterpillar to Butterfly

To find your light and access your reservoir of love, sometimes you have to let go of everything that you hold dear. The identifications that you have used to define yourself may have to fall away. You may have to forgive yourself for past mistakes in order to grow and become more self-confident. When you ask yourself, "Who am I?" you may not be able to use the descriptions that you used yesterday. As you rigorously work on yourself to become a better you, you may need to let much of the old you fall away. That you can't know exactly how you will evolve can be a frightening prospect. Enter faith. When you rustle up the courage and faith that assure you that you will become the best you if you put your heart in it, you will be able to walk through the unknown and come out renewed.

The most striking and universal image of the metamorphosis that is possible for each of us is the transformation that a caterpillar undergoes to become a butterfly. A caterpillar lives in a protective shell, foraging for food on the ground and finding its way. This unassuming creature lives largely unnoticed by many of its companions in nature. It blends into the earth as its entire being intuitively prepares for the next phase of its life. At the point when it is about to transform, the caterpillar envelops itself into a cocoon, a protective encasement that serves as a perfect incubation environment. Only when ready, when fully developed, does the butterfly within the caterpillar emerge. In order to become its magnificent Self, a living being with extraordinarily beautiful wings that allow it to lift off from the earth and flutter about in the sky, it has to let go of its old Self. The caterpillar is no longer when the butterfly enters the world.

Where are you in your life? Are you a caterpillar preparing to emerge into a more beautiful and greater you? Are you willing to let go of that part of you that you no longer need in order evolve into your magnificent Self?

Things Fall Apart. Let Them.

I asked myself these questions with great intensity in the summer of 2000. At that time, I had experienced tremendous success, but I wasn't sure what or who I was. My definitions for my role in life and my accomplishments seemed to have evaporated, and what was left was unclear. I remember walking up lower Fifth Avenue one summer afternoon, having just left what would become my new office. I had finished moving from a space that had been filled with boxes of memories—memories of good times with my family, sweet times with my colleagues, brittle times with my past employer, hurt times with loved ones. I had thrown away paper after paper and box after box of things and allowed them to return to the universe and free me from whatever clutches they had been invisibly holding on me. As I headed a few blocks north, I ran into three beautiful men. The first is a colleague and friend who years before had sat with me to strategize his departure from his job. Having left my job a year or so earlier at that time to start my business, I had had many suggestions for him on how to maximize his potential to win and win big. His strategy had paid off, and he was filled with stories of how his career was unfolding. The other two fellows I had met at different times. One had grown up around the corner from me in Baltimore and had dated my sister Stephanie when they were teenagers. He had come to New York to pursue a career in fashion, as I had done some years earlier. The other fellow, whom I had also met before, was his assistant. These two shared their good fortune—that they were moving to L.A. to work on a huge film. Life was great for these men, and I was so proud to know them and to witness their success.

As I left them, I also felt extremely sad. What had happened to my strategy? In that moment, I couldn't see even a glimmer of my success. Instead, I saw a vision of the boxes in both spaces that were left to tackle. I saw the multitude of issues that I was still facing in order to set my life on course—to choose my own Truth. And I remembered in that moment why I was feeling so off-center, what at least one source of the hollow ache was that seemed to be walking ahead of me, beside me, in front and in back of me, within me, as I made my way up the street. That day marked the one-month anniversary of my losing the precious baby that I had been carrying for the previous three months. Like a fresh wound, I revisited my loss. I felt the emptiness again as if it were brand new. This was the first time in my life when I could not quickly shake off a tragedy and move on. It was taking time. And during the time it was taking, I felt as if my whole world was crumbling in. As I continued to walk up the street, refocusing on the work at hand, knowing that I had to find a way to *do* what was on my long list, I had the thought: Let things fall apart.

Accepting My Life

I have been programmed for my entire life to keep it together. It has been like a mantra. *Keep a smile on your face, girl, and push on. You can do it. You can recover from whatever is before you. You are a survivor. You can keep the pieces together.* I am often reminded of Billy Crystal's classic *Saturday Night Live* skit as the character Fernando when he proclaims, "It's better to look good than to feel good." Being a fashion girl, I had claimed that tricky wisdom years before. Put on a good face. Dress up. You can do it.

On this particular day, I realized that I could only do one thing: accept that a part of my life had died. More than my precious child, I could see that many of the thoughts, ideas, concepts, and things that I had felt so attached to also were leaving me and that was somehow okay. I had heard that sometimes our whole foundation has to shake to its core—that the whole house of cards has to fall down in order for us to build back anew with strength and staying power. Is this what was happening to me? And more, how was I to choose my own Truth at this turning point?

My instinctual responses hadn't been working. The phone tree was not yielding inspiration toward freedom. The therapist I had engaged since the loss of my child was helping, but not fast enough. My meditations had been few and far between. I was lost in a swirl of agitation, seeking any possible way not to have to sit with myself. I was afraid to allow myself to just be. Then what? Aha! *Let things fall apart. Have no fear. Everything is in divine order.* These words began to echo within my being. From the deepest part of me, I could tell that I was at a turning point that was going to make all the difference in my life. I was going to *see* a new dimension of my Truth and learn to embrace it. But first, I had to allow all of the things to dissipate that were unnecessary. Oh, how afraid I was. What was about to happen?

Choosing God

I had the thought that this was the moment when I had to choose a conscious and fully committed relationship with God. Never mind that I had been actively committing to God for many years. This was new. I had to accept that it was God in His divine presence within my own being that I had to embrace. That as I had been shown time and again, no one, no matter how well intentioned, *no one* else could do for me what I needed to do for myself. I realized that the fear I was holding onto for dear life was that I would lose all of the people and possessions and relationships that were so meaningful to me if I dared choose God. Somehow in my mind, choosing God meant surrendering my whole life to the Lord, and that meant losing everything that had previously been important to me. What would my life be like then? Would I end up literally being alone—the very state I feared the most?

Although I had contemplated surrender and what it meant, I had no true understanding of the concept. Deep down inside, I think I knew that surrender wasn't bad or negative. But because I couldn't see the fruits of it since I hadn't yet done it, I feared it.

I am happy to report that I did not perish or become a pariah. Instead, my life changed. Because I did not have the physical or mental energy to get caught up in other people's stuff—or even my own for that matter—I had to slow down. When I did, I got to see how I could live a refreshed and more fulfilling life. Surrender began when I allowed myself to consider what my life had been like up to that point and what was no longer necessary for my well-being. For years, I had been a doer. I had excelled at everything that I had attempted.

In school from the earliest days, I had been an A student. I was especially proud that I had been able to sustain that record nearly blemish free for my entire educational life. What had propelled me to drive so hard toward academic excellence? For starters, retreating into my books had become my shield against the caustic tongues of taunting children. While they played, I studied. That my father—the one for whom I was named, the one who had himself graduated with highest honors as his class's college valedictorian—expected me to bring home perfect scores didn't ease my self-imposed burden any.

Because the pain of growing up was so deep for me, I promised myself by the time I was thirteen that I would never have children. I thought it would be unconscionable to bring another living being into the world to suffer the trauma that I had undergone. In many other eyes, I'm sure that my life looked ideal. I grew up in an upper-middle-class African-American neighborhood. My father, the Honorable Harry A. Cole, was a legend in our community, a man of honor and integrity. My mother, Doris Freeland Cole, was equally revered. A kindergarten teacher, she retired when my younger sister Stephanie was born so that she could devote all of her time to our development. Susan, Stephanie, and I had it great. We had what we needed—not with so many extras but certainly with great comfort. Most of all, we had each other's love.

Letting Go

Knowing this, I ask myself why it was that I was unhappy. It wasn't a daily malaise; indeed, I explored my creativity and freedom with great excitement. I was smart and got a chance to examine what that meant with the most tender and consistent support from my mother. Where I excelled was in my studies. Where I failed again and again was in relationships with others. I didn't argue well, so it was hard to have a prolonged conversation with my father, the ulti-mate debater. And outside of our nuclear safety, my lithe form served as a focus of admiration as well as a dartboard for others' sport and convoluted envy.

I did not have the social skills to fight the street fight that some kids incited. More damaging, I did not have the courage to walk away from "friendships" that were clearly unhealthy because I wanted so much to belong. It took many years and more experiences than I care to count for me to grow beyond those childhood challenges. Thanks to my mother's consistent support, I got to see that I could rise above all of the issues that had been holding me back. Only, many years later, when I was to have a child did I realize that I could be a good mother. Only when I had to face grown-up kids with a new version of mali-cious words did I discover that I didn't have to let them hurt me. Only when I embraced my spiritual path did I get the reinforcement that I needed to know for sure that I was great as I was. Only after every experience that I had had up to the moment that I met those fellows on the street was I able to see that I didn't need any of that stuff anymore. I could let go of all of it and allow my true Self to emerge.

ASSESS YOUR LIFE

GO BACK to your earliest memories of things that worked well and those that stood in your way. Consider how you have loved yourself in your life and when you have denied yourself love. What obstacles have stood in your way? What can you learn from your experiences that will enable you to embrace you as you are?

The exercise of looking into your life is a powerful one. It is not meant as an exercise of torture. No matter how embarrassing or disheartening you may imagine some of those experiences that you have tucked away in the recesses of your mind to be, when you bring them into the light of day, you can become free of them. It may mean that you will want to fortify your spiritual practices as well as engage professional support from a therapist or healer. The objective of this exercise is to see the progression of your life so that you can understand how your opinions and reactions have been formed. Once you gain a clear under-standing, you can work to change any unhealthy practices or habits. When you truly learn a lesson, you can then live it.

Look in the Mirror

To love yourself, you have to know yourself. How often do you honestly pay attention to yourself? In the course of any day, how aware of yourself are you? Chances are you look in the mirror to brush your teeth, wash your face, brush and style your hair. Men give face time to shaving and grooming, while women apply skin care products and makeup. And yet the question remains: *How aware of yourself are you?*

For women mirrors are often the bane of our existence. We confront them in dressing rooms with varying degrees of animosity. Depending on what we are trying on, even women with picture-perfect physiques go from self-conscious to downright depressed. We've been so well programmed to believe that something has got to be wrong that we often look at ourselves with criticism that clouds our retina. We don't really see the person who is being reflected back. Some retailers are so manipulative that they install mirrors that distort the human form, either elongating it to make us look deceptively smaller or expanding it to trick us into believing we are bigger than we happen to be. Dishonesty has never worked, no matter who the perpetrator may be. The greatest perpetrator, unfortunately, is ourselves. How many times have you looked in the mirror and you knew, without question, that a garment simply didn't fit, yet you bought it anyway in the hope of losing weight so you could wear it?

A Reflective Exercise

When you choose to live an honest life, you are also choosing to see yourself for the being you really are. A mirror can be a great support. Pull out your mirror now to do the following exercise:

- *Look at your face in your mirror for several minutes.* Don't look away. Keep your gaze on your face as the seconds tick by. Notice what you see.

- *Write down your findings.* How would you describe yourself to another person? How do you look? Who did you see in the mirror? What kind of person are you?

As you sort through the impressions you had when you looked at yourself, did you find that you liked the person in the mirror? Were you critical or loving as you gazed at the one who was gazing back?

Repeat the exercise, this time looking at yourself as a reflection of inner light. Look for the light in you, which can be seen by the mood or expression on your face. Can you see it? Describe the person who is reflecting that light. And then compare your descriptions to one another.

In order to contribute positively to the world, you have to take a good, honest look at yourself and your life to see how you can improve your own being. By offering yourself love and compassion, tenderness and attention, you can illuminate the goodness in you and then share your brilliance with others.

The Ties That Bind

It's easy to give somebody else advice. I've found myself in situations where I have happily offered guidance to someone I truly care about. "Oh, all you have to do is give that up, honey. Then you will be fine. I promise." Have you ever heard yourself shrugging off a loved one's problems in such a way? When we are on the outside looking in, a person's problems can seem so obvious; we belive the solution is staring us—and them—dead in the face. *Just stop. Don't do it. Give it up.* You've heard those messages before.

There's another one that predates these modern-sounding odes to sanity: "For every action there is a reaction." Whether we consider the laws of physics, the universe, or spirituality, we will see that it is impossible to be free to stand in the Truth if we are bound by anything unhealthy. We know this. Yet our stuff can be so hard to get rid of. Why else would there be so many people suffering from such a wide assortment of addictions? I believe that many of us have tricked ourselves into thinking that we need something outside ourselves in order to be whole.

What can we do to become free of the things that bind us? A great sage who wrote some 2,000 years ago, Patanjali, suggested that it is essential that we ask ourselves about our actions and thoughts. He asked: *Does this add to, or diminish, the obstacles to my enlightenment?* By applying this question to those bad habits that have seemed to bind you, you can begin to see more clearly just how your own efforts are either helping or hurting you. When you do not consider the effects of your actions, deadly things can happen.

An ancient Indian text, the Bhagavad Gita, speaks to this:

> *Thinking about sense objects*
> *Will attach you to sense objects;*
> *Grow attached, and you become addicted;*

Thwart your addiction, it turns to anger;
Be angry and you confuse your mind;
Confuse your mind, you forget the lesson of experience;
Forget experience, you lose discrimination;
Lose discrimination, and you miss life's only purpose.

Ask anybody who has participated in a twelve-step program, and you will hear this reiterated. Clinging to something detrimental outside yourself guarantees misery and confusion. Ultimately, it can lead to the complete loss of perspective on the Truth.

Vanessa had a relationship with a friend that extended over several years. From the start, she believed she was "in love" with this man and decided that she would prove her love by writing to him. Week after week, she wrote her version of love letters to him, professing her undying commitment to their relationship. Week after week, she received no response. She accelerated her letter-writing campaign, making her overtures ever more flowery and descriptive. Over time, she became obsessed with the image that she had of her life with Matthew, even though it did not in any way resemble the relationship that currently existed between them. Her professions of love eventually turned into anger and ultimately deteriorated into rantings. Just as the Bhagavad Gita describes, this woman's attachment to her fantasy took over. Most tragically, as is true of all other addictions, her pursuit never brought her to her goal.

When telling this story, Vanessa described how acknowledgment of her insanity began to free her. Moving past her initial shame, she discovered that the Truth of this friendship had nothing to do with romance. In order for her to experience true romance in her life, she could finally see that she had to give up the obsession of her relationship fantasy with Matthew and allow herself room for an actual connection with someone else to manifest. Living in the eye of the fantasy had been keeping her own Truth at bay.

Set Yourself Free

When you are in the throes of an obsession, what can you do? First, you have to cease all contact with that person or the object about which you are obsessing. Second, replace the addictive behavior with something strong and positive that you enjoy. You can use the principles of meditation as a guide. To still your mind for meditation, you have to quiet your thoughts. Singing or chanting is one means of focusing, taking the attention away from the thoughts and focusing it on singing God's name. Another option is to watch your breath, paying attention to the power and vitality of the breath that fills your own body. When thoughts come up, instead of following them, you can choose to watch your breath as it moves in and out of your body.

Try it now. Take a seat, and close your eyes. Breathe in deeply, and breathe out long. Once again, take a deep breath in, and release it slowly. Allow your thoughts to slow down as you focus on your breath. The breath is the most powerful natural part of your being. It keeps you alive, and it can keep you sane.

In addition to engaging the breath, you may want to consider some other tools for releasing your obsessions. The key here is to find ways to support yourself, to fortify your own innate strength. To check the merit of your option before you choose it, take a moment, close your eyes, and ask yourself in the space of your heart whether you are making the right decision. Here are some ideas:

• *Pray.* Literally get on your knees if you need to, and ask for the burden to be lifted. Call a compassionate friend rather than the object of your obsession or someone who will not be supportive.

• *Write letters to the person, but don't mail them.* You may want to burn them as you invite the attachment to be released.

• *Seek counseling.* If you can't get past a love affair, a gambling habit, a drug addiction, or any other type of hold on your life, find the professional support you need, and embrace it.

• *Do something to help someone else.* Join a charitable organization and offer your time. Participate in an activity after work that helps to clean up your neighborhood.

• *Get busy.* As the saying goes, "The idle mind is the playground of the devil." Don't give your mind the chance to take you into a living hell. Keep it busy with positive activities—singing songs of love to God, teaching your children to be strong and brave, or exercising.

• *Forgive yourself* for being in this uncomfortable place and remind yourself, "This too shall pass."

You may want to read a wonderful book that has helped me tremendously in this area. It is called *What's on My Mind* and was written by a monk in the Siddha Yoga Meditation tradition, Swami Anantananda. This book provides exercises for dealing with jealousy, lust, anger, and other vagaries of the mind. The exercises are designed to lead you back to your center—back to the inner strength that each of us has but that we sometimes forget.

Don't Let Yourself Get Distracted

Our lives are busy. Many people I meet and know tell me that they are often weary at day's end, because the activities that fill their days take up so much time and energy. Whether it's work, parenting, talking to friends, or otherwise handling their business, their lives are full. Of course, in cities, the busy life is commonplace. In some ways, it's considered the promise of the great metropolis. Ah, the lure of never having a dull moment! Even in rural communities, people are busy with the hard work of farming and land development, as well as figuring out how to care for the family and community. Beyond productive busyness there is distraction. What my Daddy used to call the "idiot box," the television, has occupied more people's time than perhaps any other activity thus far created. Indeed, most American homes boast of multiple sets that make it possible for individual family members to select their particular programming while others enjoy their favorites at the same time. Television, video games, music, and other activities are exciting forms of entertainment, but they can take us away from ourselves. They frequently steal the precious moments that could be available for us to examine our lives and set our course anew.

I often think of *Walden,* written by. Henry David Thoreau, an unusual man for his day. Thoreau was a well-educated man who decided that he needed to allow himself the opportunity to experience the value his life had to offer, to find a spiritual awakening. His itching to discover the true meaning of human life compelled him to steal away to a secluded and beautiful location, Walden Pond, in Concord, Massachusetts. During his stay there, Thoreau carved out time to pay close attention to his life—his thoughts, his imaginings, his environment. He chose to eliminate the distractions that made it so easy for him to become numb to the greater calling of humanity.

As a result of Thoreau's voluntary retreat, he came to appreciate his life in the company of nature and to fine-tune his values. In turn, he was able to in-articulate what was important to him, even in the face of ridicule and potential arrest. Thoreau decided not to pay taxes, because he did not believe it was honest to support a government that condoned and supported slavery. Knowing that he might have to serve jail time, he stood firm in his own beliefs nevertheless.

How many of us dare to follow our beliefs? Even more, how many of us know what those beliefs are? Do you have a clear understanding of what your values are and how your actions support or deny your belief system?

Make a Plan

Every day you can actively explore your life. Armed with this information, you then can make a strategy for the next day. I recommend that you take time to be still before sorting out your plan. By stilling your mind, you can invite grace to guide you to the proper next steps. Meditation anchors you in the present moment, where you have the ability to make decisions and effect change for yourself. By becoming quiet, you can hear the wisdom that emanates from within to direct you in the moment and for tomorrow. When you allow that inspiration to come into your awareness, you can capture it and record the actions it inspires so that you can create concrete steps to follow tomorrow.

Each day I begin with a plan that I formulated the night before. The way you come up with your plan is to review your day before going to bed. What happened today? What worked? What needs improvement? What did you learn? How did you benefit from the experiences that you had? How did you handle yourself through moments of joy and challenge? What would you like to incorporate into your day tomorrow? What do you need to accomplish immediately and in the long term? What steps do you need to take in order to fulfill your goals?

Make a List

Daily self-inquiry is a powerful tool in reviewing your life and becoming clear about what your thoughts, words, and deeds demonstrate. It also helps you to let go of self-guilt about mistakes said or done during the day. By paying close attention to the way that your life unfolds, you can maintain a sense of how to be in the moment. You do know your life. You know yourself.

This may seem like a tall order. To know yourself well enough to anticipate how to respond in your own best interest in each moment of the day may appear at first to be daunting, as well as unnecessary. We live in a culture that has provided so many supports that many of us have clung to the false hope that we don't have to accept full responsibility for ourselves. We sometimes believe that we have the right to turn over the responsibility for ourselves to another who is supposed to do right by us. We often expect too much of other people. Yet when you break this thinking down, you can see that it doesn't make sense. Other than children whose parents are indeed responsible for their well-being, why would anyone actually hold in his or her heart the belief that another is responsible for his or her fate?

Self-inquiry guides you to such questions and also reveals your answers. But you have to stop long enough to allow your discoveries to percolate. This brings me to a pivotal piece of African wisdom. The Sankofa symbol of the Akan people of Ghana is one that invokes the process of self-inquiry in a powerful way. The classical form of the symbol shows a bird with its feet firmly planted on the ground with its head turned all the way around, looking behind it. In the bird's mouth is an egg that it is holding firmly and preciously. This symbol says, "Go back and fetch it." Go back and retrieve the knowledge of the essence of your past so that you can walk into your life in the present with conscious awareness of who you are and what your value is in this world. The Akan people know the importance of understanding the fullness of their heritage and using it as a foundation for their lives. Like Thoreau, these wise people choose to practice self-inquiry, to look at the full measure of their lives before moving forward.

Think for Yourself

Practicing self-inquiry is a way of using the life's education that you have acquired thus far. As you know, a good education encourages you to think. You pore over textbooks to learn about history, language, mathematics, science, technology, and various trades. From the information you gather, you then are required to synthesize the knowledge and come up with your own conclusions.

The principles of school learning apply to everyday life too. It is imperative that you practice using your own intellect and research skills to come to your own conclusions. You can consider information as it appears and give yourself the space to assess how it figures into your overall understanding. Sometimes information will be enlightening to you and may completely change your way of looking at a topic. At other times, it may help you to stick to your beliefs and shun stereotypical thinking or limited understandings about how people live and interact. To love yourself, you must be able to think for yourself. You must trust that within you is the ability to learn what you need to learn from every experience you have. To love your own being, you must take the necessary steps to become fully empowered as the self-sufficient, beautiful you that is the true you.

Your Journal Entry

Dearest Friend,

I know that I have to turn my attention inward. I want to be happy and content. It seems that the way to reach a state of peacefulness and joy is to find it inside of me. I want to access this place. I want to know it and to nurture it, so that no matter what happens, I can remember that goodness and joy reside within me. I pledge to examine my life and how I take care of my Self so that I can improve my relationship with me.

I love you,
Me

LOVING YOURSELF may seem like the hardest task of all. To do so through and through demands that you accept all of you—the things that you consider good and bad. You must forgive yourself for past mistakes. Be patient with yourself as you mature and change to become more positive. There's a great book, *The Dark Side of the Light Chasers* by Debbie Ford, that explores the value of knowing the things about ourselves that we often try to suppress. Instead of squashing anything into the recesses of your mind, have the courage to take a good, long look at you:

- *Find the things within your own experience that have supported your growth this far.* What are they? Write them down.

- *Review your history to learn from your mistakes and grow stronger.* Have the courage to think about the experiences you had that were the most hurtful.

- *Figure out your role in those experiences.*

- *Stop blaming others for things in the past.* Instead, focus on your role then and what you can do right now to free yourself of those unhealthy ties.

- *Give up whatever stands in the way* of living in the light of your Truth.

- *Approach one task at a time,* giving yourself the loving care and space to be able to stick to your commitment before you tackle another topic.

- *If you backslide, don't beat yourself up.* Know that you will continue to receive the lesson until you learn it.

- *Study yourself in the mirror.* Find what there is to love about you. Look at that person in the way that compassionate others look at you.

- *Find your soul and cherish that forever.* That is the true you.

4

SPEAK THE TRUTH

What we say speaks volumes about how we live our lives. And most of us speak a lot. Early in the morning, we may talk to ourselves, either through an inner dialogue or out loud. As the day goes on, we speak words of encouragement to our families, greetings as we approach or pass familiar faces, information to service workers, instructions to assistants, interactions with children, friends, and coworkers. The opportunity and necessity for conversation is vast on any given day. It's such a natural part of daily life that we seldom take time to examine what we say or how and when we say it. There's a wise saying that addresses how people communicate: *Great people talk about ideas; small people talk about other people.*

Which kind of person are you? It's likely that you have fallen into each category at different times. The lure of gossip has drawn in all but the most discerning of us at one time or another. Can you remember a time at a family gathering when somebody started talking about how a cousin had gained a lot of weight? For a few minutes, you couldn't resist chiming in. Or a coworker consistently messes up, and a group of people on his floor took a few jabs around the water cooler at his expense. Have you ever participated? It happens. It also happens that people walk away from such conversations and refuse to belittle others or fall prey to disparaging comments that are undoubtedly hurtful. Similarly, in moments of inspiration, you may find yourself discussing the merits of different philosophical points of view, the effects of new educational policies on youth, or how to balance work and family time. We talk about lots of things.

WHAT DO YOUR WORDS MEAN?

When you talk, what do you say? Do you think about the words that come out of your mouth, about their validity or appropriateness? How often do you speak the Truth as you know it? When you examine what you say, you may discover that there are any number of layers to unravel before you can understand and become the master of your words. This is true for a number of reasons. We can start with language. Have you ever thought about where the words come from that describe your experiences or how you form thoughts and then communicate them to others? What about how you process and understand ideas and concepts that are shared with you? How do you know what's real even when you are trying to figure it out?

PAINT A PICTURE

HOW DO WE RECOGNIZE TRUTH? To the best of our ability, we must pay close attention. This is why it is essential to listen when others are communicating with us. When we don't understand, it is our duty to ask questions until we fully grasp what is being shared. This is true whether we are speaking with someone who clearly does not share our mother tongue or with people from different regions and backgrounds whose experience may color their world differently from ours. When we are speaking, the best service we can offer to others is to paint pictures with our words, to be clear and descriptive.

This is one of the first lessons that I give in my presentation training courses, and so I know it is one of the most challenging activities for people to master. In order to paint an accurate picture of what we envision for someone else's benefit, we have to do a number of things. First, we must be aware of all of the details of the scene we are describing. Equally important, we must consider the listener and how that person perceives the world, as well as the ways in which the person communicates. By putting our audience at the top of our minds, we have a better chance of describing our point so that it will be clearly illuminated. Speaking the Truth is far more involved than simply stating what you see, believe, or know to be accurate. It requires communicating that information in a way that can be understood; otherwise, it will be of no value.

THE CHALLENGE OF SOCIETY

SOCIETY AFFECTS our way of understanding what is acceptable to say. You may have found the perfect words to bring a point to life, only to have societal standards and mores step in the way and discourage what's about to come out of your mouth. When we are young, this editing process is instilled by parents, teachers, babysitters, and others who scold us for saying things in less than acceptable or graceful ways. As we grow older, the rules become ingrained and we self-edit. In some instances, this filtering is beneficial. There is great value in being mindful of what we say and being in control of when we release our words. The negative side effect is that by the time many of us become adults, we have twisted our way into speaking such that others will accept our words and thoughts even when what we are saying is no longer true. This is a natural, if unfortunate, part of the evolution of becoming a member of a particular culture. A society's codes of conduct do prescribe that people behave a certain way, and that includes how we communicate. Yet too often the twisting that we do twists the Truth around into something that hardly resembles accuracy. When that happens we no longer can decipher the difference between distorting and controlling our communication.

SPEAK UP

CAN YOU REMEMBER ever uttering something that sounded like the right thing to say, all the while knowing that your statement was somehow inaccurate? If you tell the Truth, the answer is likely a reluctant yes. Manipulating the Truth is so common that it's hard to escape. What do you say when somebody asks you a question that calls for an uncomfortable answer? How do you respond if you are witness to a scene that is unacceptable to you? What do you do when you know that speaking the Truth will upset the whole balance of things? Do you play nice? Do you remain silent? What do you do?

I met a woman who told me about a situation she faced at a business conference. Beth was chatting with a group of colleagues one afternoon when she found herself in an uncomfortable position. A Caucasian woman, Beth was in a homogeneous group of other Caucasians who began to talk badly about African Americans, bandying about various stereotypes as they were talking about one of the speakers at the conference whom they did not like. As the moments ticked by, Beth got more and more upset. A senior vice president from her company was in the group, as was one of her colleagues at work. She wanted to say something but was afraid to make waves. Beth ended up doing nothing.

As she described this scenario, Beth became visibly upset. She wanted to know how she could have handled the situation differently. We talked about strategies that she could have used to address the racist comments without inciting an argument—everything from inserting her own opinion about the speaker to commenting that making generalizations about other people is dangerous. She also could have removed herself from the situation. Because Beth did nothing, her silence ended up as an indirect support for what was being said. Months later, it was still bothering her.

Beth learned the hard way that you've got to stand up for what you believe. Communicating within a web of deceit can only lead to a less than noble life. Dishonesty for the sake of getting along will ultimately eat you up inside and destroy your integrity. You cannot give in to such a practice, for that would dictate that part of your very soul must die in order for you to get along with others. Is that the promise of human life? I don't think so. At the same time, it is valid to imagine that if we dare to speak the unbridled Truth in all circumstances, we will ruffle more than a few feathers as the day goes by and end up numbing people to our message. For example, if in every conversation, I chose to address the many-layered issues of discrimination that have harmed people of African descent at nearly every turn in history, I would end up being ostracized. That doesn't mean that I don't or won't wage that battle, just as so many before me have. It does mean that I pick my moments wisely so that my assertions and revelations will be most effectively received. If you harp on the merits of healthy eating while you are sitting at the table with someone who is consuming the unhealthiest meal, your wisdom will likely fall on deaf ears. You will be wasting your breath. Casting your pearls to swine is just as irresponsible as lying.

Where is the balance? With the intention of living an honorable and honest life, how do you break free of untimely, inaccurate, duplicitous, or dishonest communication and continue to respect and support others?

BECOME A STUDENT

ONE WAY TO DISCOVER balance is to adopt the attitude of a student. This frees you from the weight of believing you have to know everything up front. Rather than standing as an expert or in judgment, you can approach life eager to learn. Why should you know the answer to every question right off the bat? Arrive at each moment with the question, "What am I to learn here? What is the Truth?" Pay attention to what's going on. Take in the whole scene. Before coming to a conclusion, make an informed assessment of the information before you. Do your research if you don't have the answers. This will prevent you from jumping to conclusions. I can't emphasize this enough. Too often people rely on word of mouth to guide their steps. Because they heard something from someone, they think it's got to be true. They're often wrong. In school, you learn to exercise the muscles of your own brain. You engage the regular practice of challenging the information that is presented to you. Whether it appears on the news, in a book, or even from a trusted family member, run it through the sieve of your own growing understanding. If the information doesn't make sense to you, don't repeat it.

Gladys moved to Denver after spending several years in her hometown of Cleveland, Ohio. She moved with her daughter to get a fresh start in her life. Right away, she joined a church and became active on the choir. Gladys was a single mother with a voluptuous figure. Right away, people at church became suspicious, wanting to know who this woman was. Based on her appearance and her status as a single mom, some of the older church members deduced that she was a floozy and began to talk about her in a disparaging way. Whenever she stood up to sing at church, a contingent of parishioners rolled their eyes, angry that she wore what they considered to be provocative clothing in the sanctuary. One church member did some digging and learned that Gladys had been an exotic dancer when she was in Cleveland. This information only made things worse. A core group of the church's membership decided to write her off.

But Tamara, another single mom at the church, didn't go with the rest of the group and decided to get to know Gladys herself. Over time, the two of them became friendly, and Tamara learned about Gladys's history as well as her hopes and dreams today. Gladys was trying to make the best of her life in a new town. Tamara witnessed how well she took care of her daughter. Overall, she could see that there was no reason to label Gladys at all. Rather than reporting back to the group, which would only start up the rumor mill again, Tamara chose to befriend Gladys and let time tell the rest. After several months passed, more parishioners got to know Gladys, and many of them changed their views.

TOOLS FOR HONEST COMMUNICATION

COURAGE, compassion, and simplicity are antidotes for the disease of dishonest speech. By mustering up the courage to stand firm in our convictions, we gain the ability to discern what we actually believe. By exercising compassion and offering our deepest respect for others as we interact with them, we can avoid being noxious or otherwise destructive toward them. And by being straightforward and unencumbered, by being direct, we can cut through the many fabrications that we so creatively weave instead of stating the plain Truth.

Choosing TRUTH

We can free ourselves from the constrictions of speaking within the shackles of others' beliefs and perceptions. We can stand firm in our own understanding of what is real and true, no matter where we are.

To accomplish this mode of communication requires practice and discrimination. We can observe children for clues. Little ones can be great examples for how to live honestly. When it comes to speech, they may be the best teachers. How many times have you been in the company of a child who tells it like it is, regardless of what someone else might think? Without malice, without strategy, the child simply utters what is true about the situation before him or her in the moment. Because it comes out of the mouth of a child, the overarching Truth that resounds as a result is heard—even if an apologetic P.S. is ascribed to it by a parent, such as, "Sorry, you never know what young people are going to say today!" We take in much of what children say because *they* say it. Their joy and wonder attract us. Because we have not yet built up an internal guard against their words, we are able to hear them.

Can you think of an example when a child revealed something significant to you? Take a moment to remember. What was going on at the time? What did the child say? How did you feel? How did you respond? Were you able to accept the wisdom offered?

Right away I think of my nieces and nephews in Baltimore. When my husband and I visit our families, the children come running—for both of us, but especially for my husband. Before the front door is all the way open, we can hear them chanting, "Where's Aunt Harriette? And where's Uncle George?" They like to see me, but they *love* to see him. Why? As my niece Kori Morgan pointed out, "Uncle George plays with us all day long." She spoke the Truth. George is incredibly generous with the children. He rolls around on the ground with them, letting them tug at him and do flips over his back. He races, plays trucks and dolls, rides bikes, colors with crayons—whatever their fancy—for as long as he can. And they love him for it. They love being with me too and I do play with them, but not nearly at the energy level or capacity as George. So when I come to visit by myself and I see the momentary long faces that ask, "Where's Uncle George?" I don't let my feelings get hurt. Instead, I get the gift of a reality check. I can step up and fill his shoes and shower them with his brand of love or offer my own more fully in his absence and enjoy the reciprocal delight that comes with that.

We can easily see what's real if it is reflected to us in such a straightforward way, through a child's words. When we see it, we can then respond in any number of ways. If our response is honest, we can experience clarity and peace in the moment. I know that my nieces and nephews yearn for interaction and that the more I give, the more they will fill with joy. I gain greater respect for my husband for being so willing to be with them and give every ounce of his energy to match theirs. I also take time to examine how I can be the loving aunt that I am without feeling the need to compete with my husband for their attention and love.

I point this out because it is just as easy for an adult to become jealous of a child's affection or wrecked by their innocent, and sometimes incisive, commentary. Adults are "supposed" to know better. We are "supposed" to have the powers of discrimination that enable us to understand the dynamics before us. This is not always true. Many adults have told me about situations in which they have become emotionally distraught because they got caught up in reacting to what children have said to them. This has been true for parents, grandparents, teachers, and neighbors—basically anybody who interacts with a child. How do you respond when a child looks at you and says, "Wow, you've gained a lot of weight!" or "I don't want to talk to you right now," or "I wish you wouldn't . . ."? Instead of looking at the simplicity of what's there and responding in an appropriate, uplifting manner, even the most well-meaning people can become defensive.

This may be because they are caught off guard. As adults, we commonly work to couch our thoughts and feelings in packages so that how we say what we say will be palatable to the person receiving the information. When someone breaks that mold and says flat out what's on his or her mind, then what? Personally, I have found it both agitating and refreshing to communicate with people who tell it like it is, depending on their intention as well as my state of mind at the time. Sometimes as hard as it may be to hear what the person is saying, I am able to listen and benefit. On those occasions, my respect for the person—and for myself—often grows. In other instances, I feel devastated that someone deliberately chose to hurt or embarrass me. Tone is just as important as the words being spoken.

As you can see and have surely already witnessed in your life, there's a fine line here about how to communicate the Truth. I am not recommending that you toss away discretion from now on when you communicate. Striking a balance is the goal. Finding that natural space between raw Truth and graceful, honest communication is the way that we can choose the Truth responsibly when we speak.

Filter Your Words

I have learned the value of contemplating my words before speaking. By doing so, I am better able to speak consciously, aware of what I am saying and how I am delivering my message. I ask myself these questions before speaking: *Is it true? Is it necessary? Is it beneficial? It is timely?* Just imagine if you stopped in your tracks, took a deep breath, and contemplated these questions before speaking. What if the filter for your words were these four questions? Imagine how effective and honest a communicator you would become. It works whether you are in a boardroom making a pivotal presentation or speaking with your children. This model will support you when you are addressing a volatile situation in your neighborhood and when you are talking about issues of intimacy with your partner.

Rather than stepping into the role of naive child, you will be using your cognitive skills to discern when to speak and what to say. During the moments when you are deciphering how to proceed, you will be able to exercise silence in place of rambling thoughts that spill uncontrollably from your lips. Instead of lying in order to soften a blow to someone about yourself or a situation in which the person is a part, you will be still. There's nothing wrong with silence, you know. It is a central tool in the pursuit of Truth.

Practice Silence

A powerful practice is the act of *not* speaking. Many spiritual traditions recommend that true seekers devote a certain period of time each year to silent contemplation. During this time, the seeker does not speak. Instead, it's time to listen, and it's amazing how much you can hear when you dedicate all of your senses to that activity. If you remain silent long enough, you get to clear your mind of all of the clutter that can fill it: superfluous thoughts, worries about work, questions about the future. While silent, you gain the breathing room to be just with yourself. Being silent means not only not speaking but also supporting your silence by the nature of your environment. Turn off all electronics, and just be with yourself. Give yourself the present of your own company, and see what wisdom emerges.

You can also practice silence when you are with others. For example, just because you are asked a question doesn't mean you have to answer it. If you believe that your response will not be of value to the moment, you can remain silent. You may want to offer a smile, a nod, or another gesture that indicates to the other person that you heard what was being said. You may also want to move on in the conversation, changing the subject to more fertile ground while not addressing the point that you believed deserved passing over. It takes practice to master the art of silence so that you and those with whom you are communicating remain comfortable. As you engage this activity, you will see how helpful it can be in allowing you to be kind, honest and appropriate when necessary.

Know When to Speak Up

Silence can work to your detriment as well. A resounding theme that comes up when people debate the value of being honest is this: *I will be alone. No one will love me anymore.* The fear of being alone is a huge part of the human condition. Of all the topics that have come up over the course of my communication work, this tops the list. What's amazing is the great lengths to which people will go in order *not* to reveal the Truth if they believe that it will leave them alone. People marry partners they don't really love. They stay in jobs that clip their creative wings. They tolerate coworkers' disrespect in order to keep a buddy in pocket. They turn a blind eye to abusive relationships hoping that one day things will change.

What happens if you stop a cycle of silence that is unhealthy? Silence can be a blessing as well as a disguise for dishonesty. How do you use it? By not revealing information that would bring light to a situation, are you actually lying? What is your responsibility in a situation to bring forth the Truth? When you have been faced with a questionable situation, what do you do? How often do you shirk your responsibility? How often do you skirt around something that you were supposed to handle because it's easier to just let it go and say nothing?

A woman from Kansas explained that fear of losing her marriage led to a silence that she regrets to this day. Mary was married to an abusive man for twenty-five years. During that time, she had a child who was sexually abused by her father from the age of eight. Mary noticed the signs: her daughter, Jessica became introverted; she cowered from her father when he was in the room; and she began to wear baggy clothes. Meanwhile, Tom was physically and verbally abusing Mary. He would beat her from time to time and constantly bad-mouth her in front of Jessica. Mary often thought of leaving. Even after she believed that something was going wrong with Jessica, she was too afraid to say anything. She didn't know if she could make it on her own, so she kept her mouth shut.

It wasn't until after Jessica grew up and moved away that things began to change. In college, Jessica sought therapy to help her deal with her emotional issues. While in therapy, she remembered what had happened to her in her home, and she confronted her mother. At first, Mary denied that any abuse had occurred. After a while, though, she allowed herself to recall what had actually happened in her marriage and her family. Although James had softened over the years, he continued to abuse Mary verbally. With her daughter's support, Mary sought counseling. Now she's learning to speak up for herself. She has yet to decide if she will press charges against her husband or file for divorce, but she is committed to figuring it out.

Practice Integrity

Denial is powerful. When it is practiced rigorously, people lose sight of what is real; then it becomes impossible to speak the Truth, because they no longer can see what that is.

I was riding from the airport in Minneapolis, headed to my hotel, when I noticed a huge pile-up on the other side of the highway that had occurred moments earlier. A small pickup truck had rammed into a rental moving van. The front end of the pickup was smashed, and the driver and passenger were clearly shaken. I remarked to my driver how terrible this was. He then told me a story about another recent pile-up where several cars had run into one another on a highway. It turned out that the first car was the cause of the accident—something that is commonly difficult to prove. The only reason my driver knew is because of what he had witnessed. The driver of the first car got out of his vehicle after the accident and came rushing down to the other cars. He seemed disoriented and said, "I'm so sorry. I fell asleep at the wheel." My driver scoffed: "He was so stupid. That guy should have never said that. No one would have ever known."

I questioned my driver. I couldn't understand why he thought it would be best for the person responsible for the accident to stay silent. His response was simple: "His insurance is going to be sky-high now. If he hadn't said anything, he probably would have gotten off scot-free. Heck, he may have even made some money off of the guy who rammed into the back of him." What a way to think! I decided to run this scenario by a few people to see how others might respond. Much to my dismay, many others took my driver's side. Why should the insurance company be allowed to penalize anyone? they said. Insurance companies are crooks anyway.

Like all other drivers, I have insurance and understand the realities of insurance hikes. Yet this story remained unsettling to me. I was reminded of my mother's wisdom, "Two wrongs don't make a right." As I sat in traffic, with the crushed truck and its passengers in view, I realized once again that when we are responsible for something but pretend that we are not, the responsibility doesn't change. If we cause others injury, pretending that it didn't happen will not make it go away. Stepping up and admitting our role in a situation is key to honest living.

Even when it means that you will face repercussions, if you have clear responsibility for a situation that is calling for an admission, it's essential that you speak up when the moment calls for it. If you suffer consequences, be brave. The Truth is powerful. Being willing to examine your life and accept responsibility for your actions is the sign of a wise person. When you do this, you will be able to sleep at night. You will have welcomed the freedom in your being to be at ease, because you will have done your part with dignity and honesty.

Watch Your Wake: Mindful Speech

When you speak, be mindful of what you say. Be conscious of your words and the messages that they carry. One way to practice this is to envision yourself as the captain of a ship. As you pass other ships large and small, you create a wake in the water, a trail of waves that ripple behind you. Those waves represent your words. Think about a time when you said the first thing that came to your mind. You just blurted it out, and your words were hurtful. What happened? What was the ripple effect of your words? How long did your words reverberate? Did the waves rise up and crash down on someone? Did that person's boat then veer off course? Remember the situation and the effect of your words on others. Next, think of a situation when your words were uplifting, especially if they were used to point out an error or address a delicate topic. Recall the tone of voice you used to deliver your message and your intention for sharing the information. What were the waves like then? Did they caress the other seafaring vessels? Did they gently dance across the water? This exercise is a powerful way of noticing what you say and how you say it. Think of being the captain of your own ship and the importance of watching your wake throughout your life's journey.

To take the helm and step into the role of captain, look very carefully at how you use words. Tell the truth. How many times have you spouted out something that you wish you could retract even as it was flowing out of your mouth? What about those memos at work or hastily written notes at home that you wish you had ripped to shreds and thrown away? Don't forget the e-mails that you have written in the heat of the moment and sent without careful review. And then there are the voice mail messages, the heated or desperate or lonely telephone conversations. The list goes on. Even the most thoughtful among us have had moments when we have let our undigested responses to situations lead us down a precarious path. Just because we live in a society that says we *can* do anything we want whenever we want doesn't mean unbridled action is appropriate or beneficial. What about our conscience? What about assessing the situation and making clear choices that weigh all of the variables responsibly? What about watching our wake?

We all know better—intellectually and intuitively speaking, that is. We have been taught to keep our mouths closed, to be cautious about what we say, as well as when and how we say it. Many people live long lives following these prescriptions, exercising either diplomacy or laziness in their thinking. Formulaic codes of conduct that prescribe how we should respond can also backfire. Some people reject convention and speak their minds no matter what. Sometimes they prove that society's shushing can be self-destructive, turning imposed restraint into an uncontrollable bellows of retaliatory hot air. On a subtler note, our intuition also gives us messages about how and when to reveal what's on our minds. If we are attuned to our inner voice, we will be able to recognize the wisdom that is coming to our aid and welcome it into our speech. Still, whether we fall into the conventional paradigm of following society's rules, of the potential renegade, or of speaking from our hearts, it can be challenging to remain disciplined about our actions, including what we utter.

Exercise Electronic Restraint

This doesn't mean that humanity has degenerated into a race of heathens. It does point to the nature of our culture these days. The breadth and dynamics of distraction are so pervasive that it's tough to stay the course. We've gone from being a society that only a few years ago operated at a consistent and comfortable growth rate to one that expands exponentially. Commonly available global systems turn complex means of communications into a simple touch of a Send button. Most of us can reach out and touch nearly everyone in the Western world within moments. Sometimes I hear myself sounding like an old lady when I admit such things as, "I remember when we didn't have telephone answering machines or faxes." But it's true. The common use of these devices is not much more than two decades old. Now we have the Internet, PDAs, and cell phones, and more time-sensitive gadgets are on the way.

In the midst of this barrage of technology, what happens when we are inspired to communicate with someone? What editing process do we use as we reach out to others in times of creative inspiration, anger, joy, terror, romance, fear, friendship, lust, or love? Is there a filter that we use that allows us to review our thoughts before we share them? I've asked many people about their processes with the written word. Most remark on how amazingly different their options are from a few years ago when the most common written communication option they had was by letter or memo. To be able to dash off an e-mail now takes seconds and can be done while we are, at the very same time, handling several other critical tasks (or so we think). To be able to send a note to a friend via two-way pager is even quicker. No matter where that person is, moments after you press the magical Send button, your message is there.

Communications experts have begun to recommend strongly that we limit written communication via instant messaging devices to simple, unemotional exchanges. It's best to reserve sensitive topics to one-on-one, in-the-flesh discussions where the subtleties of expression and the natural exchange between two living beings make for an organic flow of communication. Many people have complained that receiving an instant communication from somebody can stir up all kinds of unintended emotions. When a chain reaction begins that is based on miscommunication, it's startling how quickly it can steamroll out of control and result in a devastating blow—something that could have been easily avoided by a face-to-face encounter.

I'll give you an example. An artist was working freelance with a company on an intense project. The bulk of Terry's daily communication with the company was by e-mail. As Terry and her bosses faced a roadblock in their work, she got angry at the way that one of her bosses, Tom, was communicating with her. In each of her e-mails to Tom, Terry believed she was explaining what needed to be handled in a particular situation so that they could move forward smoothly, but Tom didn't seem to be hearing her (translate: reading her e-mails and understanding her intention). Terry felt that Tom's responses to her were curt, condescending, and oblivious to her efforts. And so a flame was ignited. Over the course of several days, the two of them fired off messages that grew more and more heated with each push of the Send button. By the end of the third day, feelings had been hurt, and the bond that they had formed over a long period of time had been seriously damaged. To make matters worse, because they had been fighting so hard electronically, they tiptoed around their actual conversations when they did speak on the phone or in person, so the fundamental issues never actually got addressed in a neutral, person-to-person environment. Instead, both of them huddled in their respective corners, talking to their supporters. Ultimately, they had a huge showdown, one that would have been unnecessary—at least in its magnitude—had the two of them not fired off their emotional communications in the heat of the moment and opted instead to let the issues simmer. In the end, the conversation that was required to get things straight could not be averted by the push of a button.

Watch What You Say

Are there times when you have said something that you regretted?

Bob, a director in Hollywood, shared an experience that he had on his job. He was furious with his executive producer, feeling that he was being disrespected in a particular situation. At first, Bob and his agent, the fellow who represents him, called the powers that be to find out what could possibly have happened. Then they started a full-out war of words. Bob and his agent had been venting together about the project, growing more and more impatient and angry as their thoughts raced on the subject, outlining all of the indignities of the situation. Armed with hot anger, the agent went to the executive producer and let him have it. He allowed no wiggle room for his opponent, even as he believed he was being honest. Actually, he felt perfectly safe in his stance since he was armed with the facts. Yet as the story unfolded, it became clear that there were issues plaguing the project that turned Bob's concerns into no more than a minor irritation for the producer. Naturally, this only made matters worse.

So, what happened? The strong words and actions of the agent prompted a retaliatory memo from the producer to the agent and Bob—a document that refused to acknowledge Bob's full contribution, and questioned his integrity. At this point, a clear choice had to be made. Rather than reacting immediately, Bob practiced restraint. He encouraged his agent to cool down and listen for signs of the Truth in the midst of a storm. Although Bob had written a note admonishing the company for doubting him, he decided to hold onto it for a while. Rather than reacting publicly, he discovered through his own personal contemplation that the best action to take was to exercise patience.

The restraint that Bob engaged in is admirable and basic to being able to maintain one's presence of mind in the midst of high emotions. What Bob says he did was to gather up the facts quietly, reflect on his actions throughout the project, and have faith that he would know when to make the next move. His response to a potentially volatile situation was twofold—action and inaction—though never inertia. There are discourses in the ancient Hindu scripture, the Bhagavad Gita, that are devoted to explaining the virtues of action and inaction. Both have value. Both also can lead one to the sacred place of liberation in this life. It is the attitude that one adopts in responding to the things that come our way that makes the difference. This scripture suggests that the nature of action (Bob's speaking up for what is right) and inaction (his choice was to wait) both have a place in our lives. We can discern when to follow either course by staying centered and remaining focused on the highest and therefore unattached to the outcome.

So often without thinking, we allow words to spill forth from our mouths or our pens in attack or attract mode. Whether the intention is to get back at someone, set that person straight, or lure someone in, check your motive. Can you let go of the outcome? Can you establish a place of calm within yourself *before* you make a move, *before* you say a word?

When your communication is grounded in a solid place of honesty, it is more powerful. It is also more persuasive. By taking the time to take care of yourself before you reach out to others, you will be doing everyone a great service. The nature of restraint, then, is not torturous, even if it feels that way at times. You can think of it as drawing up energy within your own being. Rather than offering it out, pouring it into the universe, into someone's ears or heart, you can redirect your energy to the space of the pure heart by turning it inside yourself. This requires that you hold back on your inclination to spew forth your discoveries. The action of restraining your emotions does bring about the strengthening of your own inner core. It allows you to speak the Truth.

Be Courageous

Speaking the Truth may mean that you will lose friends. It may require that you spend time alone. It may call for you to step out by yourself and stand up for what your heart is saying to you. If you practice staying in touch with your heart and listening to its messages, you will be able to find the courage to stand firm in your beliefs. Your need for acknowledgment will diminish as your resolve grows stronger.

That's precisely what happened years ago when Pamela put her foot down. She was president of her sorority in college when a topic came up that divided the sisterhood into two stubborn camps. Pamela knew which choice made sense to her and also that her decision would dramatically affect her relationship with these women in the future. As she pondered her vote, she thought about what it would mean to stand up for what she believed to be right even when it flew in the face of what the popular girls wanted. Pamela's first inclination was to be neutral—not to vote at all. As fate would have it, she couldn't hide her feelings or her vote. There were seven members of the sorority. The vote was split equally after six had voted, so as president, Pamela was going to have to cast the deciding vote. Before announcing her choice, Pamela searched her soul for guidance.

What would she do? Would she be all right if her sorority sisters rejected her? After a few minutes, Pamela realized that she had to follow her heart. She cast the unpopular vote and followed it up by explaining her point of view and making specific recommendations for how the organization could move forward with the new policy in effect. Pamela had feared being retired to sorority Siberia, but in fact she ended up becoming more popular. Her courage and vision proved to her sorority sisters that she was indeed their leader. They agreed in unison to follow her lead.

LIVE THE TRUTH

MY FATHER had a poem by Edgar Guest that he loved, and it reflected the way he lived his life. The poem's chorus says, "I'd rather see a sermon than hear one anytime." My father was of the mind that your actions show what you believe and how you live. The Honorable Harry Augustus Cole dedicated his life's work to the law, to interpreting it in ways that would represent Truth in the purest form he could understand. As one who had the direct responsibility to pass judgment on people based on their actions, he grew to understand the power in both action and words. He took action when it was needed and emphasized living a loving and thoughtful life. In this way, he explained, he could go to sleep at night in peace. When you act with conviction and full knowledge of what you are doing, you don't have to talk about it. Your actions speak for themselves.

A longtime friend shares this perspective. When I was a student in college and a big break was coming my way, I called him to share the potential good news. He congratulated me on the possibilities lying ahead and added, "Next time, wait until it manifests, Harriette. Then you can talk about it." I thought about his words for quite some time. I wondered what was wrong with sharing my hopes with him. Since that time, I've heard my father's and his wisdom echoed through many voices, including those of superstitions that warn of dissipating your power by revealing it prematurely. The point is not to squander your energy by talking too much. Do the work, and let it speak for itself.

THE POWER OF TRUTH

AS WALTER MOSLEY put it in his book, *Workin' on the Chain Gang,* "Truth is a powerful agent. It only needs to be spoken once. After that the world has changed." In order to hold onto our power, we must invoke the virtue of courage. Anything that is powerful needs a strong container to hold it. Truth is the most powerful reality in this world, as Truth equals God. How do we muster up the courage to practice speaking the Truth in our lives? Walter suggests speaking a new Truth every single day. If the Truth changes the world, what part can you have in that change? What would happen if you accepted responsibility for introducing a kernel of absolute and inspiring Truth into your life on a daily basis?

As we walk with the knowledge that it is our duty and our birthright to speak the Truth, we must also practice the discipline that is integral to responsible communication. We have the opportunity to establish unity in our thoughts, words, and deeds. When we learn to control our tongue, we are able to support ourselves and the many others on our path. When we gain mastery over our skills of articulation, we will intuitively know what to say and have the focus and understanding to speak when the moment is ripe for receiving our words.

Your Journal Entry

Dearest Friend,
I want to be an effective and compassionate communicator. I want to
learn how to discern right from wrong. I want to understand the Truth in
any given situation. I want to have the courage to speak honestly with all
the strength of my being. I ask that you support me in my search for hon-
est speech. With your help, I know that I can master this great practice.

I love you,
Me

THE ART OF SPEAKING HONESTLY is a noble one to master, and you
can do it. There are some paths that you can explore in your journal that
may help you to navigate this journey:

- *Answer all of the questions posed in this chapter.* Take your time to consider each of them, and come up with examples that will paint an accurate picture of your life. Be rigorously honest.

- *Select a specific situation in your life when you made a blunder.* Now reen-
  act the situation and ask yourself if you could have been more kind,
  honest, loving or timely. How might you have handled this situation
  differently if you had taken the time to filter your words using these
  tools?

- *Contemplate silence.* When do you use silence to your advantage, and
  when does it serve as a mask for what's going on? Can you use silence
  in a way that will allow you to speak the Truth? Describe a situation
  when you have used silence effectively or when you intend to do so
  in the future.

- *Make a written pledge that you will pay attention to what you say and when*
  you say it. Commit to doing whatever is necessary to glean the Truth
  so that you will be able to articulate it when the time is right. Most important, commit to discovering the Truth for yourself.

5

FACE YOUR FEARS

WHAT DO YOU DO when you feel afraid? Do you stand up and face your fear straight away? Do you create a distraction so you don't have to deal with it? Do you avoid it at all costs? Many people don't address their fears immediately or directly. Whether it's dread or lethargy or anxiety that paralyzes people, something often keeps us from immediately getting to the root of our issues so that we can resolve them. It's as if fear stops us in our tracks. That's not to say that some things aren't worthy of fear. It's healthy to be afraid of the things that can harm us, such as the dangers of fire or natural disasters, the consequences of random, unprotected sex, or the threat of terrorists. Yet even in situations where a healthy fear can prevent us from making a terrible mistake or from being in harm's way, it's our response to that fear that will determine how we manage through it. For example, never lighting a stove again for fear of starting a fire is not a viable solution, nor is avoiding sexual intimacy for the rest of your life (unless you decide to become a monk), or refusing to leave your home because you have grown wary of social interaction. Even in the midst of crisis, we have a choice about how we will respond. When fear seems absolutely legitimate, it doesn't mean that we should cower from it.

REACTIONS TO FEAR

YOU MAY BE THINKING, "Easier said than done." You're right. What's required is that we give up the relationship that we have had with fear up until now. When I was a little girl, I had my own way of dealing with fear. Whenever I thought I had done something wrong, that I was going to get in trouble with my parents, or that something bad was going to happen, I would crawl into bed and squeeze my eyes shut. Each night, no matter what, both of my parents would come into my room to kiss my sister and me goodnight. On those nights when I knew that a scolding would greet me, I pretended that I was invisible.

Somehow, I got it in my head that if I didn't open my eyes and didn't respond to whatever was said, somehow it wasn't happening. I practiced this avoidance strategy for quite some time. It didn't work, of course. Sometimes my parents would wait until the next day to address the situation. Facing the fear in the light of day hardly made it easier for me. Other times they would tell me they were going to wait until I opened my eyes and responded. "You better answer me, young lady," my mother would sternly say. Even if I "got away with it," I would end up having a fitful sleep, plagued by the guilt of not communicating with my parents in the first place, especially if the fear had to do with something I had done wrong.

You may be able to relate to this behavior. Whenever things get too intense for Cynthia, a businesswoman, she says, "I take to my bed." Like clockwork, I know that something's wrong if I call her at 7:30 P.M. and her husband tells me that she's already asleep. Cynthia engages this coping mechanism to avoid what's standing before her. She does this, she admits, even though it has never worked out. Instead, the bills still don't get paid; the deadline doesn't get met; the health problems go unresolved; the conflict with her man, her assistant, or her friend remains in the purgatory of agitation. Sleeping does not lull it away.

Another incredibly accomplished woman uses a different strategy, one that I dare say she's not aware of employing. Veronica complains. When things aren't going well and she's afraid about what's on the horizon, there's obviously something wrong with the world. Somebody else has committed an egregious act upon her. Veronica moans and moans about how life doesn't treat her right. She fires off e-mails complaining about one relationship or another and how the other person obviously doesn't understand her. She gets comfortable in her fabulous home and begins a series of telephone calls, engaging all of her friends who will listen to the litany of sins that someone has committed against her. Veronica blames others instead of directly facing what's going on in her heart. As a result, she misses her own role in her life and her opportunity to change her circumstances.

These are not unusual stories. Nevertheless, some people exercise their ability to choose to step out of the hole that fear has dug for them. A father of three in Seattle found himself overcome by fear during the terrorist attacks in September 2001, sharing the view of countless parents around the country. Although Martin was providing for his family economically as well as spiritually by talking with them and being a solid sounding board, he was struck still by the fear that he couldn't shield his family from harm. During the days and weeks following the disaster, countless families echoed his concerns and often were overcome by a paralyzing fear. After realizing that he was stuck in his fear and that this wouldn't help him or his family in the long run, he decided to go to therapy to deal with his issues. A well-to-do mother of three small children in New Hampshire admitted that after the attacks, she no longer understood why she had even had children. For several weeks, she says, she was held hostage by panic. She kept asking herself, "What kind of life will there be for them?" Not knowing, she decided to quit her job and devote herself full time to nurturing her family to do what she could to make a difference in their lives.

Fear stands at full attention during disasters, and it ferrets into the tiniest crevices where you least expect a challenge. From fear of never having enough money to fear of what the next global disaster will be, fear of losing your job to fear of how your next date will go, fear of what your friends may think about you if you become a huge success to fear of dying, at some point or another most of us have allowed fear to envelop us. Even the toughest among us, at one time or another, have succumbed to its power to stop us in our tracks.

FIGHT FEAR WITH FAITH

IN SPIRITUAL TERMS, fear points to a lack of faith. When one worry after another piles up until you can hardly breathe because of the incredible weight bearing down on you, chances are you have not been taking care of yourself spiritually. The good news is that at any point along the way, at the moment when you realize that you are trapped, you can ask for help. Whether you get down on your knees and pray for guidance out of the hole you've dug for yourself or you chant and meditate, you can take action. What's important is that your action first be inward. A Bible verse illustrates this beautifully: "For God hath not given us the spirit of fears but of power, and of love, and of a sound mind" (II Timothy 1:7).

You must call on your strength when fear stands in your way. It's that power that connects you to God and radiates throughout your entire being that you need at this hour. Nobody can fix your situation for you; even if it appears, for example, that finding a new job will eradicate your fear of losing the one you just had, don't be fooled. And, as the old folks will often tell you, trading one spouse in for another only gives you a different set of problems.

What you must do is call on your spiritual reserves to fight this battle. In times when you notice that fear or anxiety is beginning to encroach on you, pay attention. Rather than giving in to the fear, consciously replace the anxiety in your mind with calming, grounding energy. Ask yourself what you can learn from what's happening to you now; look for the value in the experience.

How do you measure your life's experiences? Can you tap into the inner strength that will sustain you through tough times? Are you willing to let go of the way that you have been considering a challenge that's before you so that you will be able to find another way? Once you have carefully considered what's before you, you may want to confide your feelings with someone you trust, perhaps an elder who can shed some personal wisdom on your situation.

When I started my business in 1995, I was filled with excitement *and* fear. I had a big plan, and I was carrying it out, but I didn't know if it would work out. Although everyone in my family is successful in one way or another, no one is an entrepreneur. How would I make it? On faith, I started *profundities, inc.,* which is a personal coaching, style, and literary production company focused primarily on helping others discover how to be their best selves.

Things went exceptionally well for quite some time. Then there was a period when I didn't know if I would be able to pay my bills from month to month. I had several employees, New York City commercial rent, phone bills, and more. I got so worried that I started having nightmares. I didn't know what I was going to do. It was just too much! I did pray and work to wrestle down my fears, but nothing seemed to be working.

Here is what actually happened. Every month, just before I had to pay my bills, one of my clients would pay an outstanding invoice. In the middle of the month, whenever I was wondering how I could possibly make ends meet, I would get a call about a new project. After a while, I began to see I was wasting unnecessary energy by worrying. Since everything seemed to work out, I felt validated that I was indeed doing the work that I was meant to do. I figured I could use my energy better by planning and nurturing my business, and I began to replace fear with planning.

The fuel for my planning was an equal mixture of faith and courage. I had to believe what I already knew: that I would be okay. I had to muster up the courage to take action and use my creativity to support my vision. I came to see that my willingness to choose abundance and prosper in my work was a much more fulfilling action than being crippled by fear. I believe that I was able to climb out of my hole because eventually I had to turn inside and call on my faith. My friends and colleagues in whom I had confided hadn't done it for me. Their words had been encouraging, but I never quite got the confidence boost I needed from them. It took my own effort and focus to recognize the movement of grace in my life. You can't learn a lesson until you are open to receive it.

COMMUNICATE YOUR FEAR

AS WELL MEANING as people can be, if you are not in a position to accept wisdom that's coming your way, it will not seep in. A fellow who was attempting to talk a friend out of her increased fear of flying after the terrorist attacks sent her an e-mail imploring her not to give in to her fear. Stanley pointed out that fear is rooted in ego and that she has the power to hurl that ego away and be courageous. Boy, did he hit a nerve! The very mention of ego is a trigger for many people. It suggests arrogance and disconnection from one's source of goodness and stability. Meryl interpreted his poorly timed suggestion as cold-hearted and insensitive. Instead of being able to consider objectively what Stanley was offering to her, Meryl rejected it and him with the conclusion that the two of them simply spoke two different languages. Both were probably right.

Let's consider their situation. First, *ego* is not a bad word or a horrible judgment passed upon another. It is simply an aspect of human nature that holds onto and gets trapped in delusional thinking. The ego is the manipulative power of the mind that latches onto external forces, situations, and relationships and then uses those things to create comparisons and definitions for one's Self. The ego is the fuel that fires up fear, ever ready to stoke the flames of disillusion and confusion. For this man to recommend that his distraught friend break free of the stranglehold that fear had on her was probably intended as an act of kindness, but because his timing and tone were off, and they don't communicate using the same spiritual worldview to define their perceptions and feelings, his offering didn't serve its purpose. She could not hear what he was trying to say: that she was strong enough to overcome any negativity that stood before her, and he was unable to find the words that would either comfort her or illuminate his message so that Meryl would feel affirmed.

For these two, the potential reasons for the lack of understanding are apparent. Sometimes it's not that simple. Even when people do share a worldview, the one caught up in the turmoil of emotion may not be able to hear the call of reason. The isolation that often walls us in during moments of spiritual crisis can prevent even the most understanding and compassionate among us from getting a rope to the one wallowing in the depths of the well. That's why it is essential for the one who is suffering to search within for spiritual renewal and for an openness to communicate the nature of his or her deepest inhibitions.

ANALYZE YOUR FEAR

GETTING TO THE BOTTOM of what you are afraid of can be tough. Usually there's more than one thing on the list. I recommend that you categorize your fears to figure out which are legitimate and which are imaginary. All of your fears warrant attention. You may want to use these steps to identify what is troubling you and face them so that you can move on:

• Ask yourself what you are most afraid of.

• What's the worst that could happen?

• Compare the worst-case scenario as it relates to your fear to the concrete way that you know things actually are, so that you can rediscover reality.

• The more you concentrate on what you know or the way things actually are, the more you will be able to focus and think about reality.

• As you are standing face to face with your fears, stay on schedule. Don't allow yourself to get stuck to the point where you cannot function. Keep your daily routine, relying especially on your spiritual practice.

SOOTHE YOUR FEAR

AN EFFECTIVE WAY of going about the search to be freed of your fears is becoming quiet. When reaching out to others for support and guidance begins to be more frustrating than rewarding, stop reaching out. When the answers that you feel you need are not being reflected back at you, turn the mirror on yourself. Be still. Be quiet. Turn off the TV. Hang up the phone. Tune out any other distractions. Take a walk outside. Soak in a warm bath. Allow your true Self to come to your aid. At first this may feel strange, especially if you are prone to avoiding your issues by keeping yourself busy. Be patient and vigilant. Being alone can be delightful once you relax into you. Think about it like this: What do your friends enjoy about your company? What benefits do others gain from connecting with you? Those very qualities can satisfy you as well. Bask in your own Self. Enjoy the great person who is you!

If this sounds good to you and you could use some help in accessing that great place within yourself, here are some tips to guide you inside:

- Take a deep breath in, allowing the life-giving oxygen to fill your body, expanding your chest, your lungs, and your entire torso. Breathe out slowly, giving back to the universe the blessing of life that it is giving you. Take a few more deep breaths as you settle into your own power.

- Stand up. Plant your feet firmly on the floor, hip-width apart.

- Stretch your body by reaching your hands above your head as you inhale, engaging all of the muscles in your arms and legs, stretching and elongating your body at once up toward the sky and down into the earth as you invigorate it. As you exhale, allow your hands to return to your sides.

- With feet hip-width apart and parallel, gently swing your arms and your torso from side to side, breathing naturally with each twist. Feel your body release its tension as you twist. Return to center.

- On the in-breath, once again reach up to the sky and then, on the out-breath, bend over, allowing your hands to touch the floor. Hang there for a few seconds, breathing naturally.

- On the in-breath, elongate your torso, and on the out-breath, bend over farther, allowing your hands to touch more of the floor. (If you need to bend your knees during this exercise, do so. It should not hurt. Instead, you should feel a gentle stretch.)

- Bring your hands to your hip creases, and with a deep inhalation, return to an upright posture.

How do you feel? You have just performed very simple hatha yoga asanas, or postures, that help you to relax into yourself. If you know other relaxation exercises, you may do them now. Or you may want to sit and meditate for a few minutes. Sit in a comfortable, cross-legged posture or on a chair with your feet flat on the floor. Your spine should be gently elongated, and your eyes closed. Use your breath as your guide inside. Be the observer of your breath. Watch as it comes in and goes out naturally. As thoughts arise, return your focus to your breath.

You can contact your own inner source of power. That power which belongs to you is divine and is always present. That is the power that will support you. It can replace your fears with strength. What you must do is choose to connect with that power. As you do, you will begin to see that you have the capability to manage with grace and dignity any challenge that comes your way. No matter how simple or grave the task at hand is, it is possible to find your own inner wisdom through meditation, self-inquiry, and consistent pursuit of your true nature, practices that empower you to act responsibly and consciously. To get to this place of strength, you must believe in your power and embrace it.

UNEARTHING FEARS

SOME FEARS are not as obvious as others. Sometimes we have to peel back many layers of experience in order to get to the core issues that are standing in the way of our progress.

The Fear of Greatness

Nelson Mandela spoke about fear and its deeper meaning in our lives when he was freed from prison in South Africa after twenty-seven years as a political prisoner. In his inaugural address as President of South Africa, he said:

> Our deepest fear is not that we are inadequate.
> Our deepest fear is that we are powerful beyond measure. It is our light, not our darkness, that most frightens us.
> We ask ourselves, who am I to be brilliant, gorgeous, talented and fabulous? Actually, who are you not to be?
> Your playing small doesn't serve the world. There's nothing enlightened about shrinking so that other people won't feel insecure around you.
> We were born to make manifest the glory that is within us. It's not just in some of us: it's in everyone. And as we let our own light shine, we unconsciously give other people permission to do the same. As we are liberated from our own fear, our presence automatically liberates others.

I have contemplated these words many times since Mandela uttered them in 1994. Mandela speaks to a side of fear that many of us don't consciously realize we have. What would it be like if each of us stood confidently in our own light? The Bible says: "The Lord is my light and my salvation; whom shall I fear? The Lord is the strength of my life; of whom shall I be afraid?" (Psalm 27:1). What would it be like if we let the light of God that blazes within us shine out and over every aspect of our lives? What would we then see? There would be moments of triumph and clarity as well as situations that require repair and tending. There would be huge obstacles to overcome just as there would be exquisite treasures to enjoy. By shining our own inner light on our lives and looking at what is revealed without judgment or apprehension, we would have the opportunity to see how we want to live our lives and what choices we need to make to get where we want to go. Further, our willingness to welcome our greatness would inspire others to step into their own power.

Fear of Being Alone

Take a moment and envision yourself feeling strong. Your body is fortified from the inside out. Your mind is calm. Your breath is even. You feel confident and connected to your inner power. As you look around, you notice that you are standing in your own light, in a pool of warm light that is emanating from your own being. This light allows you to see the world accurately—those things that are nearby as well as those far off in the distance. You can see what you're facing because the light has brought it into your awareness. Imagine for a moment that this light has revealed one of your deepest fears, like the fear of spending your life alone, without a partner. As you look at this fear, you see that it does not define you. You are not the same as your fear of being alone—or whatever else your fear is. You are an incredible being, bathed in the cleansing light of your own soul.

With strength and detachment, look at this fear. What do you see? What kinds of choices have you made in your life that have been driven by this fear? Have you allowed yourself to stay in unhealthy relationships after you knew you should leave? Have you avoided true intimacy with a potential partner because you believed that the person would eventually abandon you? Have you become supercritical of every suitor instead of giving the person an honest chance? Have you accumulated a treasure trove of secret wealth that you stash in case you have to care for yourself alone? Have you belittled suitors who have had fewer material possessions than you? Have you doubted your beauty, your intelligence, or your creativity when you have been rejected? Have you chosen not to pursue your full potential in order to be attractive to a potential life partner? Have you sought a friend's partner because you couldn't find one for yourself? Have you been clingy with every partner that you've had, hanging onto the person for dear life, subordinating your personal needs and values for the sake of having a date? Have you consistently had multiple partners to ensure that you will never be without one? Have you stayed isolated from the rest of the population so that you have no opportunity to meet anyone? What have you done that is contributing to your being alone?

Fear of Love

I want to tell you about a handsome fellow who has spent most of his adult years chasing skirts. He has gone from one beautiful woman to another, wooing her until she is totally in love. One such woman was a student from France who was going to college in the United States when they met. For them both, it was love at first sight. Neither could bear to be separated from the other for more than a day at a time. When she called her family abroad, he was right there talking to them about how much he adored their daughter.

A few months into their relationship—which, by the way, did not exclude him from seeing the occasional woman on the side—the French family came to visit their daughter. Finally, they would get to meet her knight in shining armor. The only problem was that the fellow got cold feet. All of a sudden, the relationship had become far too real, and so instead of meeting her and her family for dinner, he disappeared. He didn't resurface again until the family was safely back in France. What was his fear? His closest friends who have seen him play out similar scenarios year after year suggest that his parents abandoned him at a young age, and he never has come to terms with his fear of abandonment. His efforts to get women to love him work, but his fear of having them leave him always seems to stop him just before he crosses the threshold of allowing himself a committed, loving relationship. His misleading actions leave behind trails of broken-hearted women who can't begin to understand what they did wrong.

Only when you are willing to face your own actions that have fueled your fears will you be able to neutralize them and move on. You know the saying that history repeats itself. I believe that this happens because we don't learn the lessons that life is working overtime to teach us. Why not look at your fears as opportunities for growth? Whether you are afraid to be alone or have other fears, such as not having enough money to survive, not being attractive, not being smart enough, or being considered arrogant because you are smart, know that you can look at this issue in a different way. When you face the fear from a space of strength and conviction, you can review how you have handled the situation in the past instead of falling into old patterns. You can evaluate your previous actions and assess what worked for you and what didn't. Pay attention in each moment—as a witness to your life—to notice the dynamics at work and filter out the beneficial from the destructive.

RELEASE YOUR FEAR

CONSIDER A NEW APPROACH—that of being gentle. Starting with yourself, imagine what it would feel like to give yourself a break. Instead of beating yourself up about something that you didn't handle well, something that is completely out of your control, or something that remains out of reach, be kind to yourself. Whatever happened or is in the midst of happening, choose to address it with the tenderest approach you can muster. You can express your great love for yourself by engaging your willingness to stop for just a little while to reexamine the situation. Remind yourself that you are inherently good and that your deep-down interest is in finding a way to live in true happiness. Hug yourself— literally—and tell yourself just how much you love you as you are right now with whatever flaws and obstacles you are facing. Next, look at your other relationships—with your physical space, your family, your coworkers, lovers, friends, and enemies—with a gentle heart. Ask for the vision to look on every aspect of your life through the prism of that soft golden light that continues to emanate from your being. Practice gentleness. Coupled with courage, it will reduce and then eliminate the fear that once crippled you. Practicing gentleness in each moment will enable you to rise above your fears, to see them dissolve, and to act out of love for yourself and others.

THE COMPANY OF A BEAST

I WAS TRAVELING in Zimbabwe some years ago on a project for *Essence* magazine. Our group had just gotten off a boat, and we were headed to a building that was not far off. The photographer with whom I was working suggested that we have a bit of an adventure. Rather than walking along the cleared path, he recommended that we travel through the thicket that was just to the right of us and still on course with our destination. I was game. And I was fearless—in nature, no less. I trusted Dwight and was also feeling a deep trust resonate from within, which made me feel confident that I would be protected.

We took off. Along the way, each of us noticed different things. There were the unusual bushes that we don't have back home. A sense of peace hung in the air and hushed us as we walked along. We walked with eyes wide open, seeing the wonder of nature with each step. At a certain point, I had the sensation both that I should be still and that I should look to my right. Dwight was some distance away. As I stopped walking and turned my head, I saw a most unusual sight. A wild boar was standing very nearby, grazing in the bush. He had gnarled horns, strong legs, and a benign-looking face. He was big. Perhaps sensing my discovery, Dwight turned around and instantly was at my side. For the briefest of moments, we continued to look at the magnificent beast, and then Dwight gestured for us to move on.

As we charted our course out of the bush, I was faced with something that has plagued me in the past. How was I going to allow my state to be from then on? I had been afraid of animals for years. Dogs usually sensed this and sniffed my heels with greater vigor than others nearby me. Cats sometimes hissed or made an extra-special effort to rub up on me—both of which made my skin crawl. I knew that if I demonstrated fear when in the company of the boar, even on the subtlest level, that we could be in danger. We had been warned about the ferociousness of these wild animals. They had been known to horn people in the bush. "Oh, how foolish," I thought. "We should have stayed on the man-made path. Why did we have to chart our own course?" As I briefly pondered various awful scenarios while still walking, I recognized in that moment that I was in a great state—one of wonder, respect, and gratitude. Dwight and I had had the courage to go on our own adventure, to clear our own path through that particular stretch of earth and time, and we had made an awesome discovery. We had been in the company of one of God's animals who allowed us to be very close, to witness its power and beauty. This boar had trusted us as we had trusted him, and so we could enjoy a peaceful moment together.

Your Journal

Dearest Friend,

It is natural to experience fear. There is nothing wrong with you when you notice fear welling up within. Instead of acquiescing, you can face it. God does not give you any challenge that is too great for you to handle. Remember this as you look at your life. Have the courage to examine everything in your life, including the things that make you afraid. Now's the time to go for it!

> *I love you,*
> *Me*

YOUR JOURNAL ASSIGNMENT for this chapter is several-fold:

- *Examine your life carefully to see what your fears are.* Make a list of the things that come to mind as real fears—no matter how small or large they may be.

- *Look at the impact of each of your fears on your life.* Be specific as you write down your findings. No matter how silly or painful your revelations may be, write them down.

- *Ask yourself what lessons you can learn from the fears that have been in your life.* What wisdom is emerging from these situations that have been so uncomfortable in the past?

- *How can you engage gentleness to relieve you of your constriction?*

- *Write down the inspiration that comes up for you.*

- *Sit quietly for a few minutes with your eyes closed.* Take several deep breaths, inviting the air to enter your body fully, expanding your lungs out toward the universe, and slowly introducing the air back from whence it came. As you sit, ask your heart for its wisdom. Ask for the inner guidance to tell you how you can break free from the fears that have been plaguing you. Be still, and listen for the answers.

- *Begin to write whatever this meditation has revealed.* Don't censor your words. Just record your inspiration.

- *Review your journal to see what wisdom has come from your heart.*

6

LEARN TO LISTEN

ONE OF THE FIRST THINGS that we learn as children is how to listen—or it's one of the first things we are *told* to do. Listen to your parents. Listen to your teachers. Stop, look, and listen for traffic before crossing the street.

Even as children, there's a question as to how often *we actually* listen. Why else would parents end up raising their voices at their children about the same things over and over again? Perhaps there's a part of human nature that rejects direction from others, and that also shuns slowing down long enough even when the result means you can fully assess what's going on. For sure, many of us fall prey to haste, which keeps us from absorbing what's right before us. Why? Why would we do that? As children, it may be a combination of learning the discipline of focusing, something that takes time and practice to master, as well as a quest for independence—that need to assert ourselves separately from our parents as we develop. And for adults? It may be a prolonged version of the same: the "I know best" syndrome that is possibly masking a deeper question about what we really know at all.

EXAMINING LISTENING

As people who are committed to discovering how to live the best life possible, we must examine our understanding of listening so that we can use this tool wisely in our daily lives. It is our choice and responsibility to do so.

A Year of Silence

A young man made a conscious choice not to speak for one full year. At the end of the 365 days, his first words were from Shakespeare, "To thine own self be true." He explained that the exercise of self-restraint proved incredibly fruitful. He discovered that he was able to pay much closer attention to everything that was happening around him. His observations showed him specifics about what individual people need to feel happy as well as how to take care of himself and others in different situations, and how to understand better what was actually needed in a situation before acting. He described his exercise as particularly beneficial because he discovered that by simply being still for a short time, he was better able to approach a situation in a manner that would yield optimum results for everyone. There was no need for being selfish.

A Man of Few Words

Listen. This is a basic requirement of daily life, yet so many of us don't do it. I remember my Uncle Henry, born and reared in Bumpass, Virginia, a small farm town where people still move at a more relaxed pace than those of us who live in cities. Even after Uncle Henry had lived in Baltimore for many years, he maintained his laid-back way of being. That included his way of observing the world. Uncle Henry watched and listened. He was a man of few words, which made the words he uttered that much more measurable. By paying attention to others and really listening to what they said and what their body language revealed, he was able to comfort and guide all of us time and again.

My recollection of Uncle Henry is that he was a compassionate man. He noticed what inspired my sisters and me when we were little girls and would gently encourage us. When he and my father's sister, Aunt Audrey, who had an enormous amount of energy matched by ideas, had discussions, invariably Uncle Henry would listen as Aunt Audrey, our godmother, wound her way around a subject. Only when the timing was right would he add his opinion to the mix. He used silence effectively and kindly, allowing the wisdom he gained from listening to support the situation on all sides.

Follow the Conductor

I am reminded of a time when I was sitting in a meditation hall with a large group of people. We were all chanting a beautiful prayer in a call-and-response fashion. The musicians who were leading us had exquisite voices, and they were singing in perfect unison. The rest of us were following, but we weren't really paying attention, not as a unit anyhow. What happened became a great lesson for me. The lead group sang with the most beautiful unified sound. The response group sang discordantly, with some following the conductor and others following their memory of how the prayer used to sound before. The result was no harmony.

At first, I too was singing along as if I knew the music and its pacing. I had watched the conductor for a few notes and then settled into myself, closed my eyes, and just sang. Then I noticed that something was wrong. At first, I thought, "Oh, somebody's off," never imagining that it could be me. After a few rounds with the same off notes and timing, I opened my eyes and watched the conductor. It was then that I saw just how off I had been. Way off. And so I had to make a choice. The only legitimate choice was to follow the conductor, and this was excruciatingly difficult. There was a sea of other singers, most of whom were not following the conductor. And so I had to go against the grain, against the huge wave of voices singing at their own pace or somewhere in between. In order to stay focused and follow the conductor to be in tune with the musicians and, in turn, honor the music, I had to choose to offer my full attention in each moment. I had to keep an outer focus in order to allow the inner focus to emerge out of a pure and resonant space.

This exercise revealed how tough it can be to stay your course when others around you are not. I thought of work situations and how difficult it can feel to live a spiritual life in the company of others who do not share your views. I remembered times when I just gave in rather than continuing on the course that was clearly the one to follow. I renewed my commitment that afternoon to keeping my focus so that I would truly be able to hear the flow of sounds before me and be as one with that energy.

THE QUESTION BEHIND THE QUESTION

HAVE YOU EVER BEEN in a conversation with someone when you knew that there was something greater going on beneath the surface—that even though the person was asking you one thing, it was clear that some other type of information was wanted? When you understood that other information was being sought, you knew to deal with that topic. When you were unclear, chances are your communication never reached a comfortable conclusion.

This is where true listening comes in. Very few people speak directly about everything, and rarely about topics that they find sensitive or challenging. Sometimes, due to cultural differences, shyness, or ineffective communication, they don't know how to get to the point in a timely manner. Therein lies the value of listening beyond the actual words that are being spoken. As you talk with another person, do a quick assessment to determine what the person may want from you and how you can be of help—or if you choose to be. For example, an employee who is planning to come to work late may ask an employer what time he will be in the office on Monday. What the employee really wants to know is if he has the grace period of an hour or two before he gets docked for coming in late.

My sister Susan is great for getting to the point quickly. She has razor-sharp vision when it comes to looking for the question behind the question. She also is a stickler for her privacy, so she listens carefully to determine what questions she will answer. Invariably if someone asks her, "What are you doing tonight?" or some version thereof, she will respond, "What would you like to know?" Then it's up to the person doing the asking to come forth with the true question, which may be, "Can I call you later?" or "Can I come to visit?" Because Susan is so incisive, she has trained her friends and family to be more specific when we communicate with her. I find that I think more critically about what my intentions are when I am planning to be in her company so that we will end up having an uplifting exchange.

I used to think that Susan's insistence on clarity was infuriating. I have since learned that it is efficient. Essentially, when you ask the question that you truly want answered in a timely and sensitive yet straightforward way, your chances for reaching a mutually satisfying conclusion increase. And when you listen for the real question that someone is asking you and ask for clarification when you are unsure, you will save everybody time analyzing the next step. Be mindful as you practice each side of this mode of communicating that you remain conscious of both of your needs as well as the requirements of the situation at hand. Getting to the point efficiently does not call for being abrupt or unfeeling about the other person's way of communicating. Compassion and patience are essential ingredients too.

FILTER WHAT YOU LET IN

THE WORLD is filled with sounds. Cities throb with the sounds of voices, automobiles, music, footsteps, and more. The countryside sings with the music of animals, plants, and the occasional vehicle. On any given day, you are faced with a cacophony of sounds that you must decipher, accept, or reject. You have a choice as to what you allow in.

It's important to be mindful of what you allow to reach your senses. When it comes to hearing, you have to be vigilant. Infants who hear profanity all day repeat it as their first words. Children who listen to parents speak to them abusively grow up to do the same. People who watch and listen to violent movies often begin to imagine that danger will come their way. But people who choose their words wisely in an effort to uplift others assist listeners in pursuing their goals. And those who practice selective listening set their attention on hearing the positive. They choose not to dwell on what will bring them down.

There are some strategies that you can use to support selective listening:

- *Choose environments that are positive*—for your home, your work, your spiritual sanctuary, your friendships.

- *Avoid putting yourself in situations that are debilitating.* This means you can get off the phone when somebody begins to drone on negatively about others. You can change your job if what you hear every day begins to convince you that you are unworthy of success.

- *Be selective* as you watch television, videos, movies, and plays. You can choose to turn violent images off.

- *Tune people out.* Sometimes you can't leave a situation, but that doesn't mean that you have to take in the barrage of information that others may be hurling your way. Focus on your breath instead of getting caught up in a negative conversation. Concentrate on your work, and tune your ears toward that. Turn on some music that will drown out the sound.

TIME OUT

YOU CAN ALSO ENJOY peace within yourself and by yourself. This can be a hard concept to grasp and accept, yet when we do experience moments, however brief, of savoring our own company and hearing the messages that our own Self wants to share with us, it is glorious. This is true even when it takes seeming exile for us to get to this sequestered state.

I learned about the concept of time out when my sister Stephanie's children started to grow up. When a child misbehaves repeatedly and refuses to follow directions, time-out is called: for a specified period that varies depending on the age and temperament of the child, he or she must sit alone to contemplate what happened.

Interestingly enough, I've learned that some children relish this form of discipline after the initial embarrassment of being called out on a misdeed. That's not to say that a child prefers time-out, only that a good experience can come of it.

I mention this practice, because I think adults can use it too. What do you do when you have made a mistake? Do you call up the friends who will commiserate with you? Do you engage those who will be on your side? Or do you take time out to be alone in the comfort of your own space to review what happened? Do you take time out for yourself to be with your Self?

One of the most essential components of Choosing Truth is choosing your Self. You have to make the conscious choice to get to know the true you. How do you think about things? What means do you use to evaluate your thoughts, words, and deeds? How do you spend your time? Do you consider yourself good company? Do you listen for your own wisdom? Too often people don't think about these things at all, but you can and must. When you take time out to nurture yourself, mend yourself, and take care of your needs, you will benefit, as will all of the people in your life. We do not live in a vacuum. What we do affects those around us. In order to control our thoughts, words, and deeds, we need to be aware of what they are and what their impact is on us and others. Taking time out to review what we do makes it possible for us to understand the impact of our lives on the rest of the world.

Just like children who are given the opportunity—rather than punishment—of being alone to review their actions, you have to make your time alone count. As compelling as distractions may be, don't give in to them. You know what draws your attention away from your focus better than anybody else. Some of the more common activities that I've discovered as I have surveyed people are watching television, listening to music with engaging lyrics, playing dress-up, daydreaming, and napping. Rather than letting your precious time slip by, capture it. Cherish your time out as a period so precious that you want every moment to count. You can use it to meditate, write in your journal, do some stretching exercises, or do some deep breathing. Find the activity that best suits you. Then listen to hear what your inner wisdom guides you to do next.

WELCOME SOLITUDE

FRIENDS I'VE KNOWN for many years moved from New York to Minneapolis some time ago. Their life in Manhattan had been dynamic and fulfilling, yet as they thought about their future, they decided to stake a claim in a town that had been listed as one of the most promising metropolises for the new millennium. I visited them after they had been living in Minneapolis for about ten years. They had purchased and renovated a large loft space and had created a comfortable and creative living-working space for themselves. While I was visiting, Janice explained to me how satisfying their lives had become. Art and cultural opportunities abounded, and they took advantage of them at every possible turn. Work was lucrative, and the town had a stillness to it that was refreshing for New Yorkers. Jan and John had struck a balance between the hustle and bustle of the Big Apple and the peacefulness of what was still a largely agricultural state. They enjoyed their calm. Yet they still needed a bit of noise from time to time. That's why, Jan explained, they put their bedroom next to two large windows that opened onto a fairly busy street. She said that the sound of cars moving on asphalt actually lulled them to sleep. I chuckled with acknowledgment. It's also hard for me to sleep if things are too quiet.

Below the surface of Jan's revelation was a deeper meaning that I stumbled on after we left one another: you can choose what you will allow into your ear space. You can select particular sounds, like the constant motion of cars, the soothing syllables of a lullaby or a mantra, or the sound of silence.

LISTEN TO YOUR INNER VOICE

HOW MANY TIMES have you been told to trust your instincts? Consider how many times you have given others that advice. It's easy to direct others to healthy action, but not always so easy to direct ourselves. The idea of walking the talk is the nature of choosing Truth. You must envision it, fine-tune your sensibilities to its internal radar screen, and then consciously take steps to walk in the path of that vision. This requires tremendous self-discipline. These days self-discipline is not applauded or taught as it once was. We live in an age when reckless, erratic behavior is celebrated. Just look at 90 percent of the popular films, music, and television programs available globally. Bad deeds make news. "Sinful" action is the stuff of movies and soap operas. Forgiveness takes on a whole new meaning in this context, in that people aren't even actually seeking forgiveness as much as they just think it's fine to push past any unconscious deeds from their past to future options.

Unconscious action will never lead you to Truth. We must be aware of what we are thinking, what our inner voice is telling us, how we are articulating our thoughts and making them manifest through our actions. It may seem like a lot of work, but it isn't, at least not after you get the hang of it. You must learn to honor your instincts by listening to the voice inside. Learn to heed its message. I can't count how many people have given that advice to others in the course of any given day. What about you? Do you give this advice to yourself? Do you heed it? How do you know when it's that divine voice within rather than your ego talking?

At first, you may not know the difference. I didn't. The exercise I began to practice was to listen to every message that came bubbling forth from within—to stop for a moment and consider the message. One of the most common and miraculous examples I can give is a message I have received occasionally just as I'm about to leave my home: "Pick up the umbrella." Sometimes as I am leaving, my eyes will pass over an umbrella for no more than a second. In that flash, the voice speaks: "Take the umbrella." I admit that I have not listened at least half of the time. Yet nearly every time I get that message, it rains. Even more interesting is the variety of ways that I have responded to that simple command. If I listen and act in the moment, I'm fine. I stop for a brief moment to pick up the umbrella and put it in my bag. Then whenever I walk out the door, the umbrella is with me, because I have consciously placed it with my traveling things. If I say to myself, "I will pick up the umbrella in a moment, after I do this or that . . ." I often forget. Seizing the moment is key here. Is that difficult? No.

How long does it take to pause and fulfill the task of picking up an umbrella and putting it in your bag? Chances are the longest it will take is a couple of minutes, and that's if you have to find it first! The cost of not taking that simple action in the moment may be getting drenched, spending unnecessary money for an emergency umbrella, or being delayed as you wait for the rain to stop. The penalty for ignoring the inner voice is tremendous. It's much simpler and easier to heed it at the moment when it speaks.

Here's another example. I was working on a project in the Hamptons on Long Island in New York. The project was action packed and required all of my focus and attention. As I was preparing to go to a morning meeting, I looked around to see what I would need to bring with me, since I wasn't sure when I would return. I was staying about twenty minutes away from the production site. This particular day was a very warm one in August. As I glanced around the house, I noticed my jacket. My eyes lit on it for a moment. Then rather than picking it up, I said to my husband, "Honey, do you think I need a jacket?" George, whose body temperature always seems to be warmer than mine, said, "No. You should be fine." And so we were off. When we got to the production site and I got out of the car, immediately I regretted my decision. It was about ten degrees cooler there than at our house, and the wind was blowing. I had on a sleeveless top, and I felt chilly. Instantly, I saw my mistake. *A:* I know myself. I know that I must provide for warmth. I do not function well at all when I am the least bit chilly. *B:* My husband and I do not have the same internal thermostats, so there would be no way that he could judge what I needed more accurately than I could judge for myself. *C:* Relying on my husband was giving away my power. *D:* Not listening to the voice inside that showed me my jacket and indicated that I bring it along was foolish, as my unconscious action ended up squandering precious time and energy. Ultimately, I got back in my car and drove the twenty minutes back to my house to pick up my jacket. The mistake of not listening cost me forty minutes of driving, a few dollars of gas, tremendous aggravation, and a delay in the beginning of production on my job. See how expensive it is not to listen?

These were simple examples. Let me pose some tougher ones. Ask yourself any of the questions below that may apply to your life. Write down your answers in your journal honestly and openly. See what your answers reveal:

- Have you ever accepted a job that your instinct told you was wrong for you? If so, what happened?

- Have you ever held onto a friendship long after your intuition told you to cut it off?

- Have you ever been in an intimate relationship when you intuitively knew you should never have crossed the invisible line to sexual intimacy?

- Have you ever made a purchase even after that voice within urged you to reconsider?

- Have you ever agreed to do something that your very being was telling you not to do?

If you answered yes to any of the above questions, follow up by asking yourself what happened to you after you made this unconscious choice. If you are wondering why I am calling it *unconscious,* let me tell you. When we are at one with our own consciousness, we are awake to the subtleties of our lives. We know intuitively how to move forward carefully and with precision. Consciousness is what enlivens us. Being connected to universal consciousness allows us to be at one with our own Selves, with others, and with the world in which we live. When we make choices that hurt others or us, chances are they are in some way unconscious choices. Being able to see the potential outcome of our choices in advance is what fuels our conscious awareness. When we ignore the voice within that is there to guide us and we do something anyway, we usually suffer in one way or another. As you answer the questions above, consider if and how you may have suffered after making a decision that ignored or denied the voice within.

THE HIGH PRICE OF IGNORING YOUR INNER VOICE

IT SEEMS THAT the busier our lives become, the easier it is to ignore the gift of insight that is ours. Slowing down long enough to hear and heed our own message seems impossible sometimes. Chances are, though, that if you revisit situations in your own life where you have not paid attention to your internal base of knowledge, you will want to make a change.

Rebecca shared a powerful story with me of how not listening to her inner voice caused her years of difficulty. In her early twenties, Rebecca married a man she didn't love—at least not as her life partner. She did love this man as her friend, and she believed that he would take care of her, which was what she felt she needed more than anything else. Soon after marrying, Rebecca knew she had made a mistake. The soul connection wasn't there. In the effort to stand by her man, Rebecca made a number of key decisions that would affect her for years. Among them was acquiescing to purchase a piece of property that she thought was a bad decision. Rebecca says the voice inside was screaming at her not to purchase this property—and instead stand up for herself and her own instincts and say no. The voice inside told her that saying no didn't mean that her marriage would be over, but that it simply meant that she didn't agree with the decision to purchase the property. The voice of "reason" told her that she would be "bad" if she didn't do what her husband wanted her to do, especially if she wanted to try to reconcile their differences. Rebecca cosigned on the property. A short while later, Rebecca and her husband split. One of the points of contention during their divorce was the property. Once again, rather than giving up the property that had been an albatross around her neck from the first day they purchased it, out of spite or possibly fear, Rebecca asked to keep the property. The voice inside was still screaming no, but she didn't even hear it. Over the many years since, Rebecca has suffered through one bad tenant after another, rarely receiving her rent on time, if at all. In retrospect, Rebecca says had she listened to her inner voice, she probably wouldn't have married the man in the first place, which would have caused them both far less pain and suffering. Even so, she could have stood up for her beliefs and not agreed to sign her credit over for what felt in her heart like a bad financial deal.

We always have to pay for our mistakes. Amazingly, the voice within is a voice of knowledge. It does have the wisdom to set us straight in the moment. Our job is to listen and heed our own advice.

UNDERSTAND YOUR BOTTOM LINE

A THIRTY-FIVE-YEAR-OLD WOMAN found herself in a bind when she had to break her engagement—the second engagement she had broken in her life. Marsha is a smart woman who knows what she wants. She is professional and attractive, and committed to her spiritual beliefs. She has always wanted to marry a man with whom she can share a spiritual life, someone who will want to go to church with her and be active in their spiritual community. After years of becoming disillusioned, however, Marsha began to think differently.

Marsha explained that she has been active in church ever since she joined a couple of years ago and has been trusting of the congregation. That began to change as male members of her church tried to run games on her just like the men she had met who had no faith at all. One man who wanted to go out with her was married, and another was seeing three other women who all went to church with Marsha. Then one of the ministers in her church struck up a friendship with her. Naturally she trusted that he was well meaning. Reverend Fred wanted help writing a speech, and Marsha was a professional writer. Since she didn't have many real friends in her town yet, she valued the opportunity to be of help and get to know a respected member of her community. That changed when Reverend Fred switched gears on her. He started to talk about sex when they were supposed to be talking about his speech. Next thing you know, he propositioned her about having sex with him—an offer she flatly refused.

Marsha was disillusioned and began to believe that her husband may not end up being a member of her church at all. Shortly after that, she met Doug in an Internet chatroom. Quickly they discovered that they had mutual interests and after a few months decided to meet. The two of got along great despite their ten-year age difference (Marsha was older) and their religious differences. Marsha was Baptist, and Doug was a Jehovah's Witness, although not a practicing one at the time. Within six months, the two had taken several trips together and believed they were in love. Doug proposed. Knowing that there could be trouble down the line because of their religious differences, Marsha requested that they seek premarital counseling before committing to a date.

All was going really well until September 11, 2001. With the disasters at the World Trade Center and the Pentagon, Marsha and Doug became more vigilant in their spiritual practices. One day when the two of them got together, Doug had literature from his Hall out and was heavily engrossed in study. He explained to Marsha that he still loved her, but that he knew now that he had to become more actively involved in his religious life. This was a huge blow for Marsha. She loved Doug and also knew that she wanted a husband who would share her spiritual beliefs—including going to church with her with regularity, observing the holidays that she deemed valuable, rearing their children under the same religion, and so forth. Although Doug pleaded with her, pledging that they could still work things out, Marsha says she knew it was over. "I knew in my heart that I wanted a man who would always be at my side, especially during times of spiritual need. I told myself I didn't mind that he had a different religion at first, because everything else was so great. Even though I knew all along that I wanted to marry a Baptist man who was just like me, I had learned that this didn't always work out, so I figured I could make it work." Ultimately, Marsha said she had to listen to the voice inside that told her that she could not compromise on such an important decision. This didn't mean that she valued Doug less. After all, he was fortifying his spiritual life too, which she greatly respected. It meant that she recognized what her requirements are for a lifetime commitment. Although she is in her mid-thirties, Marsha said, "This relationship was much better than the last one I had, so I'm doing all right. Plus, I believe that God has chosen a perfect partner for me. I just haven't met him yet."

TRUST YOURSELF

AS YOU GO through each day, countless opportunities present themselves for you to make a choice. Just as in politics, there are often lobbyists on either side of a situation arguing their points for and against a particular action. Sometimes the lobbyists are people who verbally and physically work to convince you to do one thing or another. In other instances, the lobbyists are in your mind, like those classic images you have seen of the angel and the devil resting on each of your shoulders. Do you notice them?

Take the giant step of confidence that allows you to trust the voices within. Pay attention so that you can tell the difference between the quick-fix voice of the ego and the intuitive voice of the soul. The soul's message will consistently bring you to a place that is solid and strong. It will not force you to lose friends who are beneficial to your life. It will prompt you to walk away from harmful situations even when the next step is uncertain. It will guide you to your true destiny. Within you rests the knowledge that you need to live an honest and magnificent life. Listen for that knowledge, and let it lead you to your Truth.

My Journal Entry

Dearest Friend,

How often I have listened to the sounds that distract me. Now I want to listen for those sounds that will uplift me and set me on course. I want to honor the voice inside that has wisdom to share with me. I want to hear what people are really trying to tell me. I want to make my body a clear vessel so that I will be able to hear that which will support me in my life as I also work to support others.

I love you,
Me

CULTIVATING THE DISCIPLINE of listening is a great virtue. When you hear what is meant for your ears and understand it, you can be much more effective in your daily life. You can honor time well and care for your own well-being with great ability.

- *When you listen, hold onto the messages that resound for you.* Write them down in your journal so that you can refer to them later. The wisdom may come from a casual conversation with a letter carrier, with a child, across a movie screen, with a colleague, or from your heart.

- *Listen with discrimination.* When you feel respected, open the doors to your heart so that you can hear what is being presented.

- *Be selective about what you allow in so that you can preserve your energy.*

- *Notice unlikely sources who may provide useful information.*

- *Respect your inner voice.* Heed its messages. Take some time in your journal to remember times when you have paid attention to that voice. What happened? What were the results when you ignored your inner wisdom?

- *Take time out to be with yourself.* Listen to the messages that your own heart and soul will reveal.

- *Develop trust in yourself.* Review your life day by day. Notice your choices and the inspiration you had for making them. Give yourself credit when you listened to the knowledge within, as well as to wise advisers, and your choice was valuable.

7

DO YOUR BEST

ISN'T IT FUNNY how the things your parents told you stick in your mind for years to follow? This has certainly been true for me. As I go about my life, I get little reminders of the wisdom that my parents worked to impart to me at the perfect moments. One of these bits of wisdom is the simple phrase: *Do your best.* Both of my parents consistently encouraged us to put our best foot forward, to reach into our inner reserves and offer our greatest ability to every task before us. Whether we received a passing grade or the top marks in class, we were instructed always to put our full effort into the project at hand.

Over the years, I have followed this wisdom. Sometimes I overcompensated, making the supreme effort to be perfect at everything I did, a practice that inevitably backfired. Other times I just strived to give each day my all. I can't say, though, that this was always a conscious activity. More, it was something that was ingrained in me, so I just did it. In my early years, I thought that everybody lived this way, but now I have witnessed all sorts of behavior from people. While some folks work to excel seemingly with their every step, others make an art form out of expending the least amount of effort possible to get by. If you choose to be so efficient in your life that you do not waste energy, you can accomplish more. If you waste time by slacking off, you're hurting both yourself and those you may be required to serve. Aside from the people who are basically lazy, there are people who choose to attach themselves at the hip to others, allowing unknowing victims to carry their weight by handling their business for them. It can be argued that all of these people are doing their best in the moment. Maybe that's how they were taught to succeed, or it's the only way that they have figured out to get ahead. In these instances, however, the best may be a complete compromise from what excellence is. This may be why educators sometimes grade on a curve. They consider the "best" to be relative to the actions of others. Yet people who are seeking to live an honest and fulfilling life cannot measure their effort in relation to others.

MAKE THE COMMITMENT

TO DO YOUR BEST, you must engage your full effort—mental, physical, and spiritual. But what happens if other people don't share this view? How can you stay strong when slackers abound, or melancholy sets in, or some other distraction gets in the way? Here's where the discipline of keeping good company comes in.

When I worked at *Essence* magazine, there was a period when some of the staff were suffering from low morale, a condition that happens periodically in any organization. During that time, my team was busy working on the lifestyle section of the magazine, figuring out ways to celebrate the many modes of living that African-American people enjoy. Because I was leading a team, it was my responsibility to find a way to lead us all into a brighter, more positive mind-set. Through this period of growth and conflict, I looked for allies. One of my greatest allies was my friend Jonell Nash, the food editor. She and I worked together and supported each other through the various ups and downs that we faced. One evening as we looked over our work, we questioned how effective we were in that moment as well as what we could become in the future. We reminded each other of the lessons our parents had taught us when we were growing up. And then we had an inspiration. We agreed that we would make a pledge. Right then and there Jonell wrote down the fruit of our inspiration: *To do all that I can do—to be the best that I can be. (Otherwise, what's the point?)* That evening the two of us giggled at ourselves, at our acknowledgment of the obvious. Why else do we live on this beautiful planet, if not to offer it our very best? Refreshed, we completed our work and went home.

I never threw that little piece of paper away. It rested on my desk as a reminder, and as I moved my business from one location to the next, it got tucked away. When I began writing this chapter, it resurfaced. How apropos! What would be the point of a human life if we didn't treasure the gifts that we have been given and use them to their fullest?

LOVE GOD

I REMEMBER talking to my grandmother on the occasion of her hundredth birthday about the meaning of life and the possibility for happiness in a world that seemed to have gone bad. I was searching for answers. I knew that there was a greater purpose in life than treading water in a sea of despair. When I asked Little Grandma about the desperate state of the world, she said, "The problem is that they are not loving God. When you love God, everything will be fine. What you have to do is love God." Clearly she had done this in her own way. It didn't matter that she had retired only a few years earlier or that she hadn't enjoyed some of the luxuries that other people have experienced. Little Grandma had a fantastic life filled with joy and love. She meditated every day, sitting in her rocking chair holding silent communion with the Lord. Carrie Freeland knew God. As far as she was concerned, the only way to do your best was to place yourself in God's bosom and trust that you will be guided to fulfill your destiny. She firmly believed that happiness is ours for the taking, because it is a gift from God.

A woman from Des Moines, Iowa, says that during her childhood, she learned the value of doing her best when she had to do chores. "If I didn't do them right, I learned that I would have to do them over again," DeLora explains. She remembers dusting one day without paying attention. When her mother spotted her, she said, "Dust like you are dusting for Jesus." At first, DeLora thought this was funny. In her ten-year-old mind, she couldn't see how Jesus would be paying any attention to the dusting at her house, but now she understands. DeLora says that every task that her family did had to be approached correctly. When her father taught her how to cut the hedges, he pointed out the importance of seeing whether they were cut evenly. When snow had to be shoveled from the driveway, everybody pitched in—including DeLora with her little blue child's shovel—and made sure that no snow was left that could turn to ice and cause someone to slip.

As an adult, DeLora realizes how grateful she is for the training that she received from her parents, which has translated into every aspect of her life. She has learned to pay attention to all of the little things that go into a task, and this level of scrutiny has helped her to be good at whatever she does. Even more, her understanding of doing her work, whatever it is, for God has given her a spiritual grounding that is quite satisfying. "I realize that God does see everything." She is proud that what everyone sees, including herself, is a job well done.

SEE THE BEST IN YOURSELF AND OTHERS

HOW DO YOU share love and do your best with others? Common ways are with hugs and kisses, sweet smiles, and kind words. Completing responsibilities in a timely and efficient fashion is another way of demonstrating love. When you're feeling great, it's easy to exude love that others can experience just by being in your presence.

It's possible to do that all the time. It's just a question of attitude and perspective. We are all manifestations of God—every single one of us. By adopting the attitude of seeing the light of God in ourselves and in others, we can live in a perpetual state of joy regardless of what's going on around us. The Siddha Yoga Meditation master Baba Muktananda urged us to "See God in Each Other." Look beyond the surface of people—their attire, their hair style, their occupation, their status in the community, even their relationship to us individually. Look instead into their hearts. Believe that within each person, the light of God burns brightly. Rather than getting stuck on a distraction that can sidetrack us into judging others, we can choose to see that light and honor it. When I first heard this principle, I thought it was a pretty lofty goal, one that I might be able to live up to in my old age but certainly not at that time when I was grappling with all sorts of contrary people. I figured it was a goal reserved for "full-time spiritual people." Over time, I discovered that I could employ this attitude myself and, more, that I too am a full-time spiritual person.

I began to put into practice seeing God in each other. The tests came immediately. One day, I saw a young boy who lives in my building in Harlem. As I was approaching the entrance, I noticed that he was urinating on the iron doorway. I was aghast. My first thought was, "How gross! He has no home training. He shouldn't be allowed to live in this building. And where is his mama anyway?!" I slowed down and remembered to breathe and collect my thoughts before speaking to him. In those few moments, I allowed a few other thoughts. What could be the reason that he would resort to such an action at the entrance to his home? Because I know him, I decided to speak with him. I said, "Paul, what are you doing?" He responded, telling me that he was going to the bathroom. I said, "But this is not the bathroom. Why don't you go inside your home?" He responded, "I won't be allowed back outside if I go inside at all today, so I have to go here." My anger turned to sympathy. This little boy was doing all that he knew to do, which was a tremendous compromise of his dignity. I stopped for a few minutes and talked to him, explaining the importance of respecting the place where we live. Perhaps he could explain to his mother why he needed to come inside. If he did so in a calm way, she might understand. I suggested other options—that there are several restaurants in the neighborhood that would gladly let him use their facilities.

I didn't stop thinking about him after he left. His life was so different from mine. He wasn't learning how to be a man. As his neighbor, I had a choice. I could help him by giving him advice and offering loving-kindness whenever I saw him to help him know how valuable he is to our community. Paul clearly needed role models who could show him the way. My husband and I talked about him that evening and agreed that we would do whatever we could for him from that point on.

A woman who was working on a start-up business shared another story of resolving a difficult conflict. As she and a small team of people worked to build a new company, they were in constant conflict with the owner. He belittled all of the women and generally spoke in a disparaging way to the staff whenever anything went wrong. His off-putting behavior was terribly upsetting and demoralizing to the team. "He obviously doesn't know what he's doing," Samantha thought whenever she saw her boss in the hallway. These thoughts precipitated curt answers to every interaction he had with her, no matter what it was. After a few months, Samantha believed that she had no choice other than to quit her job.

She talked about the situation to a close friend, who asked Samantha if she could find it in her heart to look favorably upon her boss, Charles. Rather than feeding into his disgruntled ways, could she see the good in him? Could she listen for the wisdom that he must have inside? Samantha laughed, saying that Charles was past any hope of wisdom, but she agreed to see if a changed attitude could make a difference.

The next day when Charles approached her, she listened to him more carefully. When he introduced a good idea, she acknowledged it. When he spoke to her in a way that was unacceptable, she asked him if he would consider speaking to her with a different tone. She explained that it was hard for her to hear his instruction and follow it when it was delivered in a way that felt like an assault. Charles became silent. Then initially he got defensive, saying that she was too sensitive. Samantha countered, "I may be sensitive, Charles, but I want this project to work as much as you do. And I think it will work better if we support one another as a team." Because Samantha had spoken to him with respect, Charles was able to hear her. In turn, he made a sincere effort to be more thoughtful. Samantha didn't end up staying at that company. When she left, though, it wasn't because she was driven away by Charles's ways.

In each of these instances, it wasn't easy to choose the high road. This is often the case. People will challenge you in many ways; seeing and responding to the divinity that lives within them is a way that you can connect to their great qualities. This doesn't mean that you let people walk over you or mistreat you. It means that even on the battlefield of a heated issue, you can treat each other with respect. You can choose not to call another names or write the person off as unlovable or unworthy of your time or attention. You can approach him or her with the same love that you would approach someone who cannot see or hear. The other person is unable to see the possibilities inherent in whatever challenge he or she is facing. When you see the light, you can welcome the person into it. When you live with the knowledge that God lives within your being and within each person on the planet, you can invite that divine energy to step forward in yourself and others.

ELIMINATE CLUTTER

AN ESSENTIAL COMPONENT of living an optimal life is creating an environment that supports you. This means you must eliminate any clutter that stands between you and clarity. For some people, being neat and well organized comes naturally to them, or they have developed a discipline about keeping tidy that supports them in their day-to-day lives. I wish I could say this has been true for me. The fact is that one of the toughest challenges for me has been keeping my physical space organized. I have applauded myself about my ability to keep my thoughts, dreams, and strategies well ordered in my brain—using that fact somehow as a way of balancing my seeming inability to keep my papers and other belongings straight. I even remember admitting to someone that as good a student as I was in school, I must have skipped the class on organization. Over the years, I have sought assistance in managing my stuff. I have hired support staff who are good at labeling and filing. I have purchased electronic equipment that automatically categorizes addresses, scheduling notes, and other important facts in easy-to-find ways. And still, by and large, I have found myself unable to maintain the required level of order that makes what I need accessible at a moment's notice.

What I know is that giving in to this weakness is unacceptable, and so I have made the commitment to do what I must to excel in this area that has plagued me for so long. Perhaps not surprisingly, when I made the conscious decision to master the art of organization, things got a lot easier for me. For starters, I began to pay attention to the way that other people handled their possessions.

My friend Cheryl, for example, is one of the best-organized people I know. Everything has a place and is in its place—nearly all the time. Rather than ask her how she managed to stay on top of things, I decided that I would watch her in action. One summer, my husband and I spent a lot of time with Cheryl and her partner at their home-office in Manhattan and their house in the Hamptons. What I noticed about Cheryl is that she is always doing something to keep her space in order. Never is a bowl left in the sink or a paper left astray. She doesn't put off until the next moment what she can do in this one. Cheryl talked about her neatness practice once: "I just have to have things so that I know where they are. And that means I have to keep them in their place." Cheryl is a fine artist who has always maintained a harmonious environment wherever she has lived. She added, "I believe in things being beautiful. It's just as easy to make a space beautiful as not. So why not treat yourself well?"

This is basic, obvious wisdom. As with most of the other wisdom that we encounter, it's also practical. Things don't just magically find their way to their proper home. They get there if somebody puts them there. I'm reminded of a word-of-the-day calendar that my husband had when we started dating. Whenever I visited his apartment, I would flip the days of the calendar if he hadn't already. One day I noticed that the word was *in situ,* which meant "in its place." I told George how fond I was of that word and its meaning. Several years later, he reminded me of it, saying how he had been happy that I was inspired by such a meaning and that he hoped that it would inspire me to take action in my own life!

At first, I was a bit insulted and I (mistakenly) began to defend myself, saying that it wasn't just me who was messy. The two of us made our home, and we both were responsible for whatever disarray there was. As I sat with the point, however, I realized that what I needed to deal with was my own inability to take care of my personal space effectively. To choose Truth included choosing to live and work in an environment that was orderly and efficient. A housekeeper, dishwasher, or assistant was not enough. My own devoted participation was essential.

Over the years, I have learned just how important it is to organize my own life and keep it that way. This includes letting things go. In her book *The Courage to Be Rich,* Suze Orman speaks about a person's ability to accumulate wealth and the need to eliminate clutter:

> Why won't we let these items go, the useless items we keep around us? It is the profound fear of loss, which prevents us from gain. We keep so much stuff around us because we fear that if all our material possessions were taken away, we'd be left with nothing—and who would we be if we had nothing? It's this same

fear of loss, however, that cuts off the possibility for more. . . . Surrounded by clutter, you can't find what you need, see what you have, notice what you value, or pinpoint what's missing. In a rich and radiantly abundant life, on the other hand, one in which there is clarity, there is always room for more to come.

I have discovered that staying on track is easier said than done. Like every other discipline, it requires steadfastness in order to attain success. Being in the company of others who practice the discipline of living an orderly life has proven helpful for me—which brings me to my relationship with my sister Susan. Whereas I used to get angry with Susan when I visited her home in Los Angeles and she barked out orders to me about how to keep what I termed "my room" in her home, I now honor her wishes. It is her house, after all. You can imagine how much more peaceful it is to be a guest in her home when I behave in this way. It also got me to thinking about my sister and her own discipline. Although we grew up in the same home, her room and mine always looked different: hers was consistently perfectly ordered, mine artfully cluttered.

In my own spaces, I now regularly practice slowing down long enough to sort through papers and give them a home when I print them or they otherwise come in my possession. I clean out my purses, tote bags, suitcases, and other bags on a regular basis, so that they don't pile up with bits and pieces of my life tucked away, only to be found weeks, months, or even years later. One of the hardest tasks for me is to throw things away. With the addition of a paper shredder, I now throw things away responsibly rather than stuffing a garbage bag to the gills. I also get help. When I am ready to tackle a closet or an old filing system, I engage someone who is better at it than I am. With support, I then go for it. What happens is that instead of ending up with a huge pile of stuff that I don't know how to manage, I have guidance on what to do with what I have unearthed. As a result, my physical space better reflects my mental state. Since the goal is for thought, word, and deed to resound as one, getting organized is something that none of us can give up on.

What do you do? Are you a pro at keeping your physical space in order? Do you allow room for wealth in your life? If what Suze Orman says is true, we stand to gain tremendous economic advantages in our lives by opening up our environments to order. That knowledge can serve as great enough incentive to carve out the time to put things in order.

Being organized allows you to be welcoming at any moment in your life. If unexpected guests show up, you can invite them into your space without a second thought. If you need to put your fingers on a document of great importance, you can in a matter of moments. Keeping a file folder for each of your bills and expenses and financial paperwork makes your life easier. When your possessions have a home and your finances are in order, you can relax. It may take some effort to get to that point if you are not up to speed in this area, but know that the reward is well worth the effort.

HONOR YOUR SELF

CARING FOR YOUR LOVED ONES is a worthy activity. So is caring for yourself. How many times have you made a decision with the understanding that somebody else was going to benefit, perhaps even at your expense? If you look closely at your actions, how often would you say that you have done something that goes directly against your own interests? Perhaps there was something that you said or did that stood in direct opposition to the voice within that was urging you to move in another direction. What happened when you made the wrong choice?

Psychologists call the act of doing something for others even when it stands to hurt you people pleasing. Too often people extend themselves way too far in an effort to make someone else happy. The unspoken belief is that in turn the person will love them better, want to be with them, allow them to keep their job. There is a sense of desperation that frequently accompanies such actions because they are not genuine. They are not selfless acts of generosity. They have tentacles that are forever reaching out to capture others in their grasp and make them respond favorably. Unfortunately, desperation is not appealing. It's more likely to repel someone than to attract.

So how can you move beyond the grip of people pleasing? You can start by learning how to please yourself. I don't mean pleasure as in eating candy or buying new clothes to pacify a desire or sense of longing. I'm speaking about honoring your greatest Self. When you take care of your personal needs, you have a greater capacity to care for those in your presence. When you treat yourself with loving-kindness, your entire world becomes more pleasant for you as well as others. Thinking about yourself first is basic to your very existence, yet we have come to believe that this is a selfish action. Know that there is a difference between being self-sufficient and tending to your needs, and being narcissistic.

To tally up how you take care of yourself, think about how an average day passes for you. What are your daily rituals? What actions do you take from the moment you wake up until you go to bed that support your life? Make a list so that you can literally see how you spend your time. Parents commonly complain that they don't have time for themselves anymore, that their children occupy their every waking moment. Is that really true? Aren't there any moments that you can reserve for yourself in order to rejuvenate your spirit? You can and must carve out time for you. Otherwise you won't be able to do your best.

Here are some suggestions for how you can begin to honor your Self on a daily basis:

- *Wake up each morning in time to take a breath, pray, or contemplate.* The hours before the sun rises are perfect for inner exploration. If you have children, get up before they begin to stir. Over time, even if they do awaken as you are meditating, they will learn to respect your quiet time. They may even join you.

- *Exercise regularly.* This is a tough one for working people, yet the body cannot serve you unless you engage it and keep it strong. The body yearns to move. For it to function properly, it has to be active. No matter what your health or age, you can start now and energize your body so that it will be fit enough to support you in your efforts.

- *Eat well.* You've heard it before, but you have to start with a healthy breakfast. Eat more fresh and whole foods. Check out health and eating Web sites and books or work with a nutritionist to guide your steps. Make your biggest meal lunch, and eat dinner several hours before you go to sleep. This way your body will not have to work when it wants to rest.

- *Pay attention to your health.* Look at the history of your family to see what illnesses have historically plagued your people. Get regular checkups to ensure that you are proactive about your health. Taking preventative measures will serve you now and in the future.

- *Listen to your inner wisdom.* Slow down long enough to be able to hear the messages that your body is sending to you. Throughout the day, we receive subtle cues that can guide us *if* we are able to decipher them. Don't make yourself so busy that you are moving too fast to get the message. Just saying no when you feel too busy is a start.

- *Focus on the task at hand.* Make a to-do list for work and your personal life for the day. Call your answering machine at home to remind yourself to do tasks or errands you might forget. Zoom in on whatever you are handling at the moment. When you do this, you will be able to complete the activity in record time, plus you stand a much greater chance of being accurate the first time.

- *Walk with confidence.* Remind yourself that you are great. You are capable of handling any task before you. Let your abilities shine forth in your actions. This includes the awareness that you can ask for help when you need it.

- *Acknowledge your successes.* Give yourself credit for the accomplishments you achieve each day. You don't have to tell anyone other than yourself what you have done. It is most important for you to be aware of your progress.

- *Be aware of your mistakes.* Be mindful of the things that you don't handle well so that you can address them. Resist the temptation to sweep problems under the rug.

Assess Your Value at Work

When I started my business, I had to figure out how to charge for certain services. Because I was not selling a tangible product, it was hard to quantify how much my services were worth. I had dubbed a particular part of my work "Contemporary *My Fair Lady* Training." I had decided that I would work with recording artists, sports figures, young people, nonprofit organizations, and corporations to provide strategies and tools for fine-tuning ways that people can communicate gracefully and precisely who they are. What was that worth? I did research and got some general figures. As I was assessing my ability to provide this service and its market value, I met with a music industry executive who gave me some great advice: the best thing I could do for myself was to consider a price and then whatever I came up with, multiply it times three. She said that women, especially African-American women, commonly undervalue themselves. By asserting an aspirational fee for my work, she told me, I would step into that value and make another dream come true.

It took a lot of courage even to consider this plan. I asked myself, "Who do you think you are asking for a price like that?" Still, I dutifully wrote it down. When interested clients called to discuss fees, I took a deep breath and went for it. To my surprise, some clients immediately said yes. This boosted my courage. Others asked to negotiate. Still others passed. Over the years, my rates have increased, but I never forgot that day—the day that I upped my value. It was great, because even when I agreed to negotiate for a fraction of that figure, I continued to grow into a stronger alignment with what my gifts truly are.

Remember the Value of Experience

Years ago, there was an artist who was commissioned to create a painting for an art connoisseur. Weeks passed and the buyer waited. After several months, the buyer paid the artist a visit, demanding the finished product. Indeed, the buyer wanted the artwork right then and there. The artist gathered up his art supplies and sat down. Within minutes, he drew a spectacular image and handed it over to the buyer in exchange for the healthy fee that had been previously negotiated. The buyer marveled at the beauty of the drawing. Moments later, he balked. "I commissioned you for a work of art. Why should I pay so much money for something that took you only minutes to complete?" The artist looked the buyer squarely in the eye and explained, "You have paid for a lifetime of experience."

What do you bring to the table that has worth? Take time to contemplate what knowledge you hold. You may be surprised at how vast your reservoir of experience and ability is. Until you examine it, it may be hard to quantify. That's why a résumé or listing of your achievements and employment history is important. You can start with an informal list that you create in your journal that identifies your skills in one column and your professional history in another. Add another column for civic duties and at-home responsibilities. Often, homemakers discredit their abilities, yet who is the champion of multitaskers if not a stay-at-home mom or dad? Record the things that you are good at doing. Research the market so that you can find out specifically what the industry bears for your area of expertise. Be willing to compromise in the beginning. You may even find that you want to volunteer in order to gain experience. Even when you don't get paid actual dollars for your work, know that this does not diminish your value. If you adopt the right approach, you will be adding value to your overall worth by apprenticing under someone with more experience. The goal is not to bully your way into receiving a particular fee or recognition for services. First you must step into a complete understanding of your value. From there, you can set your sights for opportunities that will support your vision.

Stand Firm in What You Believe

It *is* possible to stick to your guns and succeed. When you offer your best and others can see the quality shining through, you have better legs to stand on in any negotiation. You will not be given every project that comes along, but that wouldn't happen no matter what. The biggest benefit from doing your best and learning to assess your value is that you will begin to respect yourself more and more. Gaining respect for yourself will bring you peace.

A photographer friend of mine is a true artist who works in the commercial world—a situation that can often lead to great conflict. Over the years, he has held an innate understanding of the value of his art even as he has earned a living within the framework of the publishing industry. The best thing he did for himself early on was to hire a competent agent who represents him in financial dealings. When a tug-of-war over pricing begins, the photographer as artist operates from a distance, informing his agent of his requirements and allowing her to handle the rest. I worked with him on a big project once and had the opportunity to witness the dance of negotiations firsthand. It was an incredible learning experience for me. With the kindest, most respectful demeanor, this fellow stood his ground. He allowed a certain amount of wiggle room in the negotiations, but certain points were not up for compromise. Ultimately, the publication had to decide if it was willing to commit to working with this photographer. It was clear what the quality of the product would be. The only question was if the client was willing to pay the price for the work.

HONOR TIME

DEPENDING ON what's going on, I have responded to time in different ways. *There's never enough of it. How can I stretch it out so that I can accomplish all my goals? Why do I have to get up so early? I can't wait for this moment to pass. I wish this moment would last forever. Wouldn't it be great if time could just stand still? I will never forget this magnificent time.* The thread that has run through most of my thoughts about time has been its fleeting nature. Unlike many other commodities, time does not stand still.

As we think about our lives and how to bring greater value to each experience, our contemplation cannot be complete without a thorough consideration of time. How we negotiate our lives in relation to time is something we need to examine and evaluate. I was once asked a simple yet powerful question: "What motivates you to wake up?" As I sat and thought about it, I realized that I'm not always motivated to wake up. Sometimes as I'm traveling between sleep and wakefulness, I choose to stay in the realm of sleep, even when I really need to get up to start my day or attend to a responsibility. At different points in my life, my motivation to awaken has varied. For instance, when I've been excited about the potential for a project about to bear fruit, I'm up and raring to go. Conversely, if

I'm feeling dread about having to handle a difficult situation, I've found myself dragging to get out of bed. Cold weather has served as a trigger for clinging to sleep, just as a bright, sunny day has beckoned me to dance with it. Until being asked this question, I can't say I had ever given the subject any serious thought.

It quickly became obvious to me that there was something greater and more profound about the experience of awakening that I needed to explore. On the one hand, there's the amazing blessing of being able to wake up in the morning at all. It is a gift to become alive to the new day. That alone can, and perhaps should, be enough to motivate anyone to allow the waking-up process to happen. Beyond that basic fact is a far greater point: in any moment, we can wake up to that moment. We can become keenly aware of the moment we are occupying and thus be conscious of space and time. Rather than trudging through the very situation we are in, we can notice it, pay attention to its many details, and live in it offering our full life force right then and there.

Don't Squander Time

Imagine a situation where you can quickly see the difference between honoring the moment you are in or somehow numbly moving through it without even realizing you were there. My friend Marcus was standing in line at the bank waiting to make a transaction. There were many other people in the line, which meant a long wait. Marcus decided to place some calls on his cell phone and got so engrossed in his conversations that he forgot where he was. When he got to the teller, he began fumbling for his papers and ended up dropping everything on the floor. As he gathered up his things, he could feel the piercing glances from the long line of people who were still waiting to be served. Because he had not used his time efficiently, Marcus ended up wasting his time, the teller's time, and the time of all the other people in the queue. He could easily have gotten himself organized *before* engaging in conversation on the phone. Then he would have been ready to handle his business when the teller was ready for him.

Honor Time as God

Years ago, I received a valuable pearl of wisdom: *Honor time as God.* Consider time to be the same as God. I contemplated the possibility. What would my time look like if I honored it, if I actually treated it with reverence?

You know the saying, "Youth is wasted on the young." *Isn't it true?* Time seems to stretch across incredibly vast terrain when we are young as well as when we are happy; we take so many things for granted when we are healthy and able to do whatever our minds and hearts propel us to do. But what about the other times? Consider how you measure time and its importance in your life. You might start by keeping notes in your journal. Whenever you find yourself referring to time in a judgmental way, take note. Jot down what you are saying or experiencing. For example, if you are headed to work and you had intended to run an errand on the way but didn't allot enough *time* to complete the task and get to work on *time,* jot it down. What about giving yourself enough *time* to eat and digest your food before getting on the phone to follow up on a task that you didn't have enough *time* to handle earlier? Even the most efficient multitaskers among us often find ourselves in a veritable juggling act with time. Oh yes, we try to stretch a few more seconds out of this experience or that. Whether it's the length of stay in the bed before getting up to start the day, the amount of focus we squander on obsessing over relationships, money, or food, or the hours we sit staring in front of TV or otherwise not thinking, many of us live virtually unconscious of the precious nature of time.

Consider time as a cog in the divine wheel of life. Just as we understand God to be that pulsation that created the universe as well as each of us, we can envision time as the guiding force that regulates the seasons of the year and of our lives. Time is eternal as well as imminent. Over the ages, each civilization has sought to identify the parts of time, to break it down into measurable components. No matter how these parts have been delineated, what remains true is that there are twenty-four hours in each day, and no matter how we fill that space of time, it continues to pass in the same increments. To honor time can mean to value each individual moment. We can remain aware. We can learn lessons as they present themselves. We can honor deadlines. We can treat one another with respect when we are together. We can listen when the moment calls for silence and respond when our hearts tell us it's right. We can eat and sleep when our bodies require it. We can walk with the knowledge that every step is planted in time. Every movement reverberates throughout the world. We matter. Each one of us is an actor in God's play. Through the movement of time, we are able to fulfill our roles. When we offer our very best to each moment, we will be able to give ourselves a glorious standing ovation.

Your Journal Entry

Dearest Friend,

I want to do my best all the time. I see that this doesn't have to be looked at as a chore or a burden. I can approach my life as a grand opportunity to be great. I can call upon my inner reserves to celebrate my abilities in every moment. I have the courage and strength to live a powerful life that is valuable to me and to others. I intend to fulfill my life with joy and conviction.

I love you,
Me

DOING YOUR BEST is a prerequisite on the path to freedom and happiness. Yes, it means that you don't have downtime per se. Your time for rest requires your best effort, just as your time for play and work does. Think about how rewarding it can be for you to pour your energy into each aspect of your life so that it can be great. You can have a balanced life if you give it your all. As you consider this, you can address the following topics in your journal:

- *Contemplate what it means to do your best.* Have you been able to give yourself the love and support that you need in your life? When has this worked? When have you fallen off? How can you become more resolved to do your best?

- *How do you treat others?* Can you identify opportunities when you can be more loving and compassionate toward your friends and family? What about the people who make you uncomfortable? Can you practice seeing God in them?

- *What is the state of your affairs?* Are you organized in your physical environment? What about in your mind? Do you need to work to remove any clutter that may be infringing on your ability to flourish in your life?

- *What is your relationship to time?* Do you respect time when you pay your bills or answer your phone calls? Do you honor your responsibilities in a timely fashion? Can you improve in this area?

8

NURTURE YOUR INNER SMILE

THINK ABOUT AN AVERAGE DAY and how you express yourself from morning to evening. What is your general attitude? Are you happy or sad? Content or agitated? Energetic or lethargic? I've asked this question of many people, and the range of responses has been vast. Many people admitted that they wear a poker face during the day so that others can't read what's on their minds. Others gauge the room they're entering to see what the emotional temperature is before deciding what facade to wear. A few said they genuinely wear a happy face with a cheerful smile most of the time. Some confessed that they superimpose a smile when they are feeling self-conscious. Others simply let what they were experiencing show itself on their face. What is your answer?

When you stop to analyze your facial and physical expressions and how or whether they represent your true state, you may find that what you have thought about your presentation in the past is not equal to what is accurate. You might be surprised at how common it is that people's thoughts and feelings don't match their expressions at all. A tight lip may not always mean disdain just as a bright smile may not reflect happiness.

TEND YOUR TRUE SMILE

KYLE, AN ACCOUNTANT from Atlanta, explained that for years he had been given the brush-off by casual acquaintances, especially women. He couldn't understand why. Kyle reasoned that he is a nice enough guy, good looking, comfortably successful, honest. He admitted to being shy, feeling nervous when he approached women for dates, especially in public places. But, Kyle said, he still made the overture. The problem was that people rarely responded positively to him. After a while, he began to generalize and disparage women, saying that women these days are just gold diggers, not interested in a regular, nice guy.

His perception began to change when one of his buddies gave him some advice. Matthew explained that he had a friend who might be a good match for Kyle. As Matthew talked about Kyle's attributes to her, however, the woman, who knew Kyle, remained stuck on her initial impression of him. She was leery of going out with him, because Kyle always seemed to be in such a bad mood; he always had a dour expression on his face. Kyle was shocked. As he thought about it, he figured that it must be his shyness that was making him frown and appear as introverted as he felt. While Kyle thought he was putting himself out there to meet new people, his expression was actually keeping people at bay. Knowing that there was someone who might be interested in him gave Kyle a bit of confidence. Over time, he learned to loosen up, build courage, and demonstrate his interest in others and in what's going on around him rather than shy away into himself. Because this was brought to his attention, Kyle began to notice how he was feeling on the inside and how immediately his feelings were reflected on his face and in his demeanor. As he relaxed, it became easier for Kyle to express his joy, and to his delight, it became a lot easier to enjoy positive interactions with people.

Finding a smile is not always the challenge for people; a smile can unwittingly serve as a mask just as readily as a frown can. For me, a smile has worked both ways. For my entire life I have been one who smiles. Like my mother, my smile can be contagious, spreading to those I contact and inspiring them to smile back. Unlike my mother, I have sometimes used my smile as a shield. A perfect example is a number of years ago when I was going through a very rough period. I was definitely not happy. Still, I was walking around the office smiling as usual when I had a casual encounter with a colleague. This woman, about fifteen years my senior, was an insightful and incisive writer not known for warmth. As we saw one another in the hall, she stopped me and looked deep into my eyes. A few minutes later, she called me into her office. I thought, "Oh boy, what did I do?" Her reputation didn't give me confidence about entering her space, but reluctantly I did. In the kindest voice, Judy said to me, "Harriette, what's wrong? That smile may be fooling somebody else, but I've seen it before. It's not your happy smile. You're covering something up." I felt tears welling up in my eyes. She had found me out. I thought I had been keeping it together so well. How could she tell the difference between one smile and another? At that point in my life, I didn't know there was a difference myself.

It wasn't until many years later that I encountered this question again. I was dealing with a devastating health problem and had reached out for help. As I began the dance of therapy, my therapist and I were talking about something very serious when he interrupted me and, with a puzzled expression, asked, "Why are you smiling?" I became silent. After a while I responded, "I don't know. I always smile." He probed, "But why are you smiling now? Right this minute?" I didn't know. As I thought about it, I remembered that I actually often go beyond smiling and even laugh when traumatic things happen, I learn of horrible news, or I face distressing situations. These facades have served as my trusty defense for years. After a few times of having the disconnection between my feelings and my expression pointed out to me, I began to acknowledge that every smile is not a good smile. Every laugh is not a joyful laugh. By looking behind the veil of my smile, I have become better able to notice what I am masking that is begging for examination. Over time, I have become much better at revealing a true smile.

So, again, I ask you, When do you smile? Do you know if your smile is real or is hiding something? As I have asked around, I have found that many people use a smile in the same way that they use a straight face: to cover up something. In the best of worlds, however, a genuine smile that rises up from the depths of your being reveals something precious: the powerful light of love and Truth that dwells within you. Finding that inner smile is integral to Choosing Truth.

WELCOME YOUR TRUE SMILE

WHEN DO YOU SMILE? Do you know when you feel that sensation of joy and love bubbling forth from within you that spills over into your outward expression? The search for your true smile, of recognition of the greatness within your own being, is what we are interested in unmasking. Your true smile is intelligent and compassionate. It comes forth appropriately and makes others feel comfortable and at ease because it is real. Best of all, it starts with you. When you tap into that space of love, peace, and goodness within your own being, you can radiate that power out to the rest of the world. No matter what the circumstances, no matter how challenging the situation, that steady anchor within you that connects you to the rest of the universe can shine through.

Remember a time when you allowed that sunshine to flow from you. Maybe you were walking down the street headed to work, or perhaps you were standing in a soft rain looking up at the evening sky. Were you witnessing a tender moment between a parent and child, or kicking off your shoes at home after a full day's work? Recall a time when you allowed yourself to experience the goodness of a moment to its absolute fullest, and within you a feeling of peace warmed your being. That's the experience that triggers your true smile.

Sometimes it's hard to muster a smile even for your family and friends. I love this statement, which has been attributed to Maya Angelou: "If you have only one smile in you, give it to the people you love. Don't be surly at home, then go out in the street and start grinning 'Good morning' at total strangers."

REFRESH YOUR EXPRESSION

HOW CAN YOU MAKE your expression match your feelings? Try this solution. Although this exercise may sound superficial, it actually reaches right into the core of a person. When you find yourself gazing at one thing for an extended period, whether it's into a camera or at a person, at a post at work, or at co-workers in a meeting, look away for a moment at something else before bringing your gaze back to your point of focus. While you are looking away, take a deep breath in, filling your lungs. As you exhale, let go of the tension and self-consciousness that may be tightening up your jaw and your face. Try it now. You can use a mirror for this exercise. Do a couple of rounds of deep breathing. When you return to the mirror, notice the subtle differences in your face. Your eyes will be more alert, your jaw softer. The natural lines in your face will be relaxed. All of this happens because you have invited your full attention to re-aligning your exterior to your interior. So often we are disjointed. Our mind is thinking one thing, while we find our voice speaking another, and our body doing yet another. When you study yourself, you will see how common it is for mind, body, and thoughts to work at cross purposes. As you begin to become more aware of the subtleties that are happening within you, you will be able to adjust yourself so that all three can and will work as one. Then when you want to smile, you will. And when a smile isn't appropriate, it won't find its way onto your face. Indeed, you may no longer find yourself in a situation that is unacceptable in the first place.

There are other ways to release the clutches of deception. You can give yourself permission to leave a situation that is stifling you. You can choose not to put yourself in an environment that is compromising. You can weigh the options before you and assess the practical approach. You can reflect what you really feel. A reserved expression, for example, may be best in a tense situation. Similarly, a serious demeanor may be right when you have to give direction. Just because you aren't smiling doesn't mean you aren't loving or friendly. To lock into the space that will let you know the appropriate expression, you can practice dispassion. Then, no matter where you are, you can step out of the swirl of emotion and intrigue that challenges you to fall off center. As you observe a situation for what it is right then and there, you can act lovingly toward yourself and others.

LOOK IN THE MIRROR

HOW ACCURATE do you think your facial expressions are at reflecting what you are feeling? Most of us don't realize when our outward expressions are out of sync with our inner feelings. Obviously, we have to become aware of the disconnection in order to change it.

A portable mirror (for women *and* for men) can be a helpful tool on your journey to self-discovery. You can make a conscious effort to see yourself through and through rather than just your exterior. At home, it's helpful to have the capacity to look at yourself from three directions. Invest in a large mirror— full length, if possible. Stand or sit in front of the mirror and look at yourself. Notice the different facial expressions that you naturally make. You can start by evoking different emotions. Think about something that makes you happy. Now look at your face to see how you present that particular feeling of happiness. Next, think about something that makes you agitated. What does that look like? Call up curiosity, admiration, impatience, anticipation, gratitude, irritation, and boredom. Pay attention to the ways in which your expression changes as you experience different emotions. When you talk on the phone at home, be in view of your mirror. Can you detect times as you are talking when your demeanor may be unnatural or in some way not reflective of how you are actually feeling? It is only when you can see that what you are feeling in your heart and what you are showing through your expression are different that you can change.

Once you begin to notice, make the conscious effort to adjust your presentation. This may take some courage and persistence. If you are talking to someone on the phone and want to end the conversation, why not say as much? Very kindly, you can let the person know that you need to go and that perhaps you can speak at a later time. If you have no intention of calling back soon, don't promise or allude to doing so. If you don't intend to communicate in the future, put a clear end to the conversation. This is a challenge that many people face with telephone solicitors (as well as nagging friends and relatives). Because they don't state from the beginning that they are uninterested in whatever the solicitor is selling, they face repeated calls. If you deal with a situation honestly, in the moment, you will have handled the situation to the best of your ability.

MAINTAIN YOUR INNER SMILE

HAVE YOU EVER NOTICED the music that can dance in someone's voice, even your own, when that person is happy? The natural levity that bubbles up when you are joyous on the inside likes to expose itself through each of your syllables and gestures. People can hear smiles as others speak even when they are not physically in the same place. Can you remember a person now whose voice has a natural smile in it? Recall a time when the two of you spoke. How did you feel after being in that conversation? Just as you can get someone to yawn if you audibly yawn, you can also trigger a smile if you are honestly wearing one.

You probably have seen this with children. When they are happy, their state is contagious. Their entire bodies dance with the joy in their hearts. What's more, when children are young—before they learn the codes of conduct of civilized culture—their smiles are guaranteed to be genuine. The quality of Truth that shines from them proves that they exude love. Wouldn't it be great to hold onto that state regardless of the circumstance we are in? This leads back to the practice of dispassion. It is possible to stay centered in your inner joy. Even when you are feeling sadness or pain, the core of joy within you does not have to dissolve. Your light can shine through you accurately if you practice turning your attention within.

This is why I believe meditation is so important. We return to this fundamental practice many times throughout this book because it is a direct way to lead you to the space of Truth within. Meditation reveals the strength that lives within us. It points out the issues that we need to address. It identifies the difference between our experiences and who we really are. It captures the essence of joy within us and invites us to reside in that place of happiness that is our true home. Meditation shows us our Truth—that the divinity within us is the wellspring of our happiness. Things may happen in daily life, but that pulsing source of love in our own hearts does not subside. By meditating, we can feel that ever-present comfort and cultivate an inner smile that radiates naturally from us in a manner that is at once protective and liberating. From it we gain confidence. What's more, the grounding and clarity that we receive through the disciplined practice of meditation help us to recognize the inner smile in others as well. Imagine if we looked at one another and sought out the Truth rather than rely on stereotypes or other limited views of each other. That is where we can actually connect with people honestly.

LET YOUR JOY RADIATE FREELY

SUCH IS ONE of the great lessons of the famous doctor Patch Adams, who created the Gesundheit! Institute, a healing center in Virginia. He believes that people can be cured through love and levity as they receive medical treatment. George and I had occasion to meet and work with Patch a number of years ago. We were doing a photo-documentary with another friend for the International Design Conference in Aspen, Colorado, that explored the human body, the environment, and fashion in a futuristic way. For this project we invited conference participants and locals to appear in photographs that illustrated different aspects of human life in the future. Patch agreed to participate, and before we got to him, he heard that we had been shooting nudes. Naturally, he wanted to be shot nude too. Patch loved himself as he was and celebrated his being at every turn. The shot that he composed with us was of him nude in a newly appointed living room that had been scavenged together on top of a mound at a city dump. There reclined Sir Patch in his tall, middle-aged, not perfectly toned body having more fun than any other photo subject that day. As he laughed with us, he explained that his objective in life is to experience joy—the joy to be alive, to be creative, to see beauty in everything in his presence. That joy, Patch asserted, makes everything shine beautifully. It frees us up from being self-conscious. And, what's more, as he demonstrated to us, that magnetic joy brought a huge smile to our faces as well as all of the people who got to see his witty, liberating images.

GIVE YOURSELF A HUG

WE EXAMINE the many layers of our lives so that we can access that inner reservoir of immense joy and serenity that is perpetually present. Look within for that source of love and joy that is always there. Know that it can be tough to remember to go inside even as we maintain the best intentions. There seems to be so much out there to latch onto, so much abundance within others and in different ports of call, that it can be hard to sustain an inner focus. And yet we learn time and again that the love that we all crave is already within us.

A friend has had a compelling message on his answering machine for many years: "Give yourself a hug." When I first heard this message, I thought, "Oh, how clever—and corny." Once, for the heck of it, I physically followed his instruction. I got off the phone and tenderly wrapped my arms around my body, humming and swaying with my eyes closed. As I stood dancing with my Self, I felt a smile creep across my face. I hadn't begged it to come out and play. I hadn't thought of it at all. I wasn't trying to perform for someone else's delight or approval. I was loving me. And in the process, the most exuberant and simple expression of love emerged. The inner smile came to greet me as I loved me. That day, as I greeted others and fulfilled my many responsibilities, I glowed with my own inner smile of recognition and joy.

Because I gained so much from this simple message, I wanted to understand its origins. Rashid explained that when he was a child, his mother had been emotionally unavailable to him. His Aunt Edna came to the rescue with some essential tender loving care. Rashid says, "She knew I needed a mantra and a mother. She knew I could supply the mantra, but the supplying of the mother was giving yourself a hug." Rashid continues, "I have never known a mother's embrace, but I do know the embrace of a mother-aunt, a mother-grandmother, and friends. As a boy when I was going home and I was a little sad that I had to go back, my aunt used to tell me, 'Don't forget to give yourself a hug.'" As Rashid grew up, he never forgot this message: "The feel of a child having his arms wrapped around him is his conscious experience of being in the womb. The more you hug yourself, what a great hugger you become, because you know what it feels like. You don't have to be alone, because you have two arms that can embrace you." Thank you, Rashid.

My Journal

Dearest Friend,

I feel so happy when you share a genuine smile with me. Your joy is so beautiful. Even when everything isn't going perfectly, I know that you can find your joy within and let it out. When you do I feel so grateful. It makes my heart sing.

I love you,
Me

DEDICATE YOUR JOURNAL ENTRY to a gentle exploration of your inner smile:

- *Ask yourself what your inner smile looks like.* When do you feel that smile coming forth? What can you do to encourage it to manifest?

- *What stands in the way of your smile showing itself?* What can you change in your behavior that will enable your joy to be present all the time?

- *Devote a week of daily meditation and contemplation to accessing that smile that lives inside you.* Take note of what you experience during your quiet time, and record your insights in your journal. At week's end, look back to see what you have learned.

9

WORK WISELY

A FEW DAYS after the September 2001 terrorist attacks, my husband came home and told me that two of his colleagues had resigned. In the wake of the unrest that shook so many to their core, these two professionals with long-standing careers had a change of heart. I know these women. They are smart, seemingly wise, and sound thinkers. That's why their decision initially baffled me. I wanted to know, "Why now?" George explained that each of them essentially said the same thing: that the disaster made it clear to them that they had to make a choice. Work no longer had the same meaning that it had held the day before. One wanted more free time, so she decided to pursue her talents on a freelance basis, with full knowledge of the potential risks of going it alone when employment statistics were spiraling down. The other opted for a total career change. She wanted to start fresh and decided that the moment to go for it was now.

Does it take a disaster to reassess your life, especially how you work? Many people have shared that when they have had a near-death experience, lost a loved one, or dealt with some other dramatic incident, they have stepped back to consider what's really important in their lives. One woman, Patricia, realigned her life plan in her early twenties, at a time when many people are experimenting with what their lives may become. She had been a happy-go-lucky child, full of effervescence and fun. What prompted her youthful drive and focus? Patricia had leukemia as a teenager. After struggling for a couple of years with chemo, radiation, and slow healing, Patricia decided that if God blessed her with continued life she would make it count, and so she did. She went from her hometown to a great college and then moved to New York to pursue a career as a writer. Patricia plotted her course, making sure that each job she had would allow her to write about things that mattered to her. By the time she reached forty, Patricia had published two novels and was a proud mother. Although she wouldn't go so far as to call her life perfect, she said it was fulfilling. She chalked her successes up to her brush with death years before. "I learned early on that I had to take what God gives me and do the best I can with it," she said. At age 42, Patricia died after cancer returned to plague her body. All who loved her know that she lived a full life.

ASSESS YOUR WORK

WHAT DO YOU NEED to reevaluate your life and how you spend your time? Can you take this very moment to look at your work and determine if it counts? Do you like your job? Are you happy with how you spend the majority of your day? What about your waking moments inspires you? What is a drag? Do you wake up in the morning enthusiastic about the events and tasks ahead of you? Or do you lament the duties that you are beholden to fulfill? Do you recognize that you have the power to change the quality and activity of your day if you want to do so?

When the news of George's colleagues settled in, I was so impressed that I called my mother to tell her. As I recounted the bravery that these two had exhibited and the awe that I felt about their choices in the midst of such uncertainty, my mother piped up, "Well, that's exactly what you did when you started your business, isn't it?" I had forgotten. It's true. In 1995, I left *Essence* magazine after eleven years and started my own company. When the opportunity to fulfill my dream of being an entrepreneur arose, I drummed up all the courage I could muster and took that giant step into pursuing my own dreams my own way. I did have a good plan. A year ahead of time, I worked with my attorney to get incorporated. I roughed out what I intended to do. I found affordable office space. I secured a substantial contract to support me before I made my departure. I suppose I had forgotten how brave I had had to be at that time. Having my mother's reminder helped me to bring my own life into perspective. It also reminded me that making one decision at one time in our lives is not enough.

Choosing to spend time working on that which fulfills your spirit is a constant effort. From moment to moment and project to project, you constantly have to evaluate how you are using the human resource of *you* to determine what steps to take next. Just as in every other activity, vigilance is required here too, especially because there is rarely a job that is guaranteed for life anymore. You might feel a sense of urgency to have a job (preferably a good job, sometimes any job) because you have responsibilities. You may have student loans, children, a mortgage, school tuition, a car loan, or medical expenses to consider. In our society, even for the person with the simplest life, the reality of bills is often enormous, and it seems that no matter how much you make, you can easily need more than you've got. So it is wise to keep a lookout for fluctuations at the workplace as they relate to financial security. That doesn't mean that you have to stay put in a job that is fueling frustration, boredom, or unhappiness. While I am not advising you to throw caution to the wind, I am suggesting that you consider your work life differently than you may have up to now.

Fulfilling Work

How do spiritual and emotional fulfillment fit into the equation? Can you imagine making a life-changing decision based on that? A thirty-two-year-old investment banker, Satya had been on the fast track at her Wall Street firm for many years. She was smart, quick, and creative. She was happy brokering deals and making lots of money for her company and herself. Satya has a bubbly personality that makes her a joy to be around. Everybody seems to like her, and her bosses loved her productivity. One day, about seven years into her career, she had a change of heart. For quite some time, she had longed for a spiritual life, for something that would bring meaning to her existence. Accruing stocks, bonds, and dollars in personal investments looked good on paper and certainly gave her a cushy Manhattan life, but it wasn't enough. At the height of her career, Satya gave it all up to devote her life full time to her spiritual pursuits. Vowing to live a monastic life, she has become actively involved in her spiritual community. Still the cheerful hard worker, Satya says that now she feels like she's really doing her work. She brings all of her creativity and financial savvy to an international non-profit organization that is committed to uplifting humanity.

Satya's example is both extraordinary and extreme. You may be like her and find that you want to change your life completely and devote your time to spiritual pursuits or another noble ambition. Or your growing awareness of your desires and needs for personal growth may be more subtle. Your shift in work—if indeed you are due for one—may be far less dramatic, if not less significant. As you discover your own place in the world of work, don't compare yourself to others. You are you. Only you can truly know what's best for you.

Frustrating Work

I have had many little shifts over the years that have helped me to sharpen my understanding of what I am to do in this world. I was working on a television show a few years ago that was incredibly frustrating for me. For many reasons, the project was not working. I wasn't able to do my job in a way that came anywhere close to satisfying my creative talents, and at every turn, friction flared. I knew I needed to leave, but it was hard to take that giant step. This project, although time-consuming, represented a steady paycheck for my business. I was able to work on other efforts that were important to me during that period—when I was able to carve out free moments to spare—because I had extra income flowing in. Also, I was (and remain) very interested in television as a way to communicate positive messages effectively. Although uplifting TV wasn't the promise of this program, I figured I would learn a lot about the inner workings of the medium, so it would ultimately be worth it—or so I reasoned. Still, I was unhappy. I was almost always cranky. I suffered from severe headaches. My staff was irritable. As the leader of a team, I had to do something. I knew what I had to do, but didn't quite have the courage to step up and do it.

One day I was racking my brain about the situation as I was flying home from Los Angeles. During the flight, I began to read some words of the philosopher Henry David Thoreau. Jumping out from the page were the very words of inspiration I had been seeking. In an essay entitled "Life Without Principle," Thoreau contemplated how we spend our lives:

> Most men would feel insulted, if it were proposed . . . to employ them in throwing stones over a wall, and then in throwing them back, merely that they might earn their wages. But many are no more worthily employed now. . . . It is remarkable that there are few men so well employed, so much to their minds, but that a little money or fame would commonly buy them off from their present pursuit.

As I read, I thought about how I was spending my time. I realized that I had gotten sidetracked. I was earning good money, something I felt I needed badly at that time. I was learning about the television industry, an arena that I have spent some time in and have wanted to enter more fully. But truth be told, these were rationalizations. I didn't need to do *that* job. I was supposed to be working on my writing and I already had a writing project that I was contracted to complete in a fixed amount of time. Like too many times before, I had accepted a project that ended up occupying too much of my time and energy and delayed the more important, integral, soul-satisfying work that I had already committed to completing. When I stopped for a minute and thought, I was shocked to see that I was doing exactly what Thoreau had observed. As principled as I fancied myself to be, I had allowed a little money to draw me away from my more important goal.

Having a grace period of more than five hours in flight, I reevaluated my situation. What was really important to me? I knew it was my writing. How could I get out of my contract without causing a problem for the show? Ask to be released and, before leaving, organize all of my duties so that it would be easy for someone to come in and take over. That is exactly what I did. I went in and shared my intentions with my staff. Next, I went to my liaison at the show. There was no need for trepidation; the transition worked seamlessly. As I walked away from a healthy paycheck, I walked toward my greater purpose with full faith that I would be able to provide for my needs.

A very basic lesson that I have been encouraging myself to follow is *to commit fully to those activities to which I have dedicated my life.* If we personally make a commitment, naturally we should honor it at least until we make the decision to make a different commitment. Otherwise, what's the point? In this society, making a commitment has become a national activity for New Year's Day. We approach the contemplation and assertion of our New Year's resolutions with great fanfare and conviction. Still, nobody's actually expected to keep them all year. In fact, by the end of a week or two, many people have fallen off the discipline of whatever it was they started. In some cases, they can't even remember what it was. Indeed, newsmakers find fodder for stories in our amnesia, encouraging us in silly and creative ways to stick with it. "Don't give up. Keep on going," they chant. Yet the percentage of those of us who actually do stay committed still falls way off in the end. Has that ever happened to you? What about in a work situation? It only makes sense that you should choose wisely how you spend your time and what your work will be and then give your full consent to doing it.

DISCOVER YOUR TRUE WORK

WHAT IF YOU DON'T KNOW what your work is to be? Some people are blessed to have dreams of their life's work that they follow like a blueprint. Others figure it out early on during their formative years. Many more carve their path along the way, not necessarily knowing with certainty that they have a particular calling. If you haven't got it all worked out, it's okay. I've given advice to any number of people, from those who are pursuing prosperous careers but still aren't sure of what they are ultimately supposed to do, to young people who are floundering.

Wherever you are in your work life right now, it's fine. Look at your situation closely. Do you have a sense of what is working and what isn't? Do you have ideas about what your next steps might be? Invite your own wisdom to guide you; engage your own intelligence and intuition as you plot your course. As with all other activities, this requires listening to the voice within, which undoubtedly is attempting to give you guidance. Pay attention to what's before you. Quite often a gem is sparkling right in front of our faces, but we're too busy checking out the horizon to notice. Now's the time to notice what's going on from all angles.

Whether you are looking to change your job or not, here are some guidelines to help you assess your situation:

- *Look at your own work objectively.* In your journal, make two columns—one for what is satisfying for you about your work, the other that details what is off the mark. Be clear and complete. Include everything from your specific responsibilities to the work environment, coworkers, office dynamics, dress code, commuting time, health benefits, and so on. Do this even if you are the business owner. You still want and deserve a certain way of life. You have to figure out if you are providing that for yourself.

- *Don't blame anyone for anything that's not working.* Blame never works in anybody's favor. It doesn't matter if you're blaming yourself or another; the emotional energy required to fuel blame is both exhausting and destructive for you and for many more than you may ever know.

- *Accept responsibility for your role.* Instead of blaming, figure out what your part is in any situation that is bothering you. For example, if your officemate consistently comes to work late and you have to cover for him by doing part of his job, stop getting mad at him. Stop enabling him too. Let him know that you will no longer cover for him and that he will have to suffer the consequences.

- *Master the job you have.* Even if your specific role is not what you aspire to do, master your immediate responsibility first. I nearly got fired from my first job out of college because I resented having to do what it required. I didn't want to type or answer phones. I had graduated college with highest honors, and I wanted to write. At first I had a bad attitude. Once I figured out that I was not going to reach my goal of writing if I kept up my various protests—including coming to work late and wearing inappropriate attire—I wised up. I got so good at my job after that that I had finished all of my daily duties by midday. Because I was legitimately available to help out with other tasks, my employer gave me a shot at writing. I was good at the task I was lobbying for and was ready to go for it when the opportunity came.

- *Exercise patience.* It can be a real balancing act figuring out if you are in the job that's right for you right now. While it's important not to get stuck in a job for too long if it's contrary to your life's work, it's also wise to give situations a chance. One project frequently leads to another. You may gain skills in a job that you loathe that will support you years down the line. Use your judgment as you do your work, remembering to be patient with yourself, your employer, your coworkers, and all of the other people with whom you interact. When you look at situations kindly and with a respectful patience, you will be better able to understand how you can best handle yourself and develop your skills.

- *Make your time count.* Give yourself fully to your work. Keep track of the skills that you are developing, and write them down. For instance, if fellow employees consistently call on you to help put out fires, make a note that you have the ability to facilitate during conflicts. Your constant self-evaluation, coupled with industry research, will provide an accurate assessment of your proficiency in various areas of expertise. If your work is currently being an at-home mom, don't discount your skills there. You are likely a very effective manager who can handle a broad range of responsibilities at once.

- *Don't consider any task too small.* We live in a society that is still based on service, even though it can be hard to tell these days. When asked to pitch in to do something that feels beneath you, do it anyway. Unless your supervisor is intentionally trying to humiliate or embarrass you—and even sometimes when that's true—you can gain the upper hand by accepting and accomplishing the task with grace and dignity. That includes anything from taking out the trash for an executive to typing a letter for a boss who has a secretary. Needs arise in the moment. The one who is willing to fulfill the need is the real winner.

- *Practice forgiveness.* At work, just like everywhere else, people make mistakes—including you. The sooner you accept that even the best-trained, most well-intentioned among us can mess up, the happier you will be wherever you are. Furthermore, even the most egregious error can be forgiven. That doesn't mean that you forget. It means you honestly accept the person's fallibility and move on. That goes for yourself too.

- *Be of help.* Even at work, even if you don't want to be there, adopt the posture of helpfulness. No matter how high up on the totem pole you go, remember that you are still a person in a community of other people. People work best when they work together. When somebody needs support, don't just stand there and let the person flounder. Step in and lend a hand. This sounds easy, but sometimes it's tough. You will need to use discrimination here. There's a fine line between becoming a crutch and being of help. If you listen to the voice inside as it directs you, you will be fine.

- *Don't laugh at others' expense.* This should go without saying, but at work, disparaging behavior can run rampant, especially if employees are bored or unhappy. If you fit either of these descriptions, you have two choices: find something to do at work that will reinvigorate you, or find another job. Don't hurt others because you don't believe you have anything better to do with your time. When in doubt, put yourself in the other person's position. How would you feel if someone or, worse, a group of people were talking and laughing about you? That vision should be enough to stop you.

- *Don't abuse privileges.* Anything from use of the telephone to extended lunch breaks can be appreciated or abused. One fellow got fired from his job because he called his mother in Brazil every day from his office phone. When his supervisor asked him about it, he shrugged it off, saying that he was good at his job, so why should they be on his back? When he got fired, he had the nerve to be surprised and offended. Arrogance is one of the worst personality traits that a person can have. It makes it impossible for you to see the Truth and often hurts others along the way. Replace such ignorance with appreciation. It's great for your job to have perks. When everyone uses them wisely, everyone benefits. Abusers should be reprimanded—and usually are.

- *Resist talking about people.* Gossip is one of the worst practices. When you are in the company of others who are engaging in discussions about people's personal or professional business, excuse yourself. If you find the conversation offensive, you can also accept the responsibility of stepping in and asking everyone to stop. When you find yourself engaging in gossip, just stop.

- *Respect your "enemies."* Let's face it. Some people are not going to be our best friends. Somebody may rub you the wrong way for reasons that are unclear, while others' motives are obvious. Treat the person who is plotting to undermine you the same as you would a disabled person who is trying to cross the street: with compassion. When people are out to get you, it's either because of some feeling of inadequacy that they have that has nothing to do with you, or it's due to friction in your relationship. Everybody does not have to be your friend. Everyone *does* deserve your respect.

- *Examine your patterns.* Wherever you go, you take your way of being with you. At the same time, every day presents a new opportunity for you to start fresh.

In order to improve your life, you have to see where improvements are necessary. Review your journal to see patterns of behavior that work and others that would be wise to discard. Focus on strengthening your strong points by acknowledging when you handle something well. Too often we falsely believe that if we pat ourselves on the back, we're being boastful. When you notice a destructive pattern resurfacing, stop yourself the moment you notice it. Instead of beating yourself up about it, which would be the same as blame, give yourself credit for seeing the pattern and halting it before it played itself out. Even if you realize your folly at the very end of a pattern's cycle, still commend yourself. Seeing is the first step toward change.

- *Be proactive.* Once you figure out whether you should stay in the position you are in, take action. If the answer is that you are where you are supposed to be, celebrate. If you realize it's time to go, plot your course and get out. Be mindful of how to handle your departure responsibly.

- *Don't burn bridges.* Suppose the worst-case scenario is a firing—yours. Even then you can keep your cool. You may have needed your boss to sever ties in order for you to be free to find your life's calling. Instead of practicing bitterness, be strategic and kind. Thank your boss for the lessons learned while you were there. No matter how bad it got, you gained tremendous knowledge from the time spent there. Rather than blowing up a bridge with your emotions, mend it with the healing powers of your love and respect for the goodness in yourself and others.

LEARN AS YOU WORK

LEARNING DOESN'T END when you finish school. It is a lifelong process that promises more and greater revelations if you retain the posture of a student. This is especially important as you focus on figuring out your life's work. These days, the choices are so broad that it can be difficult to sort through them. There is a productive way to learn about possibilities: apprenticeship, or what we now commonly call internship. Years ago in nearly every field, students learned under the tutelage of experienced practitioners of whatever their trade might be. A cobbler taught a student how to craft shoes. A photographer taught an assistant how to perfect lighting, composition, and styling. A professor taught a teacher's aide how to educate students.

These days many people participate in formal and informal relationships with businesses and professionals so that they can learn details about their fields of interest. Interns gain experience from those who have greater wisdom than them in the particular area and ascertain whether this field is right for them. The person offering the internship gets to pass his or her knowledge on to someone else, thereby participating in the universe's requirement that we give and receive. A small business gets the added bonus of human resources that it might not otherwise be able to afford.

No one is too young or too old to be an intern. I was speaking on a panel at a women's conference in Chicago when a woman of about fifty years addressed the group. Mary had worked in the same job for more than twenty years, and she was bored. She said she wanted to make a career change, but she was afraid. I recommended that once she identified a firm of interest, she contact the human resources department and offer to volunteer. Taking the approach that any potential employee would, she could request an interview to find out what the company's needs currently are and indicate how she might be able to help. She could offer her willingness to help out in any way the company needed. If she got the unpaid internship, she was to work on that job as if it was the most precious job she had ever had. Whether she could do the job full time by quitting her current job or part time while maintaining her current employment, she was to give it her all. Even if this position never turned out to be permanent or paid, it would give her concrete experience that she could put on her résumé.

There are all kinds of reasons for people to decide to make a change in their work lives. Whatever your reason or circumstances, anything of value is possible to achieve if you put your mind to it.

SEEK OUT MENTORS

As you find your way in work, it will serve you well to have wise ones in your court. There is always someone who has more experience than you who can lend you support in times of need. As you look for someone who is willing and able to be your mentor, be clear about what you want. Although a mentor can become a friend, that is not the goal of the relationship. You want a mentor who knows the ropes in the particular world of work you have chosen. Your mentor may be someone who grew up in an environment similar to yours and who has transcended that life and feels comfortable in many different settings now, or your mentor might have been a trailblazer in a field that you are entering.

When you believe you have identified someone whom you would like to have as your mentor, state your request to have a mentor-mentee relationship clearly and respectfully. A young woman once asked me to be her mentor during a period when I was extremely busy. Because I am committed to helping others, especially those who are building their lives, I agreed, with conditions. I let her know that we could speak once a month and that it would be best if she thought about what she wanted to talk about in advance. In that way, we would maximize every minute that we spent together, either in person or on the phone. It ended up working beautifully—for both of us. After about a year of connecting in this way, Lori figured out what she wanted to do with her life and told me that I had been of help in guiding her to her life's work. I fine-tuned my understanding of the knowledge I had and was enormously grateful to be able to share some of what I had learned with someone who could and would benefit from it. We continue to stay in touch. Lori created her own events planning company in Boston. When she runs into snags from time to time, I hear from her, and we talk about how she might handle the challenge before her. She also touches base when things are going well.

Some mentoring relationships occur on the job. A budding editor from Louisiana came to New York to work for one of the largest publishing companies in the world. He was more than a little intimidated. The day he arrived, he was summarily shown the way to the mailroom; even though he was well dressed, the guards assumed he was a messenger since he was African American. Todd was flustered but was not to be deterred. He had arrived with the name of an executive at the publishing company, also an African-American male; a family friend had said this man would be a good person to contact. Todd called and asked for a meeting. That may have been the best decision he made in his early days at that company. Mr. Johnson, a senior executive, had long before committed to supporting newcomers, especially those who might face racial prejudice. He helped to calm Todd down and then talked with him about strategy. The two met regularly for the first few months, and their conversations shifted from how to be a Black man in a mainstream business to how to position oneself to excel in that particular corporate culture. Todd didn't always agree with Mr. Johnson, and that was okay too. What Todd gained from this relationship was a confidant with whom he could discuss his vulnerabilities and questions without fear of reproach or disclosure to his boss or other staff members. Now that Todd has been on the job for several years, he says he's a lot more comfortable and confident. He attributes much of his ease to his trusting relationship with Mr. Johnson.

CHOOSE YOUR WORK

THERE ARE TIMES when the road seems to fork, and it's not so clear which road to travel. What do you do? Years ago, I got a powerful answer to that question. I was still working at *Essence* and was offered the opportunity to become the fashion editor. Since I was a little girl, I had dreamed of fashion and had spent a considerable amount of time pursuing it. I had been a runway model. I wrote fashion articles from college onward. I styled photographs for all of my lifestyle shoots. This was a golden opportunity—except that by that time, I was fully immersed in my spiritual life and not as concerned with the world of style. I couldn't understand why this opportunity was being presented to me at that moment. I contemplated the offer deeply. The wisdom I received was: Whenever you have a choice, choose that which will bring you closer to God. If each of your choices is equal, do what's practical. That's what I did. I didn't think that being the fashion editor of *Essence* was going to trigger a spiritual revolution for others or for me, but it was the practical choice. Because I had a strong spiritual grounding and the magazine is spiritually inclined, I was able to bring my growing sensitivity about the interior world to my work. Ultimately, my choice did help to bring me closer to God, albeit circuitously. I gained great experience in documenting style and what it really means to women deep down inside. When I opened my own business, I was able to attract clients who want to look great and also want to feel good from the inside out. My commitment to my spiritual life and to learning how to honor women's ongoing interests in their physical presentation has led to a powerful foundation that I use now to support women (and men) in their pursuit of personal beauty and Truth.

TAKE LOVE TO WORK

In "LIFE WITHOUT PRINCIPLE," Thoreau makes another powerful point: "You must get your living by loving." No matter what field you choose, Thoreau suggests that you can approach it with love. A teacher who is intent on changing a child and molding her into something "better" may not be taking an honestly loving approach, whereas if he chose to enhance the skills and talents that the student already has as he also introduces the student to new ideas, he would be doing her a tremendous service. A construction worker who cares about how he grounds beams as he is building a residential high-rise ensures that each part is in perfect alignment so that the building will protect the people who will inhabit it. An assembly line worker in a food-packing plant can bring loving awareness to that job. Knowing that every jar or can of food will be used to nourish someone can serve as inspiration to package it with great attention and care.

Do you believe that you operate in a loving way on your job? What does loving look like at work? To be loving in any environment naturally inspires kindness, compassion, thoughtfulness, forgiveness, and integrity. Do you practice these virtues during your workday?

What about the fear that sometimes stands in the way of love, especially at work? Even the kindest people, those who really do apply virtues in their daily lives, sometimes find it tough at work to stay in a loving, open state of mind. Here's where an attitude of service comes in. When you do your work as an act of service, fear is automatically dispelled. Sensitivity replaces arrogance. Strength fortifies floundering. Approaching your work as a loving act of service actually makes you more powerful, even though on the surface it may seem to wash over you with a softening wave.

It's easy for someone in a bad mood or who is irritable to affect your mood at work. It's a challenge to stay bright and open when the conditions are less than optimal. Many of the people whom I interviewed for this book told me that when it comes to work, they use different standards than they do in other parts of their lives. They do whatever it takes to win at work. Rarely did their stories celebrate stepping back and seeing how they could be of service. Instead, at work, it was okay to lie if it meant the day would go more smoothly. And a lie meant anything from saying you arrived at work much earlier than you actually did to making a series of lengthy long-distance calls during office hours and charging them to the office account. People took credit for work they hadn't done in hopes of getting a promotion, while others cushioned their company entertainment expenses with costs for personal adventures. There were stories of people who stole office and even bathroom supplies to support at-home business or household needs, all the while rationalizing their actions. This is the antithesis of love.

BALANCE YOUR WORK

How do you reconnect with your source of loving if it feels as if it's all dried up? Beyond the possibility that it might be time to change what you do, it is also likely time to reevaluate how much time you spend doing what you do.

Chances are that you aren't balancing your time well. How much time do you actually spend on the job? Even the best job isn't worth 90 percent of your day, is it? Wisdom about this particular Truth frequently comes from the mouths of terminally ill patients who recognize that it's not worth it to work every single day of your life without taking any time out for yourself. When you die, what happens? Usually you are acknowledged by your remaining coworkers and immediately replaced.

I participated in a workshop for business leaders a few years ago that shed some light on how to discover balance regarding time and approach to work. There were people from many different fields of interest gathered—from educators to entrepreneurs, financial consultants to artists. Together we looked at ways in which we could do essentially what Thoreau espoused: pursue our work lives through the lens of love. We practiced talking through crises using a loving voice and looking for the lesson in the most extreme circumstances. We searched for ways to honor all of the people who came into our purview, even when we didn't believe we had enough time to do so. I thought about this workshop recently as I was sitting at my desk working. As I took a break from typing (something I have trained myself to do out of respect for my body), I looked to the right of my computer and saw the physical treasure that I gained from that two-day event. It is a tiny, framed document that tells the fruit of my contemplation about the meaning of work. It says: "The essence of work is service. Selfless service is love. Work is love." I smiled as I read my words. I remembered how a few minutes of meditation had yielded such a perfect message for me, one that I have held onto ever since. My wisdom for my work. What is your wisdom for yours?

My Journal Entry

Dearest Friend,
I want my work in this world to count. I intend to offer my time and effort
to something that truly matters to me. I want to support the world in a
significant way. When I reach the end of my days, I want to be able to
look back and know that I worked wisely.

> *I love you,*
> *Me*

As you write in your journal about work, take your time so that you
can be thorough.

- *Look at how your parents envisioned work.* What did you learn from them
  that has had an impact on your work ethic?

- *What jobs have you held over your life?* From the earliest project you may
  have had, such as delivering newspapers or working in a family-owned
  store, remember what you learned from each experience.

- *What dreams have you had about how you imagine your life to be?* What do
  you need to do to make that happen? What type of work is necessary
  for you to accomplish your dreams?

- *Make lists and graphs.* List your existing skills and education. Then list
  the jobs you would like to do, and compare what you have written to
  see how your existing experience could translate into new pursuits.
  Speak to someone currently doing the job you would like to have.

- *Look at the pros and cons of your work experience to date.* Learn from your
  triumphs and mistakes.

This contemplation can be an ongoing one. Over time, you can get to the
core of your heart's desires as they relate to work and then ensure that
you pursue them.

10

SLOW DOWN

―――――――――――――――

JUST PONDERING THE IDEA of slowing down can be hard for some people. We live in such a fast-paced society that many success-driven people believe that they have to muster up more energy to keep going rather than to pause to take a breath in the midst of their busy lives. Yet taking time out to reflect is vital to managing your life effectively. In order to know what choices to make about the smallest and grandest issues, you have to be able to examine them with your full attention.

CHOOSING TO SLOW DOWN

I LIVE IN NEW YORK CITY, the city that never sleeps. Perfectly suited to a driven person like myself, this city encourages its residents to expend endless hours of effort on an idea, project, or activity. One is given permission in this town to push forward, to continue even when the obvious alternative is to slow down and take rest.

When I broach the topic of slowing down to people in New York City, invariably I get a steady flow of creative excuses for why it just cannot happen. One woman, an interior designer in her mid-thirties, claims that she has worked overtime to figure out how to take a rest, only to discover that her efforts at planting the seeds for time out have only made her more worn out. I've noticed actors and waiters, editors and photographers, investment bankers and accountants who all claim that there's just no way to jump off the fast-moving train, for if they do they risk losing it all.

Pondering these presumed realities about living in the Big Apple, I have had to consider my own lot with greater precision. I have had to ask myself, "Was it after I moved to New York that I became so driven? Was it the fast pace of this international quick-pulsing city that quickened my own step?" The Truth yields a resounding no. I have been pushing myself creatively and otherwise since I was a child. Upon reflection, I had to admit yet another Truth: I may have selected New York because it serves as a fabulous excuse for my natural behavior.

Excuses, I dare say, do not last forever. When I was pledging my college sorority, my line sisters and I had to memorize the following saying: "Excuses are the tools of the incompetent, built on monuments of nothingness, and those who specialize in them seldom amount to anything." We were instructed to take this assertion into our being and own it, to consider its meaning and abide by its wisdom. Nearly twenty years later, it came out of the recesses of my memory to my rescue.

Over the years, I had been prone to physical ailments like chronic bronchitis, some other form of upper respiratory failure, or severe, debilitating headaches. Any one of these awful maladies would strike me at precisely the wrong moment. Why? When is there a right moment to become debilitated? Never. There's not enough time! I have also suffered terribly from insomnia. I have sought to discover the perfect potion or ointment—something that would relieve me of my symptoms, so that I could steal some rest and be able to push forth at full speed come morning.

One night as I tossed and turned trying to sleep, I realized that my dreams had actually awakened me. These dreams were filled with creative solutions to my most immediate challenges. Rather than trying to go back to sleep for another hour or two, I invited myself to get up, go to my computer, and record my dream messages. Among the dream treasures was this: Only by slowing down would I be able to see clearly what actually lies ahead of me. In the swirl of images that had been dancing before me moments before this revelation, I had been seemingly attacked by all kinds of emotions—panic because of how one client had been manipulating me, fatigue because of how many days and hours I had been working without pause, anger thanks to a buildup of swallowed frustrations that I had been unwilling to let out for fear of exacerbating an already volatile work situation. Only in the stillness of nonaction could I begin to unravel the essence of what my life looked like in that moment. I had to be still long enough to see how the pieces were fitting together, and then, without judgment, I had to determine what action was appropriate to take next. This wasn't an easy process. It required tremendous self-restraint and discipline. I had to force myself to be still long enough to see clearly and objectively, long enough to allow the full wave of emotions to pass over me and drift off, leaving me in a space of peace and comfortable resolution.

From that still space, I could see. With clear vision, I can make choices that are based on what's real rather than on an emotional reaction. As I become planted in my own Truth, I am able to claim a remarkably perceptive vision that allows me to see precisely how to move forward. The challenge is learning how to sustain this place of clarity. As always, it has to do with choice. What are the choices that I can make in order to see how to move forward effectively?

In this instance, the choice to slow down was also recognition of my role in my life. I had been stuck in the dangerous mode of doer. I believed with all my heart that I had to "do this" or "do that" in order to be successful. Over the years, I have discovered that the false sense of control that is derived from doing cannot sustain me. Any attempt to juggle all the balls of my life at once without acknowledging the support and direction of God is foolhardy. When the balls start falling down, which they inevitably do, it is then that I see that I am not really the doer at all. Yes, I have to put forth my own effort to stay on course. More, though, the divinity that guides my life, that lives within me and also as the entire universe, wants to lead the way. When I slow down, I can see that. When my vision becomes clear, I can rest in the cradle of God's love so that I can be strong enough to forge ahead.

A writer-filmmaker living in Los Angeles shared a similar story. A calm and kind man, Alex says he used to get frustrated all the time as he was pursuing his career. He would have a plan in mind and put forth an enormous amount of energy trying to make it happen. But after a few years, he began to feel completely burned out, and his career stalled. Alex finally called it quits. He figured Hollywood just wasn't for him.

Before moving back to his hometown, he took a break. He visited the neighborhoods in L.A. that he had previously not had time to see. He took long walks around a beautiful reservoir near his home. He wrote in his journal about his ideas and experiences. He went back to church. Slowly but surely, Alex realized that his career *wasn't* finished. Instead, he discovered that when he had a creative idea on a particular subject, invariably he would run into somebody who was the perfect person to talk to about the idea. This happened over and over again, and after a while, Alex regained confidence in his professional vision, this time with the bonus of seeing that there was a power at work in his life that was interested and willing to support his every step. What he had to do was slow down enough to be able to recognize it.

WELCOME REST

HOW DO WE FIND TIME to slow down once we become adults and have multiple responsibilities? Back in kindergarten, we had a special time during the day to rest. Being quite a busy girl even when I was five years old, I recall finding it difficult to slow my little brain down and go to sleep like the other children. Because we had about a half-hour to lay our heads on our desks and be still, I was able to master it. What a delightful experience that nap was! It came at the perfect moment every day: just before we began to squirm in our seats too much, we received the delightful invitation to rest ourselves completely.

An invitation to rest. How often do you receive those now? From whom do they come? If you have children, do you find that they are quick to ask you to relax with them or by yourself rather than taking them to soccer practice, the mall, or over to a friend's house? Does your boss come in and say, "Oh, let's just take today off so we can rest"? What about *you*? When you are tired, do you slow down? When you know you need to rejuvenate, do you take care of yourself, or do you just keep moving, operating on the belief that you have to do what you have to do?

What about taking a nap? Imagine shutting everything out for a certain period of time when you just let your body rest, exactly as you did in the kindergarten. Whether it's for fifteen minutes or a couple of hours, a nap can prove incredibly beneficial when you welcome it at the time it is needed. My cousin in Baltimore is a schoolteacher. Patricia tells me how rewarding and stressful it can be to work with young people all day long. It takes a lot of energy to keep them focused and interested in learning. By the end of the week, Patricia is beat. Already past the thirty-year mark of her career, Patricia also knows the importance of taking care of herself along the way so that she can really be there for her class. That's why she gives herself the gift of a nap. Sometimes it's on Saturday afternoon; other times it's after work before it's time to have dinner. Pat says that sometimes she feels guilty for stealing that precious time for herself. She quickly adds, though, "It's important. When I'm that tired, the only thing that makes sense to do is rest." Our bodies do tell us when we need to rest. They send out signals that encourage us to slow down well before disaster strikes. The more in tune we become with our bodies, the better able we will be at heeding their messages and honoring ourselves.

FOLLOW A SCHEDULE

DISCIPLINE IS THE INGREDIENT that makes it possible for us to savor a balanced life. Knowing when to begin and end activities helps to create order in our lives. Parents work to establish discipline in their children. Teachers seek order in their classroom. Employers create parameters for work hours as well as deadlines for projects. There are many supports that help to carve out patterns for people's lives, but these are not enough. Rather than following someone else's plan for living, we must create our own. Only we know what we need to accomplish during our waking hours on any given day. Only we understand what forms of discipline will afford us freedom to relax in our lives. You may want to make a schedule that you follow throughout the day. Most important is to create a cut-off after which you will not work. This goes for entrepreneurs and those climbing the corporate ladder alike. There is a time and a place for everything, including when we are facing challenges. The sooner we learn to manage our time and efforts, the sooner we will be able to enjoy each moment. The philosopher Bertrand Russell had a lot to say about the human quest for happiness and the challenges that stand in our way. In his book *The Conquest of Happiness,* he wrote:

> The wise man thinks about his troubles only when there is some purpose in doing so; at other times he thinks about other things, or, if it is night, about nothing at all.

We can be wise. We can choose to move on to the activity at hand even if a particular topic has not been resolved. As Russell explained, the best way to move forward is by using our brains when we can be effective and allowing our minds to rest when the time is right. Think of turning water on and off. Water, just like your thoughts, will flow freely when the spigot is open. When the spigot is completely closed, the water stops. When you control your mind, your thoughts can be stilled completely. At first, it may feel as if you have a leaky faucet, because thoughts seep through. The more you practice being fully present in the moment you are in, you will see that your ability to close off the "thought valve" will strengthen.

MAKE A TO-DO LIST

AS WE BECOME MASTERS of our bodies and minds, we also start to lose the feeling of guilt that may crop up when we are juggling what feels like a hundred things. When we cultivate a balanced life, we find more and more that there is enough time to do everything that we have to do. The superfluous activities fall away, leaving space to accommodate what is truly the requirement. And these requirements include taking care of your Self.

The process of retraining ourselves toward balance also allows us to let go of the propensity for self-blame. Unless we choose to stop blaming ourselves for all of the things that we want to change about ourselves, we will remain stuck in how we have lived rather than how we are living in this moment. Feeling guilty for not mastering balance in our lives is not productive. I know how insidious the feelings of guilt and self-blame can be. When you look at your laundry list of things to do for the day or the week, you sigh; it doesn't seem possible that everything can get done. Now you want to add rest and relaxation to your daily activities! You can do it. Create a to-do list. Write down, from most important to least, all the things you need or want to accomplish,

My to-do list used to go from one to thirty or more items that I had to handle for various work projects. Work came first and my family second. My personal life did not appear at all. When I began including my whole life on my list of daily activities, things changed. Now on my daily to-do list, I include everything I can think of, from remembering to drink water to finishing an article whose deadline is near, as well as carving out an hour for exercise and another for meditation. In this way, I have begun to redesign the way that I live. Instead of feeling guilty at the end of the day, I can look at my to-do list and take pride in the items that have been checked off as completed. I can also see clearly what I have left to tackle the following day. Facing what I have created as my own goals is liberating. I can see for myself what needs attention and what I can remove from my list. Best of all, I no longer need to feel guilty for what has or has not occurred. Instead, I can choose to handle each task in an appropriate period of time.

LISTEN TO YOUR SELF

ONE OF THE MOST effective ways that you can restore energy and peace of mind to your being is to meditate. Think of it as your way of plugging yourself into an energy socket that recharges your batteries. When we are living our lives, we are either depleting our energy supply or drawing on someone else's supply in hopes of filling our own tanks. When we meditate, we restore our supply of vital energy.

In one sense, meditation is the practice of focusing your energy on a specific point and absorbing your attention there. But if we don't give ourselves enough room to breathe and just listen to the voice within ourselves, we won't have the ability to access our inner knowledge. Meditation is a doorway to that inner knowledge. Resting our thoughts, feelings, habits, tendencies, beliefs, fears, and apprehensions in the comfort of meditation relieves us of whatever is standing in our way. By focusing inward and inviting our entire being to become still—to rest in its pure state—we welcome the emergence of our own Truth.

TAKE TIME TO FOCUS

A FASHION CONSULTANT in New York told a wonderful story of how meditation turned her day around. She was feeling overwhelmed by too many responsibilities that needed to be handled at once. Each morning she woke up on edge, afraid that she hadn't given herself enough time to accomplish her goals. Luckily, she remembered to meditate. For one full hour, she sat down and focused her energy inside. She gave herself permission to stop thinking about what had to be done. She promised herself that she was doing herself a favor. "Trust me," she quietly said. As the thoughts came up, she shooed them away. As the anxieties bubbled forward, she breathed that much more deeply. Returning to the life-sustaining breath that supports her every move, Phyllis felt her body on the inside and out becoming stronger. By the time she was finished, she says she felt completely ready to manage her day. Tension had vanished, and in its place were courage and conviction. From that centered space, she was able to make better use of her day than she had all the other days of the week when she hadn't meditated.

Meditation takes you to the source of your very own being and creates a nurturing space for you to rest in the heart of you. I consider it the ultimate resting place. You don't have to go anywhere to do it. You don't have to spend money in order to engage it. Meditation is nondenominational. Anybody who practices any spiritual tradition can participate. It is an equal opportunity life enhancer. And one of the tremendous benefits that people gain from practicing it is a renewed body and mind that supports the Self.

HAVE FUN

GIVE YOURSELF PERMISSION to have fun. Slowing down does not always mean being still. It can also mean changing your pace. Think about how you spend an average day. Now extend that to a week. What do you do for fun? Can you imagine adding an activity to your menu of options? Before you allow any of the reasons that you can't do something fun right now, give yourself permission to dream. Out of your imaginings may come the perfect solution. You do have to give yourself room to envision it.

A woman in New York wrote to me once about her new relationship. She had met a wonderful man, and the two of them hit it off. She was single without children. He was the divorced father of two. Both had pretty busy lives, but they were trying to make space for each other. Sherry began to complain, though; she said Max didn't know how to have fun. Sherry liked to go out to dinner and to the theater, while Max didn't have time or extra dollars to entertain her in that way. Although Max did regularly invite Sherry to his house for a home-cooked meal, with and without his children, she was not satisfied. In fact, she was starting to believe that this relationship wasn't going to work out. Before she threw in the towel, I recommended that she take action rather than remaining seated in her frustration. There had to be some activities that they could do together without spending a lot of money. Sure enough, when the two of them got creative, they came up with a few months' worth of choices—from going to a matinee at the theater to seeking out an affordable new restaurant from time to time to taking a walk together in Central Park. Sherry says it hadn't occurred to her that she could figure out a solution to their problem or that money didn't have to be a deal breaker in their relationship. A few months into their relationship, she says they had grown to balance their time together with their other responsibilities, which made everybody happy.

You can be happy too. Instead of dwelling on what's not going right, incorporate recreation time into your life. What does fun look like for you? How often do you dedicate time to having fun? Even if you don't yet place true value on fun, trust that it is important to shift your perception. Life is supposed to be joyous. It is a precious gift that can bring lightness and wonder to every moment. In order for this to manifest in your life, you have to choose it. Accentuate the positive. Look for the fun in each moment as well as the special activities that you reserve to make your heart dance. As you do this, you will see how readily any moment can turn into a joyous one.

A senior music industry executive had this experience shortly after transitioning out of her job in the music industry. Juanita had been one of the highest-ranking executives in her field, running on the fast track when the industry began to weaken. Her job was one of many that were dissolved at her company. Being a savvy businesswoman, Juanita had invested well and saved some money, and she got a healthy severance package from her former employer. Money was not going to be a problem for her, so she decided that she would devote some of her new-found free time to pursuing some of her life's dreams. She took time to mourn the emotional loss that she was feeling and then visited the places that she had always dreamed of seeing. Because she gave herself permission to be a free thinker during this time, Juanita was also much more capable of developing her next career move. She trusted that her talents, knowledge, and inner wisdom would lead her to her next role.

MOVE YOUR BODY

MANY OF US live relatively sedentary lives. Being inactive for extended periods of time can have negative effects, leading to physical ailments like obesity, diabetes, high blood pressure, poor circulation, and indigestion. When you don't move your body, you aren't honoring your Self.

As we consider the importance of slowing down and allowing ourselves some breathing room, this doesn't mean that we should not do anything. Your body will support you far better if you keep it limber and supple than if you ignore it. Get up. Move around. Drink six to eight glasses of water daily. Take a walk. Go to an exercise class. Go dancing. Do *something*!

Physical activity can actually inspire your entire body to relax. It's an interesting paradox: to be able to still your mind and experience the fruits of meditation, your body needs to be open and limber. For years, I thought that the effective means of loosening up for me was to get a massage. I discovered that it was the one consistent way that I could relax. Every time I traveled, I would book a massage at the hotel, so that I would be sure to let go of any burdens I was holding onto that week. For an hour or two, I was in bliss. My muscles and mind relaxed. I was able to sleep well. All was good—except that massage alone proved not to be enough. When I finally faced the fact that my relaxation techniques had to include my active participation, I began to feel healthier. That didn't mean that I gave up my massages! When I was on the road, I simply added an hour in the gym. And at home, I began to incorporate a workout routine.

GO TO SLEEP

LIFE GOES IN CYCLES, from day to night, from youth to old age. Nature creates patterns for life that regulate how we function. Generations ago, people had little choice but to follow nature. When the sun rose, they began their day. When the sun set, their day drew to a close. With the invention of the light bulb, everything changed. Clearly we have benefited from this invention, and yet we needed only the tiniest prompting to be off to the races. We stretch minutes into hours and days into weeks, often without noticing how we are spending our time. When it comes to sleeping, we have cut into those vital hours that the body needs for restoration in order to get more things done.

What about you? Maybe you are like my husband, who has a terrific body clock. For the most part, whatever he's doing, by the time 10:00 P.M. draws near, his eyelids have grown heavy, and he's headed to bed. I used to get angry that he would sleep in this way! I wanted him to stay up and be a night owl with me, the proud insomniac. Over the years, I have figured out that his body has better sense than my own. Well, what's more accurate is that he allows his body to speak for itself. I discovered that I had denied my body, urging it to work a little longer and then go a little further. Over time, it has grown accustomed to that pace. In recent years, I have begun to retrain it to listen to itself.

How much sleep do you get each night? Doctors and scientists debate about just how much a person needs. The general sense is that six to eight hours on the average is healthy, although that does vary from person to person as well as by the age of the person. If you believe that your sleep patterns are not supporting your ability to feel fully rested and strong on a daily basis, you may want to examine how you are sleeping. Use your journal. Take note of when you get in bed each night and when you awaken, as well as when you get up. How do you feel when you begin your day? Document your sleep patterns for one month. At the end of the month, review your findings. Depending on what you learn, take the necessary steps to adjust your schedule in order for you to feel fully rested.

There are a number of basic things you can do to support yourself in your effort to sleep better. Chances are you have heard these before, but I have found that a reminder can be extremely helpful:

- *Don't eat too late.* Give yourself at least three hours between your last meal and your sleep time. This includes when you go out to eat, when possible.

- *Eat your heaviest meal at lunch and a lighter meal at dinner.* This will make it easier for your body to digest your food quickly and be at ease when you are ready to sleep.

- *Avoid caffeine after 4:00 P.M.* This is a hard one for me. I have learned that if I consume caffeine too late in the day, it's hard for me to fall asleep at night.

- *Avoid strenuous exercise near bedtime.* Opt for yoga stretches or other physical exercises that will relax your body.

- *Don't watch TV in bed,* especially not programming that will keep your mind active, such as action, horror, or violent films.

- *Read just before bed.* Poetry, spiritual literature, or other positive material is great. Read something that will inspire you to have a still night's sleep.

- *Meditate.* I can't say enough about the healing qualities of this practice. It also helps you to slip into a peaceful sleep.

If you find that your sleep is not improving, see your doctor. A holistic practitioner may be able to prescribe alternatives to sleeping aids to help you sleep. A physician may be able to identify any physical ailment that may be causing your insomnia.

TAKE A VACATION

WHEN I WAS GROWING UP, the stories I read always made Europe seem so romantic. This was in part because these people lived so far away and spoke exotic languages. That all of the citizens got to take a whole month off in the summer to enjoy their lives was equally compelling. A month off! Can you imagine what your life would be like? When I was a teenager and young adult I envied Europeans for having that luxury.

That's not to say that we didn't have our family vacations. Like many other families, mine found time to do fun things together, especially during the summer months. We took long driving trips from Baltimore to upstate New York, and to Atlanta and other points south. Usually we were headed to professional conferences that my father was attending. While he met with his colleagues, we explored the new environments, swimming, sightseeing, and meeting new people. Those memories are still vivid for me—not just the big events that we attended once we reached our destination but also the little moments in between. We were always learning something, and it was fun to learn from our parents away from school. Because of the no-eating-in-Daddy's-car rule, we always stopped and had a meal together as a family in a restaurant. This practice allowed us to focus on what we were doing—eating—in a way that promoted good health, as it also encouraged healthy family dialogue. It wasn't until many years later that I realized how precious that family time really was and increasingly how rare it has become for many families, from dual-income, ultra-busy families to single-parent households. Even single people find it hard to steal away during the height of their working years.

Vacation. Time off from work when you do what you want to do. When was the last time you took one? Many people complain that they don't have enough time or money to take a proper vacation. Even when they are feeling stressed out, they won't risk getting away. I met one woman who actually postponed her wedding twice because her work just wouldn't accommodate her honeymoon schedule! Finally, she did get married, but the rocky start created a huge hurdle for her and her husband to face before they even crossed the threshold of their new home. I know a chorus of professionals quick to count how many years they've gone without significant time off. Some wear this passage of time as a badge of honor.

If you see yourself in any of these stories, you may be feeling anxious even thinking about taking a vacation. You can start to change your attitude about this by giving yourself a break. You do work really hard. Finding time to give to yourself is not always easy. I certainly have found it challenging at different points in my life. Recently I came across some wisdom on this topic from Bertrand Russell, who says, in *The Conquest of Happiness,* "The more tired a man becomes, the more impossible he finds it to stop. One of the symptoms of approaching nervous breakdown is the belief that one's work is terribly important and that to take a holiday would bring all kinds of disaster."

A spiritual or nervous breakdown is not our goal, nor is fleeing from work, from a marriage, or from some other relationship. If you are one of those people who find it hard to set aside time just for you, I encourage you to approach the whole notion differently. Maybe you don't have a month to devote to downtime, but you can probably carve out a long weekend or even seven days straight when you can do whatever allows you to relax.

Just as you plan for work, plan for time off. Imagine what you will do each day that you have allocated to your personal pursuits. Select your destination, which can be anywhere from the island of Tahiti to your own backyard. Make an itinerary that includes time for all of the goals you want to accomplish, including just being still. Especially if you stay at home, be sure to consider how you will spend those precious hours that you have set aside. Maybe you'll go to a museum, have lunch with a good friend, or take a drive out to a historic site you've wanted to visit. One afternoon you may want to shut out the entire outside world and give yourself an in-home day of beauty. Whatever you fancy, plan it and make it happen. Write about your experience in your journal so that you can relish the moments you gave to you.

CARVE OUT TIME FOR YOURSELF

REST—the ability to take time off for you—is not relegated to the rich, although some people mistakenly believe this. Once you have committed to carving out time to enjoy yourself and truly relax, you will be able to make it happen. That's what Kathy did. When she was in her twenties trying to figure out what kind of work she was going to do, Kathy says she already knew that she did not have the ambition to be a lawyer, an educator, a medical worker, or an engineer. She knew she needed to work in order to be self-sufficient, so she reviewed her options. She pursued office management training with the plan of becoming proficient in using office equipment and keeping other people's business in order. Since she had always been an organized person, she figured she would be good at this. Her choice paid off. For the past twenty years, Kathy has been able to earn a decent living without feeling bound to a particular job. She has accepted long-term temporary positions at various companies. When she doesn't want to work because she chooses to travel, she has the flexibility to do so. Kathy balances work with restful pleasure efficiently. She has set aside resources for her retirement so that when the time comes for her to rest full time, she will be prepared.

A Jamaican-born electrician who has spent much of his life in the United States created his own model for living that works for him and his family. Married with three children, Frank received the training in his youth to become an electrician, a skill that can travel wherever he goes. He and his wife have built a firm foundation for their family, which has included sending their children to college. Now in their fifties, Frank and his wife are enjoying their lives in ways that many might envy. They kept property in their Jamaican homeland, and Frank spends at least six months nearly every year on the island or in another equally exotic locale while his wife comes and goes as her work permits. As he plans for old age, Frank is building a home for his family in Jamaica. When the time comes, his extended rest will be in his ideal environment.

Rest can be interpreted accurately as time for Self. Your own creativity can be your guide for defining your time for self-rejuvenation. What's key is that you carve out time that belongs to you, where you experience little or no stress. It becomes your time to flourish.

KNOW WHEN TO RETIRE

THE AVERAGE AGE that Americans reach increases nearly every year. Although there are variations depending on ethnicity, gender, economic status, occupation, and environment, even those at highest risk in our culture outlive many who were in similar circumstances in past generations. Look at your family history. Think of relatives who have passed away. What age did they reach? How was their health? What were they doing with their lives in the days leading up to their death? As you contemplate the paths that your predecessors followed and the ways in which their lives ended, consider what you want for your life.

Things are very different now than they were even a generation ago. The formal age of retirement remains sixty-five, with sixty-two being acceptable for social security, even though you are penalized if you begin accepting the benefits three years ahead of schedule. Regardless of when you retire, social security is not enough for most people. Indeed, even with retirement funds, annuities, and other savings instruments that some of us have contributed to over the years, many people don't have enough money tucked away to be able to afford to retire when they are legally ready. The choices that many people make in their lives early on when they do decide to pursue their heart's calling don't always provide them with the necessary cushion to make ends meet during their golden years. Does this description fit your life? And is there anything you can do about it right now to make it easier for you when you reach the period when you would like to take it easy?

You can start by getting financial advice. Many employers offer free services to their staff. Banks, other lending institutions, community service organizations, money management books, and on-line services provide a wealth of information to help you figure out how to make your money stretch. Creative management of your personal resources can help you to live a life that includes full-time rest during your later years. In order to claim this golden period, you have to plan ahead, as well as be willing to make sacrifices. Talk to people who understand how money works in this country. Seek out advice that will help you to make the right decisions about your life.

This includes information about insurance. What happens if you can no longer work and the only choice available to you is to stop and rest, to heal your body? Have you made the proper choices that will afford you the opportunity to be still for the time needed without undue pressure on yourself or your loved ones? You'd be surprised at how many people become homeless when they are struck down by disabilities. Don't let yourself be one of them, and don't wait too long to set your insurance plans in order.

An insurance executive in South Carolina died suddenly in his late fifties, leaving behind a wife and three grown children. Since her husband was in the industry, Yvonne was certain that she would be set for life. Much to her dismay, she learned that her husband had not purchased a substantial insurance policy. His estate did not even cover the price of their mortgage or all of his personal bills. Although she was able to work her finances out, Yvonne was angry and frustrated. How could it be that he hadn't taken care of business?

Many people ask themselves the same question when they unexpectedly face long-term disability. Because of the feeling that "it won't happen to me," more people than you might imagine do not take the necessary precautions to support their lives. I have spoken with people who lost their homes, their credit rating, and their jobs as a result of prolonged illness, car accidents, and other disasters. Although insurance can't make up for many of the side effects of physical or mental impairment, the financial support can afford a person the opportunity to rest without fear of economic peril.

It's all about choice. We have to choose to take care of ourselves using the resources at our disposal. Although we live in a society that urges us to consume everything now, we need to exercise our muscles of restraint that will allow us to enjoy the present again and again.

My Journal Entry

Dearest Friend,

How are you feeling today? How much rest do you need? What can I do for you right now that will replenish your spirit? I pledge to take care of you. I want you to be strong. I know that means you need time to just be, to reflect, to rest. I promise to give you that time.

I love you,
Me

LET YOUR JOURNAL ENTRY flow with the love and compassion that you feel for your own spirit. Contemplate the state of your body and mind:

- *How have you taken care of yourself in the past?*

- *What can you do to take care of yourself now?*

- *Be patient with yourself and mindful not to beat yourself up as you review your life.* Even if you have never taken time off before, be happy that you can see that now is your moment.

- *Cherish the realization that in this moment you can do something special for you, that each day means a fresh start.* Do something that will replenish the wellspring of love and joy that are waiting to shine through you out into the world.

- *Pledge to give yourself the time and space to slow down and enjoy yourself.*

II

RESPECT YOUR BODY

The human body is a source of wonder and inspiration. It is a complex machine that serves a multitude of purposes. The body's most significant duty is to house the spirit that enlivens each of us. The body of a human being is resilient and powerful, an exquisitely complicated and perfectly designed vessel that supports the soul's journey in this life. The body is both compassionate and forgiving. When we get sick, we usually get well. If we get injured, most often we heal. Even when we suffer dire conditions, we frequently survive. The body's amazing ability to overcome even the most extreme obstacles in order to survive may also be its greatest challenge. Intuitively, we know that our bodies serve a vital function in our lives. And yet we often take our bodies for granted.

The vitality of the body is often something that goes unacknowledged, largely because it is so consistent. It's as if the body serves as a best friend to us, providing for the growth and evolution of our souls seemingly without requiring attention or accolades.

More to the point, in contemporary culture, many of us live in an unrealistic relationship with our body. Whereas we subconsciously know that without the body we will die, we often do not understand the fundamental Truth that the body, the mind, and the spirit need to be in a space of alignment in order for us to live peacefully and healthfully. Mistakenly, what many people pay an inordinate amount of attention to is identification with the body. Instead of viewing the body as the sacred home of the spirit, many identify with it in ways that are unhealthy, unproductive, and often unrealistic. I do not state this fact to make any of us feel bad. One of the most lucrative industries in America is that of beauty. Many women and men alike are locked into the belief that we need particular products or regimens in order to be whole. In the midst of the swirl of images that lure us into wanting to be different from how we are, we easily forget who we are. We begin to believe that we need to look different in order to be entitled to a life worth living.

Clearly, there's something wrong with this picture. Wading through the many layers of illusion to get to the true reason for having a body and understanding its role in our lives can be tough. Indeed, it can take a lifetime to become evident. Though I'd rather not admit it, I have to say that it took me the better part of my life thus far to break free from the many false concepts that I had held about my own body. For years, I felt trapped in a body that betrayed me. Instead of loving my body, I spent endless hours discovering ways to camouflage what I perceived as my deficits. For many years I was very tall, extremely thin, and naturally shy. I towered over all of the other girls, when I was young, standing eye-to-eye with the boys for most of my formative years. It was awkward to be different from the other girls. In seventh grade, the girl who was supposedly my "best friend" and who had already begun to bud into her femininity challenged me one day about my bra size. In front of other girls, she chided me, proudly telling me and those gathered that she wore an A cup. "What do you wear, Harriette?" she sneered. Not having the faintest idea about cups (I had no need for them), I accepted the bait and proclaimed, "I wear a double A!" She laughed and walked away. Never mind I didn't know that I was basically telling the truth even as I was ashamed—for being completely flat-chested and for not knowing the first thing about cup size. I share this story from deep in my closet to illustrate how immediately it affected my own pursuit of Truth. What I experienced at a young age were rejection and ridicule based on my physical body. I grew to loathe my body, feeling awkward and unfeminine.

I hid from most situations that caused me to disrobe. I figured out how to bow out of gym class—"legally," based on a health condition that was real but didn't necessitate exemption from exercise. I never pursued the one sport in which I excelled, swimming, because I dared not jump into a pool with others wearing a swimsuit for fear of further embarrassment. The most unusual turn in my movement away from my body is that I became a model. It was something that my mother and older sister had done, so it wasn't entirely foreign to me. I was tall, after all, and skinny, which is what models were. But more to the core of the matter, I learned how to adorn the body that I felt was betraying me so that it became "beautiful." I offered a carefully crafted illusion of beauty to the public in order to shield myself from the hateful slingshots of my peers. On certain levels, it worked. During my time as a runway model, I received wide acclaim for being graceful and beautiful. Since I was so "skinny" (a term I loathed), I could fit the samples, a painfully small size 4. Because my mother and father had taught me how to carry myself, I wore the clothes well—so well, in fact, that my peers in college strongly encouraged me to go to Paris to pursue modeling on the most celebrated of runways. I declined that option, feeling that being on stage in that way was not my calling. Since that time, I have worked in the world of fashion and style from the other side, as an editor who has created image by working with models and designers and as a writer who has commented on the many layers and meanings of how we present ourselves.

So over the years, I have figured out how to use fashion to help myself as well as others. In fact, I have come to describe my work with people as going from the outside in. My clients and I often start with wardrobe as I help women and men define the way that they want to present themselves to the public, and then we quickly move on to deeper issues probing beneath the surface to what really matters in their lives so that their presentation will be honest and clear.

Although I figured out how to move past those initial crippling images of myself, the process has not been easy. Ultimately, I go back to the question: Did it work? Did adornment of my own body in the cloak of fashion improve my self-image? Not enough. A mask never fully covers, does it? It was like putting a bandage on an open sore. It still hurt underneath.

SEXUAL INTIMACY AND SELF-IMAGE

WHEN IT CAME TO RELATIONSHIPS with men, I had some serious problems. It was one thing, after all, to look good in a fabulous designer dress and quite another to stand naked before a man for any reason whatsoever, especially to make love. Rather than loving my body and believing that a man who loved me would love it too, I stood very shy before my lover. Lights out? Yes. Covers pulled up? Yes. Oh, and let's not forget the requisite drink. My most painful admission in recent years is that for most of my intimate life, I chose to be in some state of intoxication before nearly every sexual encounter, from my first when I was nineteen through my first marriage. Why? Because I didn't know how to love myself, or at least the part that was attached to my body. I understand why so many women pay for dangerous breast implants. I can't tell you how many times a man who professed to love me asked some version of this question: *Where are your breasts?* I assure you that when you are about to have sex with somebody, the last thing you want to hear is a question that erases any trace of your femininity.

I have spoken to countless women with similar stories. There are the ones who keep their bras on because they're afraid that when their over-thirty breasts fall out and down, their lovers will flee. There are the ones who have lost their breasts due to cancer who fear that no man will ever love them again. And there are the sisters who have countless other body parts and shapes that they mistakenly allow to cause them undue pain and wreak havoc on their chances at true intimacy.

What happened for me was one part spiritual, one part evolution. I have read again and again in spiritual texts that identifying with the body represents wrong understanding. You know the phrase, "The body is the temple of God." From that perspective, the body is something to be cared for, adorned, and tended, but not primarily as a sensual entity. Instead, on spiritual terms, it is the house of the divinity that dwells within each of us: a sacred house whose role is spiritual. Love it and tend to it, for its spiritual contribution is the message. Move beyond being locked into the ultimate climax or connection with a lover. Conceptually, I got that, even though it was much easier to understand theoretically than to practice. Thank goodness for evolution: the older I got and the more pounds I gained, the fuller my body became. Even more significant, I have to give greater credit to my own growing consciousness. Some years ago, the body stopped meaning the same things to me that it did in my youth.

THE DISABILITY OF IMAGE

IT'S EMBARRASSING to admit that insecurities about my physical body that began in early childhood affected my own ability to choose to stand in my own Truth on such a fundamental level for years. My experience was no different from a disabled woman I recently met who said that she married the wrong man. He said he loved her and since she was severely disabled, she felt she was lucky to find anybody who was seriously interested in her. What happened in her marriage is classically tragic. Her husband abused her emotionally by regularly disparaging her, calling her names, and otherwise belittling her because of her disability. He also cheated on her—blatantly—which fueled her low self-esteem.

When you believe that you are unworthy of respect, this is the treatment you will receive. Ultimately, this woman allowed her physical disability to disable her spirit. She then became truly disabled, broken, and vulnerable—prey for one who could not love her and who could only abuse her. Several years after getting a divorce, she still feels the pain from this relationship and is afraid to consider entering into another.

HONOR YOUR BODY

I CAN'T SAY ENOUGH about the importance of building self-esteem. When you look at self-esteem in relation to your body, it means that you have to honor and respect whatever body you have been given. You have to believe in you—from the inside out—in order for others to stand a chance of loving you the way you need and deserve. Whatever your physical form, you must learn to honor it as the vessel God has given you to travel on the journey of your life. It is beautiful because it is yours. It does not define you as much as it enables you to navigate each day. When you look at it in this way, you will be more aware of treating your body with respect and, in turn, holding your Self in the highest regard.

BECOMING A SACRED WOMAN

HERE IS WHAT one young woman learned after many years of practicing an unhealthy way of thinking and living. Nikki grew up in Cincinnati, Ohio. Her mother was extremely timid, and her stepfather became a drug addict and petty drug dealer shortly after the two married. Nikki says she remembers having to shoo drug addicts out of her living room when she was eleven years old. When her sister was born, things got worse. Nikki essentially became guardian to her sister and often had to fight off her stepfather when he was high.

At about this time, she figured out that she had to escape. Her solution turned out to be double-sided: she took herself to the church and the street. Her life resembled a seesaw. She went from singing in the choir to clowning in class; drinking and dating older boys who said they loved her to reading inspirational books. She tried everything she could think of in her effort to fill the empty void. Ultimately, Nikki moved out of her home and in with her grandmother, hoping that her life would get better. Instead it got worse. She began a downward spiral of drugs and alcohol, promiscuous sex, and self-neglect. She smoked three packs of cigarettes a day, and drank Jack Daniels straight daily. Nikki says, "I was tired of being a straight A student. It didn't matter. I was still abused, criticized, and denied the opportunity to go to the school I wanted to attend, so I set out to get away from everyone once and for all." By the time she was eighteen, Nikki was a full-blown alcoholic. She says she basically bought into all of the things that her stepfather had been telling her she would become: essentially nothing.

Eventually she stumbled on a metaphysical store and came upon *Heal Thyself,* a spiritual self-help book written by Queen Afua, a holistic teacher, healer, and high priestess of the ancient Egyptian Khamitic tradition. Nikki says that when she read the book, she was immediately reminded of the princess she had imagined herself to be as a child; it was as if the ghastly spell that had been cast on her for many years had been broken. Nikki read the book, and then sought out and began to study under Queen Afua. Over the next five years, she replaced her self-destructive behavior with prayer, meditation, yoga, fasting, affirmations, and journaling. Now, instead of stepping into situations that negate her power or her integrity, she says she honors her body and her spirit. Although the process is far from over, Nikki has learned that she must value her body as the sacred instrument that God gave her. With this knowledge, she believes that she will consciously take the steps to live as a sacred woman. Already, Nikki has found that she manages boundaries better in intimate relationships with men as a result of considering her life in this way.

THE VALUE OF LIFE

WHAT ABOUT the boundaries that we form around what we do with our bodies as it relates to the creation of life? With the advent of the Pill as well as other new forms of birth control, sexual freedom has reached an all-time high. Although I am an avid proponent of women's rights and freedom of choice, I also believe that we need to take a much harder look at how we engage our bodies for sex. In order to enjoy freedom, we must also accept responsibility. This includes the freedom to choose how we will address our ability to create life.

When I was in college, just before HIV/AIDS crashed into our awareness, many young women were exploring their sexuality for the first time. So many men and women felt their first true sense of freedom as they pursued their intimate lives. During that period, many young women got pregnant. I remember that one of my acquaintances, a young woman who was beautiful and extremely popular, proudly announced that she had had four abortions in the several years since she had been having sex. As I looked at her face, I couldn't read any remorse hiding behind her smile, but I imagined that she must have had some feelings of regret deep down inside. It wasn't until I was in her same position, recovering from an abortion myself, that I understood just how devastating that action can be. When I think about the awful day when I walked out of a doctor's office after having made the decision to terminate the life that I was carrying, I feel numb all over again. At the time, it seemed like the only thing to do. I was still in college and hardly capable of taking care of myself, let alone another. Yet I knew that something was terribly wrong. In retrospect, I see that what was wrong was everything—the whole scenario that got me there in the first place. Like many other young women, I had gotten sexually involved with a guy who was basically out for the sport of it. I thought I was "in love" with him; he was simply practicing his skill at playing the field with the end result that a precious life was lost due to irresponsibility on both our parts.

Women and men who have lived through abortion say that in the fear of the moment, many just wanted to get rid of the potential problems that a child may bring. It was not until years later when their perception of the value of human life changed, when they wanted to have children and experienced complications, or when they learned about others who were behaving just as recklessly as they did in their youth, that many people come to reconsider their earlier actions. I urge all of us to be conscious of what we do with our bodies, to understand that we have the ability to bring life into this world and that there is a tremendous responsibility associated with that. Part of respecting your body is treasuring the gifts that it provides instead of squandering them. The goal is to be aware of the choices that you make so that you can affirm the value you have placed on your life and that of others.

THE PRIVILEGE OF SEX

PART OF THIS AWARENESS calls for a more clearly developed understanding of the sexual act itself. Most students learn about the mechanics of sexual intercourse in a health class. Some brave parents search for words to describe the best conditions under which two people should engage in this intimate activity. Ultimately, it's hard to explain how you can turn what is an animal instinct into a spiritual experience that honors both parties. I would like to tell the story of my friend Dekar.

When Dekar's daughter was a preteenager, he began to talk with her seriously about what sex means and how she might approach it when her time comes. This single father very frankly and tenderly explained to his daughter that her body and her life were precious gifts. He told her that the only time she should have sex is when her partner understood and respected her as the precious gift that she is. Dekar said that probably a lot of guys would try to get her to have sex with them, and sometimes it would be very tempting. He also suggested that instead of feeling guilty about considering it, she should make her decision based on her analysis of the relationship. She should ask herself the following questions: Is she ready to enter into a sexual relationship with this person, and is her potential partner worthy of such a level of intimacy? If either answer is no, that's what she should say. When the answer is yes, she should proceed with caution and protection. Because Dekar understood that seeing is believing, he also showed his daughter through his own actions what he meant. As a single father, he was dating as his daughter was maturing. On one occasion, a woman came to visit and was obviously interested in having sex with him. Dekar decided that he was not interested in her in that way and invited her to leave. Later, he and his daughter talked about what had happened. He explained that he also valued his body as precious and did not intend to give away his gift arbitrarily.

Taking care before moving into a sexual relationship is smart. Being mindful of the action you are taking means that you can take the requisite steps to be respectful of your body, your heart, and your partner. When all of the elements come together, the experience can be wonderful. This reminds me of the beginning of my intimate relationship with my husband. George and I had been dating for some time and had grown to love one another. It was as if we naturally fit together, and we were enjoying each other's company in many different ways. Just before the first time we had sex, George paused and told me that he considered the moment as a tremendous privilege. I paused and reflected. I had had sex with other men before, but even when the relationship was great, never had I heard such words uttered. George reminded me of what my parents had taught me when I was a little girl. You don't give your body to a man just because he asks for it. You don't have sex with someone in order to be liked or loved. It's the other way around. When you seriously consider allowing a man to enter your temple, your body, it should be because he has the utmost respect for you. It should be because you love one another and are committed to each other in some significant way.

Bernadette's father told her he knew that he could not force her to remain celibate until marriage, so he wanted to give her some valuable advice. He said not to date anybody more than once whom she couldn't envision as her husband, because routine can trick even the smartest person into a committed relationship. Further, he said not to have sex with anyone whose baby she wouldn't want to have. He told her that if she followed this advice, she would be as safe as he could envision for her. What this has meant over the years is that Bernadette has not had lots of dates, but those she has had have been meaningful. Although Bernadette has not yet married, she says she feels lucky that she has followed her father's direction. Unlike some of her other friends, she hasn't gotten burned by abusive boyfriends, although she has had her feelings hurt from time to time.

If you are wondering where you fit into this picture, you have to decide. Especially if you are single, it can be tough. Many people are sexually active and intend to continue their intimate pursuits. At the same time, they want to be respectful of themselves and others. How do you strike a balance? There is no one answer to this, although it's smart to start with a firm foundation that clearly tells you what you believe is important about sexual activity. Do you want to be in a monogamous relationship? Are you in a position where you want to be in more casual relationships? What do you want, and what are you willing to be responsible for in your life now? When you have assessed your position, you can take responsible action. There may be those who question your choices. The point is that you will have made them with full knowledge of the consequences. Ramona is a great example of this.

Ramona grew up in a traditional southern home where she was taught that you shouldn't have sex until you get married. She also learned as time went by that she wasn't going to follow those teachings. This didn't mean that she planned on being promiscuous. She was cautious as she entered into relationships with men. When she was in her twenties, she met a jazz musician. All of her girlfriends went crazy over him, while Ramona stayed cool. Her brother was a musician, so she knew how they could be. As fate would have it, the two really did like one another. One night Jeff invited her to come over to his place. Ramona was very much attracted to Jeff and wanted to go, but she was scared. Before they left, Jeff called her over and explained, "I just want to tell you about me. I'm married to my music. My saxophone is my wife. I am not ready to be married. I like you very much, so I wanted to let you know my story. Are you sure you want to do this?" Ramona went with him. They had sex that night and continued to be in a relationship for some time. Ramona visited him in different cities where he had gigs. Jeff was always respectful of her, treating her like a woman and a friend, not a groupie or sex partner. For a while, Ramona admits that she was more romantically attached to Jeff than he was to her. But because the relationship started off honestly, they were able to work it out. Some fifteen years later, they are still friends. Although the intimate part of their relationship has subsided, the respect and love that they share for one another has not. Ramona chalks it up to being honest from day one.

IF YOU DON'T MAKE A CHOICE
YOUR BODY WILL MAKE ONE FOR YOU

On a very practical level, we know that we have to tend to our bodies in order to be able to live our lives. What happens, though, is that the body is so resilient that its kindness often ends up deluding us into thinking that it will always be fit and firm, so we can just go on and do whatever else we want.

For many people, it takes a health crisis before they are willing to make a dramatic difference in the way that they care for their bodies. New mothers regularly talk about the exercise program that they have begun in order to lose the forty to ninety pounds that somehow adorned them during their pregnancy. People who have survived tragic accidents or illnesses admit to cherishing the new lease they have received on their lives, and they often make the decision to take care of themselves better at that time.

My husband, George, completely revolutionized the way that he treated his body after he discovered that he had no other choice. George is a photographer. Although his is a creative job, he carries and handles heavy equipment with regularity. That didn't seem to be a problem at all for more than twenty years. Then, that changed. Over the course of several years, George experienced intermittent back pain. At first, he toughed it out. Then he went to a chiropractor. He received regular adjustments and learned that he had some significant spinal concerns that could be realigned if he stuck to a physical discipline. When he was in pain, George followed the prescribed regimen. When he felt better, he slacked off. One day, my very independent husband called me from work. In a nearly unrecognizable and feeble voice, he said, "I can't walk. Can you come get me?" Never before had George asked me to do any such thing for him. I could tell that he was in trouble. I raced to his rescue, got him in a taxi, and took him home. We called a few people and were given the name of a doctor who, we were told, could work miracles and get George back in shape in a flash, and we made an appointment for the next day. When it came time to go to the doctor's, we realized the severity of George's ailment. He could not walk. There was no way he would be able to walk across the courtyard to get into our car. I enlisted the resident handyman to carry George, fireman style, and place him in the car. From there, we gingerly proceeded to the doctor.

We received no miracle that day. Indeed, a bevy of doctors later, we still didn't have a solution. We learned that George's insurance would pay for back surgery and nothing else. From poring over books on back pain, we also learned that there was a good chance that surgery wouldn't be the end of it for him. Ultimately, George went to a Chinese medical doctor who came highly recommended. Dr. Li performed acupuncture on George six days a week for four months. That, coupled with a twice-daily medicinal tea, got George back on his feet. For two more months, he went for physical therapy. Six months after that frightening day that he called me from his office, George was back at work. And the one exercise he was able to pursue, swimming, became his new best friend. As a result of his injury, George vowed never to put himself in such a compromised position again. For the past five years, he has swum five to seven days a week. His newfound discipline demonstrates the respect that he has gained for his body. George is the first to admit how truly grateful he is that he discovered the value of his body and how to take care of it before it was too late.

DEVELOP AN EXERCISE PROGRAM

YOU HAVE TO get your body moving on a regular basis to keep it healthy. Recent studies point out that regular exercise is the most effective means of staying alive. So, if you need to change your relationship to exercise, commit to changing now.

- *Walk.* A brisk or easy, steady walk for about 30 minutes a day is a good start and is perfect for people of every age.

- *Stretch.* Open up your body. Get your circulation flowing. Learn to do simple yoga postures or calisthenics.

- *Make it a daily ritual.* I started by turning on the television to an exercise show each morning because going outside to the gym wasn't happening yet. Get motivated to move your body. Once you get into it, you will want to continue.

- *Check in with your doctor.* Be sure to check your medical status to ensure that you are doing the exercises that are best for your body.

REWRITING FAMILY HISTORY

MASTERY OVER your physical being is a lifelong prospect. Knowing your family history is a key link in achieving this goal. This is why doctors routinely ask what diseases your blood relatives have had. Each time you have a physical examination, you are asked to check a list of physical maladies and your relationship to them. Do you take this seriously? You should. Doctors are not magicians. Even the most sensitive and well-trained physician may not detect something that is wrong with you if the doctor does not have full information about your health. When people go from one doctor to the next, switching because of insurance concerns or other reasons, their records don't always travel with them. As a result, many doctors have missed early diagnosis of easily treatable ailments simply because they didn't have the proper information.

When it comes to your health, you have to be your biggest advocate. Know all of the health challenges and strengths on both sides of your family. Interview your relatives if you are unsure. Talk to your parents about any childhood illnesses that you may have had that could be of significance to your health now. Keep track of your medical history, and share it with each doctor throughout your life, whether traditional Western medical doctors or practioners of alternative therapies. Sometimes allopathic and homeopathic treatments don't work together. If, as my mother says, the right hand doesn't know what the left is doing, you could end up suffering severe side effects.

Don't let ignorance stand in the way of your seeking out the best medical attention possible. This is true for everyone, including people who don't readily know their medical history. If you were adopted, for example, and don't readily have access to your records, do some research. Chances are your adoptive parents received some background information on your parentage. If you can find the agency that handled the adoption, see what information they can give you. It's worth knowing.

As you do your family research, you may find a whole new world opening up. Frequently people do not reveal their ailments. In many families, when people died of consumption, which is now known as either tuberculosis or cancer depending on the interpretation, the family didn't talk about it. If someone had a so-called shameful disease, such as mental illness, it often passed in silence. Your responsibility as your own health advocate is to probe. Here is a time when using the approach of a student will be most effective. The art of being a great student calls for creative questioning. If your family is close-mouthed about certain things, start gently. Who are your people? What have their lives been like over the generations? How many babies did each family member have? What kinds of physical or mental challenges did any of the children undergo? How long did your ancestors live? And so on. Imagine what a beautiful gift you can offer back to your loved ones in exchange for the valuable information you glean from them. You can write a story about your family's struggles and successes that you share with everyone. You can create a genealogical chart that documents the history of your family. The opportunities are endless for ways that you can celebrate the life of your family even as you search to find answers for how you can create a life of optimal health for you and for them.

This is essentially what my friend Margo did after she discovered that she had breast cancer. At age thirty-five, Margo was an energetic entrepreneur, wife, and mother of four children. Anyone who knows Margo will immediately describe her as outspoken and independent. She knows what she wants and does her best to make it happen. After a routine medical exam, Margo not only learned of having cancer but also that it was imperative to operate immediately. Since Margo came from a family of women who had suffered from cancer, she knew that her situation was serious. Her mother had two mastectomies, and her twenty-eight-year-old sister was diagnosed with and treated for breast cancer, which later progressed; she succumbed to colon cancer two years later. Margo says, "The invincible Turnquest clan had to deal with our first up-close and personal look at our mortality. My mother was never the same. There were seven siblings—now six."

Even with these revelations, it never occurred to Margo that she could fall victim to this disease. As a responsible woman and mother, Margo was shocked into accepting that she had to change her life. She began to embrace the knowledge that there is a lot of work that she needs to do on her body and spirit in order to survive. Rather than keeping her head in the sand, Margo is taking action. She is working on weight loss, exercise, and boosting her immune system as she also seeks out ways to reduce the stress in her life. As Margo works to fortify her life from the inside out, she has committed to learning more about her family's history as she also encourages every woman she meets to pay attention to her body. As Margo says, "It is the only one you get."

THE SIGNS ALONG THE WAY

WHEN YOU RESPECT your body and take consistent care of it, you stand a better chance of enjoying a good quality of life. Even when people find that they are struck down by an ailment, it doesn't automatically mean that they will learn how to care for their bodies. This is that recurring point: Just like in school, you keep getting the lesson until you learn it. This is what happened to a thirty-year-old woman who moved to Chicago from New York to begin a career in graphic design.

Donnie was eager to make her mark, so she worked hard to pursue every outlet that might give her a break. For several years, she worked twelve to fifteen hours each day, not taking time out to tend to her body, believing that she was to use her youth to forge her future.

In the midst of her mission to succeed, Donnie ran into a gypsy woman who bumped into her as she was rushing. Donnie quickly apologized and tried to keeping moving. She says, "Before I knew it, she had turned around and grabbed my shoulders. She looked at me with a pleading intensity and said, 'You are very sick. You need to see a doctor right away.'" For a few moments, Donnie stood paralyzed, then snapped back to New York City reality and got angry. She shrugged off the woman, ran off, and went on about her business.

Not long after, Donnie began to have physical problems. When her menstrual cycle came, it didn't stop. Excessive bleeding finally led her to a doctor, who discovered that she had fibroid tumors. For the next few months, Donnie had consultations, tests—the works—in order to see what she should do next. She scoured every book she could find about her condition and learned every tidbit of information available. She ultimately had surgery to remove the tumors. After healing for several months, she returned to her life. The mistake was she didn't continue to follow up on her committment to healthful living. Four years after her surgery, Donnie began to bleed heavily again; the fibroid tumors had returned. Donnie has decided she doesn't need to learn the lesson a third time. She has had to undergo surgery again to remove the foreign growths in her body, and she has vowed to pursue the diet and exercise needed in order to support a healthy lifestyle that will discourage any future invasions.

GIVE UP ADDICTIONS

SOME PEOPLE never face the facts. This is particularly true for people who are plagued by addictions—anything from alcohol and drugs to excessive or inadequate eating. One of the worst and most common addictions is nicotine. Even with incontrovertible evidence that proves that cigarette smoking causes cancer, people continue to smoke. I recently learned of a woman who has had a stellar career in the arts and could conceivably live for many more years contributing her great intellect and wisdom to her field. But she has developed lung cancer—and still refuses to stop smoking.

This overt denial of reality—or perhaps acceptance of the fruits of one's actions—gives me great pause. Why would you choose to kill yourself? If you know for sure that you stand a great chance of dying as a result of committing a particular violation against your body, why would you choose to do it? This is a question that has stumped professors, scientists, doctors, psychiatrists, and lay individuals alike. Addiction is powerful. It is true that certain substances are so immediately able to connect with the human body and tell the body that it needs them that it can be almost impossible to shake. Excess sugar and caffeine, while not truly addictive, top the list of legal things that people consume to their detriment on a daily basis. Even after people are struck with life-threatening diseases such as high blood pressure or diabetes, many often cannot control their intake of ingredients that can trigger fatal reactions when not managed.

REJOICE IN WHAT YOU HAVE ATTAINED

BETTY WAS A FRIEND of one of my best friends. By association, I was pretty sure that she was a special person, but she turned out to be even more amazing than I had imagined. I met her on the occasion of her fifty-fifth year on the planet. In celebration of her life, she was pinning the people she met with large stainless steel diaper pins that had a "55" tag hanging from them. Betty said that she was still living in her youth, enjoying every breath, and happy to share her joy with others. As I watched and listened to her, I savored a refreshing sight. It's so common for women especially to become self-conscious with each passing year; I know more women than I care to count who refuse to say their age no matter what. When I turned forty and celebrated with a party where I announced it to the world, one of my friends—a male—called to tell me that I was making a mistake. He said, "If you tell how old you are, people are going to know how old I am." My response was: "So. What's wrong with that?"

What is wrong with aging? The alternative is death, isn't it? I've been blessed with a family that has always had lots of older people in it. From a young child, I got to see the stepping-stones of age. And for the most part, people were healthy even as they progressed up the age ladder. It was a sign of honor to grow old. The wisdom that an elder attained was considered invaluable in many communities. Although I have yet to reach elder status, I know for certain that I am far wiser today than I was in my twenties or thirties. I have earned every gray hair I have, whether I care to show them or not! In the spirit of Truth, why not embrace your Self as you are and where you are chronologically in your life? With each decade, the body changes. Welcome the changes that are natural, and stay fit so that those that are unnecessary need not trap you. It is possible to live a wholesome, energetic life until the day you die. Just as Betty demonstrated as she celebrated her birthday, every year that you get an opportunity to contribute to uplifting yourself and the world is a tremendous blessing.

YOU ARE WHAT YOU EAT

IF YOU FEED YOUR BODY junk food, it will end up becoming worthless, just like junk in a junkyard. If you feed it healthful, balanced meals, it will function at an optimal level. There is a tremendous amount of information available about foods, with proponents of various types of eating rallying on each side. Rather than recommending a particular diet, I encourage you to pay attention to what you consume and learn about what your body needs. The body is intelligent, and it gives signs all the time for what it requires to function. Listen for those signs. Read about the body and food to learn what to consume at what hours of the day and how to give your body the opportunity to digest food and rest when appropriate. Your vigilance regarding the quality and quantity of food that you consume will directly affect your overall health. If it is true that you are what you eat, why not become a connoisseur of wholesome living. Eat to live.

BUILD SELF-CONFIDENCE

THE TOPIC of our relationship with our physical body rings a common chord for many people. I have talked to all sorts of people—young and old, short and tall, thin and full-figured, African-American, Hispanic, Asian, and Caucasian, male and female—and have discovered from interviews as well as my own work on myself that a key to a healthy relationship with your body is your level of self-confidence. Nobody can "make" you beautiful or not. No one can convince you that you are worthy to be loved or that your body is desirable. The range of responses that people have to their body image is as vast as there are people.

Each of us must build confidence in our own Self. The little self that I used to think I was walking around in—shy and easily intimidated and desperately seeking validation—began to fade away as I started to embrace my own power. The more I asserted myself and stepped into my Self, the profoundly strong and capable one, the more I grew to love everything about me exactly as I was. I created a new alignment with my physical body that celebrated the fact that my spirit is housed in such an important vessel. The more frequently I assumed this approach of respecting my temple, the more confident and clear I became.

Having confidence does not mean that struggles evaporate. Instead, it means that we face our conflicts with a sense of capability. What better way to start than with the house in which our spirit lives? To strengthen our confidence in our physical selves, we have to be intimately knowledgeable about our bodies: how they work, what they need to function, how they will treat us based on how we take care of them. We also need to recognize that our bodies are instruments for our spirit's work. That's why we must respect them.

Your Journal Entry

Dearest Friend,

As I grow to honor my thoughts and my actions, I must include my relationship with my body. I want to love my body as it is and commit to taking care of it so that it can support me in my life's endeavors. Help me to love my body. Help me to treat my body with respect. I pray that I will be able to be consistent in my resolution on this vital topic.

I love you,
Me

ASK ANYBODY who has stopped and started at a gym, and you will hear what you may already know: it takes discipline to respect the body. If you want to live an honest life where you celebrate your own Truth, you must examine your relationship with your body and make the necessary adjustments to support your goals:

- *How would you describe your health?*

- *What is your family's health history?*

- *If you are in a relationship,* how does it affect your physical health?

- *Do you exercise?* If so, how often? If not, will you make the commitment to do so now?

- *What is your diet like?* Do you put healthy foods in your body that will help to fuel your life? What might you eliminate from your diet in your effort to become a cleaner vessel?

- *Are you an active champion of your health?* Do you bring pertinent information and questions to the medical practitioners you engage?

- *If you have been passive in your relationship to your health,* are you willing to change now?

- *What will it take for you to embrace your body* for the role that it serves in your life and make it possible for it to serve you better?

12

KEEP GOOD COMPANY

~~~~~~

YOU'VE PROBABLY HEARD THE SAYING, "As you think, so you become." It's true. The thoughts that occupy our brains color our perceptions of the world. If we are constantly dwelling on what we don't have, we will never have. If we regularly long to be like somebody else, we will always feel less than. On the other hand, if we fill our minds with positive thoughts, we will gain confidence. If we envision our lives as productive, resourceful, and loving, so our lives will unfold. Within us resides a tremendous power that can guide us to fulfill our greatest purpose in life if we let it.

Choice is essential here. We must choose to fill our minds and our lives with thoughts, activities, and individuals who will support our life's intention, even if we are still figuring out what that is. To determine your life's intention, you can use the practices of self-inquiry, meditation, and journaling. These three in particular will support the exploration inside that reveals your life's purpose. It is true that some people know intuitively or from an early age what their duty in life is—what they are supposed to do with the precious time that they have on this planet. For others, it's a weeding process. They travel along one path and then another until one day they come to the answer. Indeed, all along the way, they may be fulfilling aspects of their life's purpose. For many, one day it's as if a bell rings from deep inside proclaiming that this is the road to take. Whenever it happens for you, you can fortify yourself by being mindful of the company that you keep. When it feels wrong to be in someone's presence, chances are that the flashing red light inside is urging you to stop for good reason. When you feel empowered and clear, it's likely that you have surrounded yourself with the proper resources to nurture your soul.

YOUR LIFE AS A GARDEN

~~~~~~

IMAGINE YOUR LIFE as a garden. Envision your home, your family, your job, your hobbies, your strengths, your vices, and your thoughts as elements of your garden. Weeding out the unnecessary and potentially destructive elements in your life is a vital component of your life's work too. What kinds of plants and flowers do you grow in your garden? Do you know how to take care of the different forms of vegetation? Do you tend your garden, discerning the difference between a wildflower and an unwanted weed? How does your garden grow?

My husband is an attentive gardener. Growing up in lush Jamaica sparked his lifelong interest in the beauty and wonder of the outdoors. George's mother and grandmother reinforced his respect for the harvest of the earth because they have always grown fruits, vegetables, and flowers wherever they have lived. Since he was a little boy, George has loved plants and wildlife, and he enjoys tending them. I have learned much about gardening from watching him.

Shortly after we got married, we moved into an old building in Harlem that has a huge circular courtyard. At that time, two dogwood trees stood in the midst of otherwise barren soil. One day after a hard rain, the maintenance crew uprooted the trees and left them sitting on their sides as they worked on repairs in the basement of the building. Following the directions of their superiors, these men "did their job" without ever thinking about the life of the trees. They neglected to cover the trees' roots or give them water. After about a week of being uprooted, the trees were replanted in their plots. It was too late. The beautiful dogwood trees perished.

For some time, the courtyard was completely barren. Not even a blade of grass grew. Soon a number of people in the building began to talk about planting a garden. One wanted to hire a professional European landscaper. Another wanted to force the building management to pay for garden development. A coalition, which included my husband and a few others, decided to do it themselves. For several seasons, we purchased flowers and trees, ground cover, and nutrients and established a charming garden. Being one who pays extremely close attention to detail, George researched the best ways of maintaining a garden of this nature and did his best with the others to get it going. When weeds sprouted, he and a small crew dug them up. They took turns watering parched leaves and blossoms in the blazing summer and kept vigil over invading insects through the fall. The garden grew, and as it began to mature, there was less need for intense maintenance. This coincided with an injury that forced George to stop being actively involved. Different people stepped in and began to tend the garden, which remained beautiful. Occasionally, George would bring seeds and plant them, or friends would donate trees and bushes.

Over time, George began to notice that some of the new gardeners didn't recognize the difference between weeds and new buds. They didn't follow the seasons or the natural timing for pruning or watering. Much to his dismay, George watched as perfectly healthy budding plants were uprooted while weeds grew free. As one innocent assault after another occurred against the grain of nature in the garden, George became angry, then hurt. Finally, he decided to say something to the people who were managing the garden, to let them know about the rhythms of nature that were begging to be followed. He also decided after that that he could and would let go. The garden was still beautiful. As this new crew of people tended it, they too would learn in time how to make it grow. George's inner wisdom told him to give the others their chance to be with the garden so that they could gain the knowledge that was there for them, just as he had done for himself.

How does your garden grow? Do you allow weeds to grow in the garden of your life as you carefully, if unwittingly, uproot valuable shoots of wisdom? One of the lessons that George learned from gardening is that it matters what gets planted next to one another. When compatible plants stand side by side, both flourish. If a predator plant grows beside a delicate flower, it will likely overtake the flower before the planting mistake is noticed.

Nature provides many lessons for us. It proves to us the importance of keeping good company on many levels. Using nature as our guide, we can look into our own lives to see just how healthy the garden of our life is.

WHAT'S ON YOUR MIND?

THE GARDEN that we have the greatest responsibility for tending is that of our own being. At the top of the list is our mind. Our mind is extraordinary. It is capable of thinking faster than can be accurately calculated by most scientific equipment. It directs our bodies to action and our tongues to speech. It tells us tall tales and reveals the Truth. It can be our greatest friend and our most ferocious foe.

Recall a time now when you let your mind go free. Where did it take you when you set out on this adventure? Were you pursuing a goal? Imagining what a new romance would be like with your secret crush? Plotting how you might purchase a big-ticket item for your home? Envisioning what your life will look like when you win the lottery?

It may be that you let your mind go free, and it went to a wholesome, supportive place. If you have been training your mind to be your friend and to be in line with your life's intentions, a free roam may have proven glorious and uplifting. For many of us, however, our minds are still in training, and when we let them go, they venture too far astray.

What we must do to stay in a healthy, constructive relationship with our mind is to tend it with consistent love and commitment. Then whatever outside elements may approach us, much like new seeds in a garden, we can choose whether we will welcome and nuture them or send them on their way.

It is possible to make choices that will keep our minds calm and clear no matter what is going on in our lives. We can choose to rest in our own knowledge of how to understand the experiences of our lives and forge ahead. There is a way to keep from being swayed by others—thoughts, people, relationships, obligations—and remain anchored in the protection and support of who we really are.

Rather than rejecting the things that happen in your life, remain steadfast in your awareness of who you are in relation to them. Instead of holding your breath and feeling tense because a problem has arisen, relax in the knowledge that you can handle the situation, whatever it is. This knowledge inspires peacefulness and delight.

To gain this knowledge, you have to review your life, assess how you've handled yourself in the past, consider the health of your relationships with others, and evaluate and clarify your intentions for moving forward. The choice—to consider thoroughly the kind of company you keep—is both essential and beneficial. It will lead you to a clear understanding of how you can choose to live in relation to others and what you may want to do to cultivate the garden of your life.

START WITH YOUR FAMILY

A STARTING POINT for this exploration is family. This is where we begin our lives, under the protective guidance of loved ones—whether parents or guardians. Our relationships with our immediate and extended families figure directly into our initial ability to nurture our lives and welcome positive energy. This is true for every one of us, no matter what our circumstances. Whereas if you grew up in a luxurious two-parent home with the best of everything, or grew up having only the bare essentials and lived in a single-parent household, whether you were adopted, or grew up in foster care, to establish a comprehensible picture of how you understand your role in the world as it relates to other people, you must examine the lessons you learned about human dynamics during your formative years. No matter how challenging it may be to do this personal investigation, know that it is worth it. Knowing your history, starting with your family, will empower you to make the choices that will support you in your life today.

One of the greatest blessings in my life is my family. Although we don't number many, we have a close bond. We know that we can count on each other when one of us is in a pinch emotionally, financially, or spiritually. Thanks to our mother, my sisters and I have no doubts about the security that one can gain as a result of unconditional love. Mommie accepts each of us for who we are. She addresses us as the adults we are, and she supports us as best she knows how. One of Mommie's consistent lessons since we were little has been the importance of keeping good company. Her point was that it is essential for each of us to surround ourselves with positive influences in order to lead healthy lives. Good company, as she learned it from her parents, meant people, environments, and ideas that support positive living. Since my father was a judge, we learned all about the consequences of not keeping good company. We saw how bad things could happen to good people when they found themselves in the wrong place. We witnessed how people's lives could be devastated when the people who were closest to them were not supportive. In the midst of many stories, our parents constantly drilled into us the importance of maintaining positive, uplifting relationships. They understood that choice to be one of the most valuable components of a successful life.

Creating Family

As I have talked to people about their families, I have heard all kinds of stories. Some families have solid foundations, where even though rocky spots do exist, the good times outweigh the bad and the bond of love is undeniable. Other people don't have it so easy. In every situation, people have the choice as to how they will live. Even in the worst of circumstances, the opportunity is there to succumb to the whims of others—parents included—or ascend to the highest heights and make the best of what you've got.

Years ago, I worked with a man who had a heart of gold. He is married with two children and had what appeared to be a beautiful, solid life. One day we got to talking about our upbringing, and I learned that he and his blood family have virtually nothing to do with each other; they have been estranged since he was a teenager. Walter explained that his family was dysfunctional in ways he refused to describe. Suffice it to say, he allowed that they did not encourage him to grow or support any of his independent thinking or feeling. As Walter was maturing, he experienced his parents and siblings as a noose around his neck. After spending many years trying to convince them to change or at least love him as he felt he needed, he chose to craft a new family paradigm. In the family that he has created with his wife and children and his wife's family, he does not bad-mouth or belittle his birth family. Occasionally, he says, they get in touch with one another. But what he had to do was to move out of what felt like bad company into a healthier environment, even if he had to create it himself.

I met a woman in her late sixties who is still going through angst about her family. As a child, she suffered incestuous abuse from her father. Although she feels relatively well healed after having undergone extensive therapy, nonetheless she says that that early trauma affected her ability to trust people in her life, especially those who are closest to her. In fact, she says when she was a young woman, she gave a child up for adoption, partly because she didn't feel fit to care for a child after having been so poorly cared for herself in her youth. Now, as her life in retirement has given her the space to reflect, she has taken a huge step. She decided to find her child and offer whatever love and connection she can at this juncture. Thanks to her prayers and commitment, this woman did find her son. They have connected, and she has offered to share her life with the forty-year-old son she is coming to know so that he can experience true family love, something she never had.

Honor Your Parents

What is your family relationship like? Is your experience with them of being in good company? Have you resolved any issues you may have had with your parents? This is an important question, because most children face silent battles with even the most loving parents. Quite often these tensions last well into adulthood. Until children of whatever age are able to resolve these issues and position themselves in a healthier relationship with their parents, friction can simmer just below the surface of nearly every thought and interaction with them. The Bible commands us to honor our mother and father. Other spiritual traditions echo this message: *Offer the greatest respect to your parents.* Do you feel that this is something you can actually do? Do you practice honoring your parents in your daily life?

If you have doubts, work through them. A practice that will support you is thinking about what role parents play in a child's life and how your parents fulfilled that role. That you were cared for to the extent that you are here now seeking ways to fulfill your own life is significant. How did your parents contribute to that? Think about this seriously. You may be surprised at what you discover. It may be that they spurred you on by offering just the basics, making sure that you were well fed and provided for as a child. Perhaps they encouraged you to go out and get a job right away so that you could learn how to support yourself. Even if they ignored you, they may have been doing the best that they could at the time. And since you are here right now looking to improve your life, you can thank them for doing the best that they were able so that you now can do the best you can.

A Releasing Exercise

If you find that you cannot understand your relationship with your parents or forgive them for whatever may have occurred between you, seek support in working through this block. This may come through contemplation and self-inquiry or with the professional support of a therapist or psychiatrist. It's amazing how many people hold onto grudges for years, finding themselves unwilling or unable to move beyond the things that troubled them when they were children. This exercise can help you through being stuck:

• *Stop whatever you are doing,* and commit your full focus to this exercise.

• *Look around you.* Notice what your life is like right now.

• *Become fully aware of the nature and quality of your world.* Who is important to you? What about them supports you? What is challenging for you?

• *What do you value at this moment?*

• *What lingering worries or distractions* about your relationship with your parents are standing in the way of your experiencing this moment fully?

• *Be mindful of your worries,* whether they have to do with the past or the future. Take stock of each of the issues that you have been harboring about your mother or your father. Examine these concerns one by one. When you look at them for the lesson they hold for you and without passing judgment, you will have a greater chance of reaching lasting resolution.

• *Welcome the present.* Give yourself permission to stand completely in this moment where you are. Invite your mind to focus on what's immediately before you.

• *Reflect on your challenges* with your parents and what they mean at this moment. Notice the freedom inherent in remaining steadfastly in the present, not allowing your mind to take you back to past experiences or potential problems in the future.

When you follow this exercise completely you will gain the ability to observe what your issues actually are now instead of what you remember them to have been. Anger and fear about your mother's deteriorating health that may cause you to miss vacation this summer get washed away because you are looking at the present. When you anchor yourself in the here and now, you will be able to make clear choices that will allow you to manage your life effectively, everything from organizing care for your mother to forgiving your father and yourself for what has passed. You will be able to come up with viable solutions to handle all the challenges that present themselves. You will not be bound by things of the past or concerns about the future. In fact, you will have the unique opportunity to sculpt your life as you want it. You will then experience a greater feeling of love and satisfaction. In essence, you will give yourself the space to be empowered in your life so that you can honor your parents and yourself at once. In a sense, this is what growing up is. When you truly become an adult, you accept that it is now your turn to be the master of yourself. It is no longer the responsibility of your mother or father. It is yours.

Respect Your Siblings

How does this understanding relate to siblings? With maturity, you can gain the skills to manage relationships with everyone, including those who grew up next to you. As any brother or sister will likely admit, however, the evolution can be difficult. Everything from loving-kindness to near warfare occurs as children grow up together. The eldest children reserve the right to be king or queen, while the others jockey for other forms of status. In the midst of intense sibling interplay, bonds of trust do generally form. Feelings of suspicion sometimes fester as well. So the question arises, are siblings always good company? The answer is no. It is possible to love your siblings unconditionally and be there for them to the best of your ability. But just as in any other relationship, you must be clear about your personal boundaries. You didn't let your little brother beat you to a pulp when you were young. Why would you let him chump you out of a huge loan as an adult if you believe he won't honor his commitment to pay you back?

Respect for siblings does not mean that you allow them to walk over you. Instead, it means that you remain committed to finding ways to support one another throughout your lives. It also means that you accept your siblings for who they are. No matter how hard you try, you cannot turn your sister into an engineer if she has chosen to be an artist. And you cannot convince your brother to lose 100 pounds if he has decided he wants to remain obese. At the same time, you don't have to enable them either. For example, if your sister's artistic efforts depend on your supplementing her income, you can stop if you no longer feel comfortable providing that support. And you don't have to feel guilty either. Just let her know that you love her but that your role in her life is not to be her bank. Similarly, when your brother comes over for dinner, you don't have to serve a calorie-rich southern spread. You can feature a well-presented healthy meal that will be as appealing to him as it is calorie conscious.

Now, let's turn the tables. What about you? When it comes to keeping good company with your siblings, you have to know where to draw the line. Revisit your childhood relationships to see what the dynamics were like when you were growing up. Do you still fall into any of those patterns from time to time, including the unhealthy ones? Can you see a way out of them? Make the decision to take charge of your life. Include a refreshed way of communicating with your siblings in this new paradigm.

I did this in recent years with my older sister, Susan, and our relationship has blossomed beautifully as a result. For a long time, we had a seesaw type of bond. Whenever I needed advice, she was right there with support. At other times, our interactions were more strained. Susan is the oldest of the three of us. In that role, she is excellent at telling me what to do. As you might imagine, the adult Harriette was not interested in that type of relationship. Without really thinking, I would either find myself ready for a sparring match whenever Susan would begin her explanation of how I should do something better than I was doing it or I would quietly retreat.

One day I got tired of it. I was so frustrated that I didn't know what to do. I felt that Susan was being extremely judgmental of all my friends as well as of my way of living. I had had enough, so I told her. I drummed up the courage to tell Susan that I was no longer willing to sit back and listen to her critical comments. She was shocked and had no idea what I was talking about. Susan was just being Susan, the way she had always been. Since I had not verbally challenged her ways—at least not very often—my response in that moment came as a complete surprise. Instead of becoming defensive, Susan told me that she wanted me to tell her the next time I thought she was being unkind or harsh. She asked that I point out my issues when they happened so that she could see if she thought I was being overly sensitive or if there was actually a problem. Because we spoke to each other openly and kindly in that pivotal moment, we created an opportunity for growth. We have moved beyond the stereotypical big sister–little sister combative roles into a mutually respectful and supportive relationship—one that would not have been possible had I not stated what was burdening my heart. We have become true friends as adults. And more, I have learned a valuable lesson: it is essential to stand up for yourself no matter what the situation. Only when you stand up for your own Truth will you know the true nature of any relationship.

Mind Your Own Business

Sometimes standing up for yourself with your siblings can mean that you agree to love one another without getting into each other's affairs. Relationships always involve boundaries, and the sooner you recognize what your boundaries are with respect to each of the key people in your life, the better off you will be.

This became evident for Marsha and Claudia, two sisters in Milwaukee, some years after they had moved away from home and established their separate lives. The two grew up in a traditional Baptist home. Over the years, younger sister Claudia relaxed her religious convictions as older sister Marsha became more devout in her practices. Claudia didn't have any issue with Marsha until the two of them got together. Claudia had moved in with her boyfriend. When Claudia began telling Marsha about her new live-in love, Marsha abruptly stopped her. Rather than listening, she began to scold Claudia about her lifestyle, quoting Scripture to support her argument against "living in sin" together. Claudia was taken aback. She and her sister had always been able to talk about whatever was going on in their lives. Now, Marsha's religious dogmatism was standing in the way of their longstanding and cherished open dialogue. For a while, Claudia retreated. She basically wrote her sister off, deciding that Marsha could no longer be her confidante. In Claudia's mind, Marsha was expunged from her roster of "good company." Marsha stuck to her guns, too, believing to her core that she was right.

Because the two sisters really do love one another, this schism couldn't last. At the next holiday when the family got together, they tentatively sat down to talk. They both acknowledged how much they missed one another. After a few hours of candidly discussing their lives and beliefs, the two agreed to live and let live. Instead of criticizing one another, they agreed that they would continue to listen to the perspectives that each of them brought to their relationship to find the wisdom there. More important, they promised not to pass judgment but instead to support each other as they also maintain their personal beliefs about how to live honorable lives.

Dealing with Family Crisis

Sometimes people cannot resolve issues with loved ones even when they are blood relatives. When that happens, it's important to be aware of the impasse and take appropriate action. It is possible to love people from a distance if that's the only way that you can have a productive life.

A family in Louisville, Kentucky, faced a challenge that nearly tore their family apart until they came to terms with it. The Smiths were a close-knit group. After the children grew up, quite a few stayed in Louisville and built their lives near their parents and other relatives. Aunts and uncles operated in traditional ways, serving as support for rearing children and helping out in various ways around the house. Everything was fine until one of the cousins developed a drug problem. As with many other families, nobody wanted to acknowledge what was really happening, although it was apparent that something was wrong. Occasionally, Lance would disappear. With his sporadic disappearances, valuables also vanished—everything from silverware to electronics and jewelry. When one of the family homes was robbed and all of the wife's jewelry was stolen, somebody had to take a stand. Uncle Jake, the man of the house, had to step up. He says it was really hard for him to let Lance know he was no longer welcome in his home, but he had no choice. After a family meeting where everybody finally accepted that Lance had a serious problem, they did their research and learned about making an intervention. Then the family as a group approached Lance and strongly encouraged him to go into rehab. They told him that they would never stop loving him, but that he had to stay away until he got the proper help.

ESTABLISHING FRIENDSHIPS

MY GRANDMOTHER used to talk to my sisters and me a lot about how we spent our time. With her musical, high-pitched voice, Little Grandma encouraged us to stay strong by having faith in God and keeping good company. This was like a mantra in our family, one reenforced by our parents and the various loved ones who were part of our extended family. When we were young, it was pretty easy. My mother took us everywhere she went. Mrs. Lancaster, a wise and sweet older woman, supervised us at home when Mommie wasn't there. Aunt Audrey and Uncle Henry, my father's sister and her husband, looked after us when my parents wanted some time alone. We were surrounded by a close-knit group of people who shared the same values and made it their business to instill those beliefs in us. Honesty, integrity, and fairness were at the top of our loved ones' minds as they interacted with us.

After we went to school, things changed. As hard as our parents tried, they could not protect us from all of the challenges that would come our way. My mother explains that she did what she could, which was to explain to us the importance of living a life of honor, and that included choosing our friends wisely. I'll never forget my mother telling us that if we were lucky, we would have one or two dear friends who would be with us for our entire lives and that we really didn't need more than that. What we needed was to take care that whomever we allowed into our inner circle deserved to be in there, because the person would respect us for who we are and stand by us in times of need. I was inspired by what Mommie said even as I was puzzled. I knew that she had fast friends—one who had been a close friend since they were four years old, one who is a blood relative as well as a friend, and others who have been by her side since they were in elementary school. Mommie is proof that one can develop and maintain powerful, loving relationships for life. What was odd to me was her admonition that the list of such loved ones would be short. "Why?" I wondered.

Don't Be Naive

Instinctively I knew that my mother's advice was sound. I followed it to the best of my ability, but like everybody else I've asked about friendships, I stumbled quite a bit in my efforts to build lasting unions. My "best friend" from kindergarten until the seventh grade dealt me a blow so low that it took me years to recover. My naive belief that she loved and respected me and would never intentionally do me harm proved to be false. Coming to terms with what happened in that relationship marked the first conscious and dramatic turning point in my life. I had to choose to change.

One day in the seventh grade just before class ended, the teacher posted the top grades for an exam we had taken. I had earned an A and was mortified that this shining grade was revealed to the whole class. (Although I was almost always an A student, I religiously hid my accomplishments from my peers. High marks earned more disdain than praise from my classmates.) The teacher called out to me as class let out, so I ended up leaving the classroom a few moments after the rest of my class. As I rushed to approach my posse of girlfriends, about seven teenagers who were my buddies at the time, including a neighbor I had known since we were born, I called out to my "best friend," whom I will call Clarissa, to ask her and them to wait up for me. Clarissa did not respond, nor did she or the rest of the group turn around or in any way acknowledge that they heard me. At that time in my life, I was painfully shy, and I spoke in a whispery quiet voice. I called out with greater force. This time I knew my voice was audible. "Wait up, you guys!" Still no response. I hurried up to meet the group, and when I reached the girl who was farthest behind, I asked her why she hadn't answered. Although I was standing right next to her, only inches away, she still didn't respond. It was as if I wasn't there. I stood still for a few moments, shocked and bewildered. I couldn't understand what was happening. Why were they shunning me? What had I done? After following them a few more steps, I turned down another hall just before the tears began to brim over my eyelids, and I went to my next class. The rest of that day I walked around in a fog. My heart was broken, and I didn't understand what had happened.

When I got home that afternoon, all I had to do was look at my mother, and she knew something horrible had happened. She urged me to tell her. From that point on, she worked with me, pleading with me to let these "friends" go. She explained that they were not the good company she had encouraged me to keep since I was a little girl. As I pleaded with her to explain why my "friends" would act this way, she suggested that I stop asking why. "Sometimes there is no answer, Harriette, at least not one that makes sense. Sometimes you just have to move on." This advice was hard to swallow, especially since we were still going to the same school and in the same classes. For some time, I continued to try to mend the fence. I learned that it had been Clarissa who had been the ringleader in this vicious act and that the other girls mainly went along. As I proceeded to protect myself by immersing myself ever more deeply in my studies and slowly building my self-esteem, I also vowed never to have a "best friend" again, at least not outside my immediate family.

Develop Healthy Relationships

With my mother's constant encouragement, I began to count my blessings. For every blow I had endured, my mother reminded me of the great things in my life, of all of the precious gifts I had been given. Together we recited blessings—everything from my love for education and the rewards it was yielding to my good health and that of my family. I added my gratitude for my sisters—Susan, who was vigilantly there to protect me, and Stephanie, who was consistently there to nurture me. At that time, Stephanie and I were virtually inseparable. Although she is four years younger than I am, she has always been a source of unconditional love and light in my life. At that time when I felt so terribly broken, I realized that I did not need my so-called friends because I had my sisters and my family. Stephanie and I spent time before and after school together. We created our own fantasy world in which we crafted stories of our biggest imaginings. We soared through our dreams and plans. Little by little, I healed from those wounds.

For many years, those wounds would smart from time to time. I still don't understand why those girls would be so cruel. What I have witnessed from many other people's stories as well as my own is that peer pressure can be deadly. In my case, I had to choose to walk away from those girls, to stop begging for entry into their secret society. Similarly, members of that group eventually had to make their own choices—about staying in a relationship that was intentionally hurting others or move out and allow their own spirits to flourish.

This brings me back to my mother's understanding that only a precious few people should be allowed entry into the temple of your heart. Only the most deserving are the ones for whom you should open the door. That doesn't mean that you become a recluse. Instead, it means that people have to earn your trust.

How does this happen? You must engage all of the tools of your inner wisdom to guide you. Look beyond what people say, and notice what they do. Observe and evaluate your interactions with associates. Guard your heart as the greatest treasure you possess. When you begin to envision yourself as worthy of respect and honor, you will attract respectful and honorable relationships. For sure, you will be thrown a curve ball from time to time; it should remind you of the importance of not taking anything for granted. Be vigilant about your friendships. Be kind and respectful toward others and compassionate toward everyone, including yourself. Notice when a relationship sours, and have the courage to let go.

Friends and Work

Sarah found herself in quite a predicament at work when she mistook her relationship with her boss as a close friendship. Sarah and Alicia are about the same age, and Sarah believed that the two of them were as close as sisters. Sarah says, "We stayed over each other's homes, went to the movies and shopped together. She talked nice to me to my face, but when the opportunity came for me to be loaned to another department in our company, my boss wasn't so friendly to me." As

Sarah's growth opportunity was taking shape, her once supportive boss, Alicia, did everything she could to discourage Sarah from taking the job. It got so bad, Sarah says, that bigger bosses started questioning what was going on. People knew that Sarah and Alicia were friends and expected Alicia to be proud of her friend's success. Ultimately, when Sarah was approved for the new position, her relationship with Alicia ended—at least in the form it once had. Although Sarah was crushed at first, refusing to believe that Alicia's seeming envy could destroy the closeness that she believed they shared, ultimately she had no choice but to accept it.

Sarah says she learned that friendships don't have to last forever for them to be valuable. What she and Alicia had shared was important to her during the time that their friendship was healthy. Just because it had deteriorated into something that was no longer acceptable for Sarah didn't change the past. Ultimately, Sarah says she was able to move on with a certain amount of peace. She knows that she once had a dear friend when she needed her. She also learned that nothing is promised forever, at least not as far as relationships with people go.

Just because someone sits next to you does not mean that she is your friend. The man who keeps catching your eye may not ultimately be your husband. The assistant who has been assigned to work with you may not always have your back—that is, support you. I don't say these things to make you paranoid. I say them to make you aware.

It's okay to make the assumption that people are inherently good. Deep down inside, there is goodness in all of us. Don't let your intention to recognize that goodness cloud your vision of how they are behaving in the moment, though. In work environments, people are looking out for their best interests. You need to know this. We talked in Chapter 6, "Learn to Listen," about looking for the question behind the question. This is critical at work. Ask yourself why you believe that people are communicating with you in the ways that they are, and why you are responding in kind. What do you want or believe you need from your coworkers, superiors, and other people at your job? As you consider these questions, you can determine whether your needs and desires are properly placed. For example, you may want friendship, whereas you need and deserve respect. You may want to be liked, while you need to be heard. You may want lasting relationships, although what you actually need are political allies.

Maintain Positive Relationships

My mother frequently talks about how small the world is and therefore how essential it is to do your best to live an honorable life. Then, no matter where you are or whom you see, you will shine. She also taught us to stick with the people in our corner. She urged us not to forget those who have been our allies as well as those we really like, because you never know when that relationship will prove to be of value to you and them.

Such was the case with two women who worked together at a national magazine for several years. When Ellen left to pursue her career at another publication, Portia stayed. They never lost touch. As a result, when a job posting came up that seemed perfect for Portia, Ellen automatically thought of her. Because Ellen knew that Portia was not only a good and loyal friend, but also an excellent production manager, Ellen had no qualms about recommending her right away for the job and helping to facilitate her interview. Trusting her intuition and her knowledge of her friend's ability made this business alliance work out.

A Place and a Time for Everything

Sometimes friendship can stand in the way of clear thinking. This was true for Edward and his friend Rick. Edward is a successful accountant whose firm needed a part-time bookkeeper during tax season a few years ago. Rick is a freelance bookkeeper who needed work and was Edward's longtime friend. When Edward learned that the position was available, he immediately thought of Rick. But Edward knew that as nice as Rick was, he rarely made scheduled meetings on time—even if they were going to a restaurant or a bar. He often came off a bit flaky when they were discussing serious ideas. Although Edward secretly doubted Rick's ability to be consistently professional, he didn't think he would be acting as a true friend if he didn't recommend Rick for the position.

Based on Edward's stamp of approval, the firm hired Rick. From the start, there was trouble. Rick was good when he wanted to be, but that was never eight hours a day. Rick relished the fact that he and Edward were working in the same place. Whenever he could, he would stop by Edward's office to shoot the breeze. Trying to be nice, Edward would chat for a few minutes and then encourage Rick to do his job. Rick assured Edward that he had it under control. After a month passed, Edward got called into the senior partner's office. He was reprimanded for slacking off in his own work and spending too much time fraternizing with his friend. Further, he was informed that Rick would be given a warning the next day: if he didn't shape up soon, he would be terminated. To save face and his own reputation, Edward suggested to Rick that he resign before being fired. Rick was insulted and became indignant. Ultimately, he got fired, and their friendship suffered a tremendous blow.

Resist Peer Pressure

It can be tough to step out of a situation that doesn't feel right to you, especially if you believe you are among friends. Frank, a college junior, can attest to that.

Frank was basically a good guy, and his close friends were just like him— guys whom most girls' mothers would appreciate. One night Frank went to a party with another group because his close friends weren't available. He knew these others in passing and knew that they liked to have fun, which included smoking marijuana. Usually, when they did that, Frank just avoided them. Even so, he figured it would be okay to hang out with them for an evening. When they passed a joint to him, he took a toke for the first time in his life. "I guess I didn't want to seem like I wasn't down with them," Frank explains. "After all, I did see them a lot, not to mention they did defuse a tense confrontation for me at a previous party, which involved guns. So I was indebted to them." After getting high, Frank went out to the dance floor and tried to get a young woman to dance with him. He says he didn't notice the girl's boyfriend standing right next to her. "If I hadn't gotten high, I would have certainly seen the obvious." Her boyfriend started cursing at him, and Frank's group jumped up to help Frank out. The problem was that their "help" ended up escalating the situation into a full-fledged fight. Frank lost two teeth and got a citation from the school when the police arrived. Frank says that deep down inside he knew better than to hang out with this group in the first place. They were not his friends. If he had gotten into a verbal fight with the girl's boyfriend when his other friends were around, he's sure he would have just apologized and walked away.

There are many stories like this—people who were in the wrong place at the wrong time or who allowed themselves to be convinced to do something that was contrary to their beliefs. Whenever people share these stories, they admit that it wasn't worth it. They also share that it can take a lot of soul searching to stand up for what they believe to be right. Your own vigilance to be true to yourself can serve as your guiding light.

MAKE YOUR PARTNER YOUR BEST FRIEND

WHEN PEOPLE MARRY or decide to commit their lives to one another, ideally they become each other's best friend. They support each other and grow together in such a way that they put each other first. In order for this to work, especially in a culture full of distractions such as ours, it means that you have to start by selecting a partner who respects you and shares the same values. This, of course, can be said about all friendships. A love interest that lasts is one based on honest caring about the other's well-being.

Old folks often talk about long-lasting relationships. You hear stories about how one finishes the other's sentence or how intuitively one understands what the other needs. This isn't just an old wives' tale. If you make the commitment to love and honor your partner for life and you stick to it day by day, a bond of intimacy can naturally form that brings you together as one. This doesn't mean that you lose your Self in the relationship. Instead, it means that you consider the best interests of the family that you have created with your partner as being of the utmost importance in any decision-making process. This type of bond develops over time. In order for it to prosper, it must be based on an initial attraction of goodness and integrity.

My husband and I have friends who have been married for more than twenty years. We often think of them as a great example of good company in marriage. Peggy and Lloyd demonstrate time and again how it is possible to allow a partner to be free to pursue individual pursuits as you support and love your spouse. For years, Peggy was a model and traveled all over the world doing high-fashion shoots and fashion shows for top magazines and designers, while Lloyd, a fine artist, was at home teaching and developing his work. Together, they created a hair salon in Harlem. They got involved in local politics and crime prevention. Both originally from the South, they turned their home into a refuge for many who have come to them for love and shelter during times of need. What has always struck me about this couple is the ease that they share with each other. It's not so much that they are problem free. Nobody is. Instead, there is an acceptance built into the fabric of their relationship that speaks to their commitment to be together and to find new and creative ways to express their individuality and their love for one another at the same time. When they talk to and about one another, it is with respect. When they share wisdom with others, they commonly make reference to each other. They are living proof that it is possible to keep good company every day of your life. If you are blessed to have a partner with whom you share your life, it is possible to look for that goodness and welcome it into your life together. When you do that, not only do the two of you benefit, but also everyone else in your company enjoys your presence.

SEEK SUPPORT

WHAT HAPPENS when you don't know how to handle a situation and you are alone? The first thing I recommend is to become still. Nine times out of ten, you will find answers to your questions, no matter how dramatic they may seem, if you quiet your mind and allow yourself to seek out your own inner wisdom.

There are times when you either don't choose to turn within, you feel that you don't have the strength to do so, or you believe you truly need help. When this happens, it's critical that you make conscious choices about what kind of support you engage. It's easy to pick up the phone and call someone who will commiserate with you over something that you know you've done wrong. If you keep company with people who will tell you anything you want to hear, you can convince yourself that you are in the right at those times when you really need to be apologizing . When you are in need, don't forget to keep good company. When you pick up the phone, reach out to those who are compassionate, honest, and trustworthy. Just because so-and-so is at home doesn't mean she's the best person for you to call right now. The same goes for a coworker who may share your worries about work with others on the job and jeopardize your future. Be conscious and intentional as you reach out for support. In this way, your actions will not betray you.

BECOME YOUR OWN BEST FRIEND

WE END where we started this chapter. How does your garden grow? As you consider each of the personal relationships that you have in your life, don't forget to include your relationship with yourself. You have to love you in order for any other relationship to work. A fellow once told me that when he was having marital problems and had no idea how to change his life, he learned a great lesson: "You have to take care of first things first. That means you have to figure out what you want and what you need. Otherwise, you can't be happy. And you will make mistakes with other people that could be terribly detrimental to yourself and others."

It's true. How can you access your wisdom on behalf of others with any consistency if you aren't doing the same for yourself? It only makes sense that you have to engage your own Self with loving-kindness and discipline. Instead of turning to someone else for support, look inside for the wisdom that you already hold. Rather than giving away your power in order to feel loved by another, hold onto it and love yourself. You have the capability to be the best company for yourself. When you step into the role of being your own best friend, then the right people and opportunities for growth will come forward to fill in any blanks.

Your Journal Entry

Dearest Friend,

I have long known the importance of being selective about whom to welcome into my inner circle. I know that it is important to keep the gates of my heart closed to all but the most trusting souls. I know that this starts with my love for my own Self. I have to trust me before I can know what good company looks like in others.

I vow now to pay attention to my own thoughts, feelings, and actions. I plan to observe my relationships from the perspective of loving myself first. I intend to welcome only those who will be nurturing in my environment. This does not mean that I will welcome only people who say yes. It means I will welcome honesty and thoughtfulness and turn negativity, gossip, envy, and jealousy away at the door.

I love you,
Me

As you contemplate what good company means in your life, you will need to evaluate the benefits of your relationships and determine how you will move forward based on that information:

• *What kind of company do you keep?* Make a list of your friends. Are they beneficial to you or not? Be specific.

• *What about your family?* Do you have a healthy relationship with your mother? Your father? What steps can you take to improve your relationship with your parents today?

• *Do you have siblings?* If so, what is your relationship with them? Can you see patterns that you can change now that you are an adult? Can you discard ways of communicating that are no longer effective for you?

• *What kinds of friendships do you maintain?* Do you have ulterior motives for remaining friends with anyone? What about your relationships at work?

- *How do you envision good company?* How would you define that concept in your life?

- *Think about your love interests.* When have you selected well? When haven't you? List your previous and current relationships and what has worked or hasn't worked about them. Be rigorously honest here. Are you willing to walk away from a relationship that is unhealthy?

- *What do you think about?* Would you consider your thoughts good company? Do you let your mind run free? Do you practice self-restraint? Are you willing to practice vigilance in your relationship with your mind?

13

LIVE IN SERVICE

OUTSIDE OF THE FIVE OF US who made up my immediate family, the person I loved the most when I was growing up was my mother's mother, Carrie Elizabeth Alsup Freeland. She was old from the day I was born, and she was steeped in the wisdom of each of her years. Little Grandma, as we fondly called her (Carrie towered at a powerful four foot nine), was a powerhouse of strength and love. She lived a life of service. Born in 1889 and armed with a sixth-grade education, she didn't have much choice as to how she would earn a living. Most colored girls of her day worked for white folks, taking care of their every need—cooking, cleaning, and washing their clothes and bodies. Carrie Elizabeth did all of that. But before she ever lifted a finger to take care of somebody else's family, she took care of her own. Every person, animal, place, and thing that came in her path became the recipient of her love and support. Although her work was so-called service work, it was her intention about her efforts—all of them—that created the respectful atmosphere of service that she offered.

My mother tells stories of Little Grandma going to the "country," Calvert County, Maryland, where she cared for her husband's mother until her death. She also cared for my grandfather's mother and other relatives. With her city work, she got to travel around the world as a lady-in-waiting, meeting artists such as Henri Matisse. Little Grandma had a full life for the 101 years that she lived. It was a life that was very difficult for me to understand. I heard the stories of her travels and witnessed the light that always seemed to travel with her. But what stood out more was how hard her life seemed. I remember how her beautiful fingers had hardened into gnarled claws from the beating they endured from scalding water and cleaning products over the years. Even after my parents and my Uncle Wendell, my mother's brother, and his family could easily take care of Little Grandma, she defiantly continued her work, until she was ninety-two years old. How I despised her employers for this. I recall being a teenager begging Little Grandma at one point, "Please stop working there. You don't need those people's money. We can take care of you." On one of these occasions, she sat me down and very sweetly and directly told me, "This is my work, Harriette. And I love my work. I love the people I work for too. There's no need for you to be angry with my employers." She continued, "One day you will have your own work. And when you do, you too should do it with love."

In that moment I could tell that Little Grandma was giving me precious advice, but honestly I couldn't hear it. All I could see was that she had cracking fingers and worn-out hands. In addition, my mother, who gave up her career to stay home and take care of our family, also seemed through my impressionable eyes bound somehow to a life of service. The notion of service as work seemed like the least desirable option, and I vowed never to allow myself to be in a position where I would have to serve anybody—not an employer, not a husband, nobody. I decided that I would be smart enough and earn enough money so that I would be able to take care of myself and would be the one who would be served. In my mind's eye, serving somebody else by definition meant that I would be compromising my own Truth.

Ha. As my mother often says, "chances go 'round." Over the years, I've had the occasion to see the folly of my thinking. When steeped in arrogance and self-righteousness, I have fully believed that I should be served *without* the need for any measure of reciprocity. As you can imagine, that type of convoluted thinking did not lead to comfortable or loving relationships. In moments of clarity, however, I have seen clear to the Truth: that the wheel moves with the greatest of ease when we all are offering our service to its motion. The remarkable bonus in those moments is that everyone is being served at once, making no real burden on anyone.

SERVICE

JUST AS IT TOOK ME some time to see the Truth in what Little Grandma taught, it also is a stretch for a lot of others. I have found that this can be true in many communities, including those of African-American people. I understand why. For generations, the only kind of work that our families were able to get was in service, whether it was hard labor or holding doors open for someone. In and of itself, this was not the problem. The issue was and sometimes still is the condescension that goes along with it. Many intelligent and capable people have endured hard looks, missed opportunities, and harsh judgments based on the color of their skin. They were relegated to service work when perhaps their hearts told them that other options were just a few steps away. Even Black men who earned college diplomas frequently ended up as porters on the railroad during the 1940s and 1950s because they were not welcomed into the practice of law, medicine, or business. Racism and prejudice are real. It was overt during the early days of the development of this country, and it streams through life as we know it today. Indeed, many Black people as well as other oppressed people of color in this country continue to reject service roles as a result of the treatment that they receive when fulfilling their duties.

Why would anyone expect "good service" if appropriate and respectful compensation and treatment are not offered in exchange? In order to build an honest level of trust in people, you have to treat them with respect—not lip-service but respect that demonstrates that you appreciate the role that is being fulfilled and you are truly grateful for the integrity and consistency with which it is being handled. Unfortunately, our culture does not regularly slow down long enough to acknowledge a job well done. Things happen seemingly without effort. The trash gets removed. The children get to school safely on the school bus. The dry cleaners get a nasty stain out of your favorite sweater. Your neighbor collects the mail while you are on vacation. Construction workers repair a huge pothole on your block. The parking attendant delivers your car unscratched.

In each of these situations, someone performed a service. When you were the recipient of one of these services, chances are you were grateful for the comfort and convenience that you were offered even if you didn't realize it. Someone cared while performing the service, and you benefited. If you look at the history of this country, it was by the service of others that every brick was laid and every building built. Often that service went both unpaid and unacknowledged. This is why the arguments are still being waged for apologies and reparations. People want and deserve to be acknowledged and respected.

Do you acknowledge the services that you receive? Do you express gratitude for those who have made your life more comfortable? It takes so little and means so much to stop for a moment and connect with the one who is helping you. One way that you can recognize the importance of your participation in serving the moment is to imagine what would happen if the service disappeared. How much more challenging would your life be if you didn't have the supports that you now may be taking for granted? What if you had to maintain your home, street, family, automobile, food shopping, and other basics without any support whatsoever? It would be hard if you had to go to the farm to pick the fresh produce, fill the hole in the road, and repair the television in addition to your day job, wouldn't it?

I have come to see just how grateful I am for the many supports in my life. Remembering my grandmother, I treat people with equal respect, thanking the mail carrier for getting me the parcels I need just as I rejoice when the computer repairperson makes a situation impossible for me seem easy. I imagine sometimes what my life would be like if these people didn't exist. It is then that I realize that every society needs its many levels of responsibility to be filled. We need each other. When we realize that, we have the opportunity to offer our gratitude for one another and treat each other with genuine respect.

ADOPT AN ATTITUDE OF SERVICE

The biggest thing about Little Grandma was her attitude. She approached every situation with the question, "How can I help?" It was her nature to look for a way to support a person or situation, and she did so with a heart filled with abundant love. As I have thought about Little Grandma's attitude, what stands out the most is her loving approach. Everything within her guided her to be of service to others.

Because I was born and reared in a family that shared Carrie Freeland's values, I got them whether I wanted them or not. My mother never passes a child or an older person—not anybody—on the street who needs a helping hand without offering it. The first time my sister Stephanie came to New York City as an adult, she was handing out quarters left and right to the homeless people who held out their hands. From the moment we were born, we were taught to share not just our possessions but, more, our hearts. The way to do that is to approach a situation by assessing the whole scene. Here are the steps I learned:

- *Stand back for a moment and survey the situation before you.* What are the needs right now? What do you need, and what do others need? What is your role in the situation at hand?

- *Ask "How can I be of help?"* Be realistic. A moment of guilt-inspired action could end up disturbing the balance in a situation. Assess what you actually can commit to doing, and then go for it.

- *Express your gratitude.* When somebody does something kind, let the person know how you feel. Your gesture may be a smile, a nod of the head, a few words exchanged, a handwritten note, a generous tip. It depends on the circumstances.

WORK-AT-HOME PARENTS

AS AN ADULT, I am supremely grateful that my mother made the decision to retire early and stay at home to take care of my sisters and me. When I was a child, I looked at her sacrifice completely differently. I thought that she was a prisoner. I was angry that she wasn't using her brilliance out in the world. Today I recognize the beauty of how she was using her intellect: everything that my mother has had to offer to the world, she has filtered through her children. I am so grateful that she and my father had the means to make it possible for her to stay home to be with us. Because of their shared commitment, we never had to wonder where we would spend an afternoon or who would pick us up from school. We never had to question if there would be a hot meal on the table at the appointed hour or if we would have support doing our homework. What an incredible blessing this was!

My mother offered her life in service to her family. Some mothers and fathers today are able to figure it out so that one parent or guardian can be at home with the children. When that happens in a two-parent household, it means that both parents are working to serve the family. This is something that goes unnoticed and often lacks respect in the workaday world. Often professional women who retire early to be with their children are ostracized by their "friends." When a dad stays at home, the ostracism can often be worse.

Just because you don't understand something doesn't mean you should denigrate it. Why not trust that people are seeking to do their best for their families when they make unpopular choices? If you are a parent who is making a choice to devote yourself full time to your children, you should be commended. You're taking on a job without noticeable reward or fanfare. The payoff does come, however, when your offspring thrive based on the consistent, loving knowledge that you have imparted to them. Your service, which is a true sacrifice, does have value. Don't ever forget that.

The challenge for working parents is to strike a healthy balance between the job and the rest of life. You must also find a way not to feel guilty for not being able to be every woman or every man at every moment. Organization is the hallmark of success for busy parents, whether you are in a two-parent relationship or a single-parent household. When you base your life on a clear understanding of why you do what you do, then you can stay on course. This means that as satisfying as your career may be, you don't lose sight of your bigger goals of nurturing your family.

Having the right approach makes all the difference. A single mother in Washington, D.C., says that she is happy she had her daughter and that over the years she has figured out ways to make their life work. Right after she became pregnant she called on the responsible people in her life to see who would be willing to offer her support. Although Carla did not marry the baby's father, he has contributed financially over the years and is an active part of their daughter's life. The biggest support, however, has come from Carla's parents and her closest friends. She created her village, in the tradition of her African ancestors, so that there would always be somebody available to love and nurture her daughter even when she was not nearby. It has worked out beautifully. Sharing the responsibility for her daughter's parenting was hard at first. Carla wanted to see her daughter's first step and to work with her on her first math problem. Although this didn't always happen, Carla has learned over time that rather than resenting the people who were helping to care for her daughter, she could extend her gratitude as she also remembered the many hats that she herself was wearing in order to keep her family going.

WHEN TRAGEDY HAPPENS

LIFE DOESN'T ALWAYS HAPPEN in neat little packages. To be able to respond well to crisis requires that you have your priorities in order or that you are willing to do so in the moment. This was the case for Dottie, a mother of five grown children, in Baltimore. She and her husband were enjoying their life together after each of their children had gone on to build a life for themselves. They traveled a lot. Dottie participated in many events in her community. All in all, life was great—until one of her sons came down with brain cancer. Mark was a successful member of Detroit's drug enforcement police force when he went to check out a headache problem and discovered that he was ill. Immediately his mother was at his side. Mark underwent two surgeries, after which the doctors predicted that he had, at best, three to five months to live.

It took Dottie only a moment to decide that she would do all that she could in her power to help heal her son. That meant living in Detroit for nine months with him as he healed from his surgeries and radiation. After that, she brought Mark back to the family homestead in Baltimore. Together with her husband, Dottie has cared for Mark for more than a dozen years, defying the doctor's predictions. Her sacrifice has been huge. Trips abroad were replaced by backrubs at home. Instead of socializing, Dottie has put herself in the business of healing, and she doesn't regret a minute of it. "I get to have my son. He is alive. He is doing the best that he can. And we are going to do everything possible to make him happy. I find myself now as mother and friend."

Dottie's story is one example of how serving the moment can be very different from what you think. When your heart is telling you to offer love and support, whether it's your child or a coworker, you may find that you are able to be of greater help than you ever imagined. Every few months, I hear stories of people who have donated their organs in order to help people live and of family members and friends who give up careers and ambitions in order to take care of those in greater need. Never have I heard from any of these people that they regretted it. Making the choice to be of service was fulfilling enough.

ANTIDOTE FOR THE EGO

IT'S AMAZING how powerful you can become by adopting an attitude of service. One of the best ways to shake off the jitters is to have this approach to any task you accept. This became crystal clear to me when I began to work on my first book, *Jumping the Broom*. I had gathered up all the research I needed to write and was preparing to do the hard part—writing the book—when I started to feel some doubts creeping in. Thank goodness, I had scheduled a meeting with a dear friend who had agreed to review my project and provide any advice or direction that she could to help.

Dianne suggested that I write my book as a gift to God and also to my audience. To do this, her recommendation was to begin each writing session by making special prayers that invoked God's grace and support. Further, I was to focus on my audience and consider what they really needed. How could I create a book that would be of the greatest value to them? Dianne told me that if I followed these guidelines, my jitters would subside. In their place would come a strong intention to craft the most exquisite and useful gift that I could for the people who would be receiving it.

She was right. My ego had been doing a number on me. Although I had been writing professionally for years, somehow my doubts had begun to get the best of me. I had started to ask myself how I could possibly be worthy of writing such an important work. When I refocused my attention on the positive and sought out ways to support my audience, everything shifted. Sure, there were still moments when I felt butterflies in my stomach, but amazingly they immediately passed when I remembered my goal: to create the most precious gift I could for the most deserving group of people.

I have since used this philosophy with all kinds of other activities, large and small, and you can too. Instead of letting your ego get the best of you, either giving you an inflated or a diminished sense of your value, consider the true purpose of the effort. Rarely is a worthwhile activity solely for the benefit of one. When you focus your attention on how you can use your skills and talents to support others, to support the moment, everything comes into balance. Then, however great your abilities are, they will inevitably be of equal measure to the task at hand.

LEARN FROM YOUR MISTAKES

COMING INTO PROPER ALIGNMENT with the value of service requires a lot for some people. Sometimes it takes a very wrong action for one to have an awakening. This was true for a twenty-year-old man in New York City who got caught jumping a turnstile in the subway. Jimmy knew what he did was stupid, but the thrill of doing something wrong got the best of him, and he jumped without knowing that any police were around. Moments after his illegal action, Jimmy found himself handcuffed and chained to a group of several other offenders. When they checked his pockets the police officers had to laugh. In Jimmy's pocket was $200 in cash.

Jimmy was sentenced to six weekends of community service at a shelter for recovering addicts. At first he hated the schedule, which required him to get up early in the morning and work late into the evening for no pay. His duties included going to a church service, followed by unloading trucks of food and supplies, lunch, and more unloading. He hated that he would be in the company of addicts. There were women with small children, women and men infected with HIV/AIDS, and many young people who looked quite old. At first, Jimmy turned his nose up at these people, considering himself better than they were. But because he had to keep coming back, he got to see them as they recovered. Over time, Jimmy saw that he was in no position to judge them. They were people just like he was. Some had lost their way, just as he had. They all were trying to find their way back. Being around Jimmy and a few of the other men who were trying to make something out of their lives ended up being a source of inspiration for those who were recovering. In the end, Jimmy says, everybody benefited. He grew to respect people who were different from him, and he got to see how his own contributions helped to make these people's lives better as they made strides to reenter the working world.

After his six-month sentence was over, Jimmy continued to go to the shelter to help out. He says he got to see that he could make a difference in other people's lives, and that felt good. As he worked to improve his own life, he saw that a way to strengthen himself was to support others.

DON'T KEEP SCORE

WHEN YOU ADOPT the attitude of giving, there is an expectation that you will receive as well. This is a law of the universe—the give and take of nature. And yet, if you pay attention to nature, you will see that an ant, for example, doesn't do a good deed because it believes it will get a paycheck at the end. It does its work because that is its duty in life. To serve the community is the role of the worker ant, and so that is what it does.

To be a vital, contributing member of your community—the world community—is your duty. Although we live in a capitalist country that prospers based on the buying and selling of goods and services, which includes your time and effort, this cannot be the only way that you look at your contributions. I learned years ago that you give because it is in your nature, human nature, to do so. When you give your best effort to whatever you do, you will be rewarded with peace of mind, one of the greatest gifts you can receive. A bonus is that you may also be rewarded with material benefits, such as wealth or possessions. Surprisingly, when you do not expect the possessions, you have the greatest power. When you are tied to the promise of expectation, you naturally weaken.

This is something that people rarely consider. When do you have the most power in a negotiation? It is when you are willing to walk away from it. When you are not feeling needy, you can stand in your own authority. Even if you actually do need something, your attitude will largely determine the outcome. Rather than approaching a relationship with the mind-set of tit-for-tat, assess your needs and your intentions. If you believe that your efforts will not be respected, don't offer them. If you believe you need to negotiate for more reasonable terms, do so. Throughout your transactions, be clear that when you do offer your effort, you do so selflessly. When you give your best to whatever you undertake, you can always stand strong with that knowledge.

Because people operate based on different understandings of right and wrong, be crystal clear in your dealings with people as to what you are to deliver, and make your requirements known. Then there will be no need for keeping score. Your agreed-on terms will spell out how you will proceed.

ONE HAND WASHES THE OTHER

OVER THE YEARS, when my mother and I have talked about what our efforts mean in the world, she has pointed out that to do our best and to give when we can is the right way to live. We give because it is our duty. We support one another because that's the way the world works. We need each other, whether we believe it's true or not. When we have the ability to help another, it is our responsibility to do so. In turn, at some other point when we need support, it will be there for us, because, as Mommie says, "One hand washes another."

SERVICE IN ACTION

At the dawn of the year 2000, I did what I have done for many New Year's celebrations. I listened to my spiritual teacher share a message of insight and direction for us to contemplate throughout the year. Included in that year's message was the question: *Are you offering your service while standing in your own Truth?* This question blew me away. I was already working on this book about how to choose Truth in our lives. Here was a question that required tremendous probing and activity on my part, on each of our parts, in order to be able to answer with a resounding *yes.*

At a certain point that year, I was working on a big project that involved many different people with varying perceptions about the creative vision. In a work setting—as an entrepreneur—I sometimes find it challenging to manage through difficulty and stay in a balanced place. More commonly, I struggle— sometimes feeling grounded, other times feeling off kilter. In order to strike a balance during the foggy moments, I put myself in contemplation mode. I often write down the various issues that come up. By recording my thoughts, I can look at them as separate from me, witness what's going on, and look for clues as to how I should proceed from a more objective perspective.

Using all of my tools of self-inquiry during this period, I searched my soul as I took part in what felt like a ferocious battle of wills over principle and power. The ego was in full effect with each person involved, especially the "boss." How could I serve my higher purpose when my blood felt as if it was boiling over with anger? How could I serve the interests of the project if my ego had been bruised and I was retaliating in a knee-jerk way? I sought the space of my own Truth. I asked myself why I was in this predicament. What was it in my personality and in my way of working that had allowed me to be in such an uncomfortable situation?

Because of my contemplation, I was able to go back to the question: *Are you offering your service while standing in your own Truth?* The honest answer is that I wasn't. When I was offering my service, I was giving it grudgingly. Plus, I felt as if I were allowing my feet to be cut out from under me. As hard as I tried and as clearly as I reasoned with the head of the project, I kept running into a brick wall. Day after day, I felt as if I was standing in a lie. I stopped believing in the project, and I began to doubt myself. What was I doing wrong? Because every interaction felt like a fight, I found myself retaliating and retreating in a cyclical way. It was exhausting on every level.

At one point, it became clear to me that I had to walk away. As much as I wanted to be part of this project, it no longer served me to be affiliated with it in any way. I was unable to offer my service while standing in my own Truth. Because the principals of this effort did not share my understanding or focus, or respect my contributions, my efforts proved fruitless.

Living in service does not mean letting someone take advantage of you. To serve the moment may require that you walk away from an unhealthy environment. In order to serve others in bringing your own special gifts to the effort, you have to be strong within yourself. You have to be clear so that you are able to offer your best without strings attached.

My Journal Entry

Dearest Friend,

Living in service is not the most popular activity these days. Trust me, though, it is one of the most rewarding. The world relies on the efforts of each one of us for its sustenance. The same is true for us in our lives. We have needs that others fulfill, just as we are able to satisfy other needs. I want to adopt a healthy attitude of service as a way to guide my life.

I want to temper my ego with selfless service. I want to think about others as I live my life and be conscious of how my actions affect those around me. I want to contribute to the upliftment of those around me as I work to support myself.

I love you,
Me

As you think about your life, consider what type of service you offer.

- *Do you pay attention to the people who help you?* Do you thank people for their service? How do you treat people who fill service capacities? Can you improve your interactions with them?

- *Do you pay attention to what is needed in the moment?* Do you hold doors open for people or offer your seat to someone in need? Do you listen when the moment calls for it? Do you support others as they are attempting to communicate a point?

- *How do you do your job?* Do you have an attitude of entitlement or of service? Do you think it's possible to rise to the top and maintain an attitude of service?

- *How can you maintain personal strength as you also take care of others?*

- *Can you imagine living your life so that every action is one of service,* even as you prosper?

14

BE RESPONSIBLE

WE LIVE IN A FREE WORLD, or so it has been described. Those of us in the West live in a democracy that politically allows us to make personal decisions about our lives and our future, but also—and even more significantly—we are born into a life to which the universe has given a huge opportunity, the ability to choose. This is the great distinction between humanity and the rest of the animal kingdom. The freedom and ability to exercise choice is a powerful gift reserved fundamentally for us. How we exercise our will to choose represents the difference between one human being and another. Whether we make conscious choices or knee-jerk ones determines the quality of each of our lives now and over time. This is true on every level of our lives. The ways that our societies are run depend on the integrity and compassion of our leaders. Our families grow based on the choices that parents and guardians make about nurturing the home environment. Our bodies serve us directly in relation to how we serve them. In every moment, we have the choice to act in ways that are beneficial or not.

As we look into our lives and examine the ways that we have responded to the situations that have come before us, we become able to assess the quality of our choices. When we dig deep enough, we can find the core reasons for the decisions that we have made in the past as well as those that we continue to make. By understanding our thoughts, words, and deeds, we gain the power to harness ourselves, focus our energies, and exercise our freedom of choice with the requisite dose of responsibility.

As a human being you have the capability to do just about anything you want. So, it's essential to remember that for every action, there always is a reaction.

Freedom requires responsibility. When you are on a search to understand and live abiding by the Truth within your heart that also reverberates through the world, your responsibility is to continue to probe until you discover how to live in that Truth and ultimately attain liberation—true freedom.

I believe that the act of Choosing Truth is integral to the search for the human connection to God. Each of us in our own way is here on this planet at this moment in time for a reason, and we are all on a search for happiness. People attempt to experience happiness in many different ways: through their relationships with others, through extracurricular activities, through diversion and distraction, through communion with nature, and through spiritual effort. All indicators point to spiritual focus as the most direct way to reach that place of recognition of our true purpose, which enables us to experience happiness in each moment.

We live in times that allow people to search for spiritual meaning in their lives without the fear of being judged as weak or fanatical (well, mostly). We live in times when people are boldly admitting that they don't have all the answers, that the endless offerings of escape have not quenched their thirst, that the something more for which they have been searching has got to be found. But where? Every spiritual tradition will tell you that only through a direct relationship with the divine can one ever quench that spiritual thirst. The logical next question is, How does one establish a direct relationship with God? And who is God anyway? Theories abound. God is love. God is the supreme Truth. God is universal consciousness. God is compassion. God is everything. God is you and I. God is that insistent and patient voice inside that points the way.

If God is the ultimate Truth, then how do we discover that Truth? I believe that the requirement for seeing the Truth, for recognizing and then embracing it, is to exercise choice. In the moment of awareness, when we see that a choice is before us, we must ask ourselves which choice will bring us closer to God, closer to honesty, closer to the purity of the universe. When we accept responsibility for our lives, we will grow stronger in our ability to recognize the choices before us and act accordingly. Just as in exercising the body, it takes practice and discipline to strengthen the muscles of discrimination and discernment. It takes consistent, conscious effort to remain aware of the choices before us and to find the strength and courage to choose that which is most beneficial in the long run rather than for a fleeting moment. There is a difference between living in the moment responsibly and throwing caution to the wind. It is up to each of us to discover that difference and then choose to live with conviction and dignity, welcoming the power and grace that each moment brings.

BECOME THE CAPTAIN OF YOUR OWN SHIP

LIFE LESSONS come in the most unusual ways. My mother used to say all the time when we were growing up, "The Lord works in mysterious ways, His wonders to perform." She would repeat this when we shared a bit of wisdom with her that we had received from an unlikely source, because she wanted us to know that God lives in every moment, in every interaction. We may not always recognize the Lord's presence, but if we can remember that God does not abandon us ever, we may also remember to look at everyone and every situation with a healthy dose of respect. When we look at the world from this perspective, even when we are in the midst of tremendous challenge, we can step into the light. We can find our way.

I experienced this concretely, in my early twenties, a few years after I moved to New York. I suppose I had always been searching for happiness and had experienced various ups and downs that had shown me that happiness is not always as easy to grasp as I thought. On the surface at this particular time, my life seemed great. My career was evolving quickly and beautifully. Dreams that I had had since I was a little girl were coming true. Yet inside I felt alone and abandoned. Not knowing what to do and feeling extremely self-conscious about sharing my vulnerabilities with loved ones, I was lost. In my mind's eye, I was supposed to be "perfect." Everything was supposed to be just so in my world. Although it may have looked grand, the truth is that on the inside I was falling apart. After many noble but nevertheless unsuccessful strides, what I chose to do was to escape. I couldn't figure out how to find happiness as I pursued all the "right" things, so I turned to other things that eventually began to undermine whatever possibilities lay before me. One very late night, I found myself in the home of a fellow who was essentially my drug dealer. I never thought of him in that way. No, I considered him to be my friend. I marveled at how he lived his life. He was content in his fifty-some-odd years. Amazingly, there was solidity about him. I'm told that there still is.

About me there was something else—a quiet desperation perhaps, certainly not solidity. On that particular late night, Sun Lee listened to me, in my heightened state of awareness, as I was lamenting the nuances of my sadness. After a while he calmly chuckled saying, "You know what your problem is? You are not the captain of your own ship." I snickered uncomfortably, thinking under my breath, "Who are you to talk? You are a drug dealer." But even then, I knew that he was more captain of his ship than I. He knew what he was doing, had chosen it for whatever his reasons and was not posturing as something else. I, on the other hand, was pretending to have it all together, convincing myself and others that I was happy and successful, that I was a good girl, the judge's daughter, the magazine editor, the dutiful wife, when all the while my world was crumbling.

Shortly after, all the cards did come crashing down. My health disintegrated, and my marriage ended. I was a mess.

More than a dozen years later, many of them sober, I reflect on that moment. How resoundingly true Sun Lee's words were. "How was it," I asked myself, "that I had sunk so low, that I had allowed myself to give up my Self?" And more, I questioned, "What happened in the interim to bring me back?" For starters, I heard the wisdom in Sun Lee's message, though it had come from a most unlikely source. On that fateful night, though I didn't realize it, my faith got stirred up a bit.

It is true that faith has been the transforming ingredient in my life. Belief in that which is greater than I am and that at once lives within me has served as the magic wand to turn things around. The turning, however, has not been easy. Even now, in the midst of continued and quite spectacular success, I must remember to hold onto that faith and nurture it in order to stay strong. To be captain of my own ship means that I must take time to know my ship, honor my ship, love my ship. It means I have to choose me. This is exactly what I have been doing. The result has been no less than miraculous. I have built a firm foundation for my life. I have a healthy and happy marriage. I am doing what I want to do in my work. And, yes, I still have to remind myself that I am in charge of me. It is my responsibility to take the steps necessary to care for my needs. When I step into the role of captain of my life, when I make that requisite effort, then the Lord can effectively lead the way.

WHAT IS YOUR CHOICE?

THIS PERSONAL DISCOVERY has led me to notice the search in others. I have begun to ask this question of people: *Do you choose yourself during the course of the day?* Ask yourself this question now. Consider how often you put other people's perceptions about you in front of your own real needs. Look at your life to see whether you honor your own Self regularly. Do you choose You to love and nurture and respect?

I promise you that if you probe your heart carefully, searching in all the hidden nooks and crannies for Truth, you will find areas where you can be more loving to yourself. You can find ever more rewarding ways to choose you. As a ship's captain pays attention to the entire body of his ship, so must you tend to the entire body, mind, and heart of You.

DON'T BLAME

OFTEN OUR LIVES just seem to happen. We have routines. Most of us are pretty busy. And time ticks by. When our schedules don't seem to allow us to complete all of the duties or activities that we have planned, we sometimes blame others for our predicament. Blame is sneaky. Rather than recognizing that we actually can control the things that we do—every single thing—we tend to blame the busyness of our lives on the actions of others. Someone or something else has encroached upon us, making us unable to fulfill an obligation, even if the duty is simply to take it easy.

When you start pointing your finger outward, chances are you would be better off pointing it at yourself. You cannot control other people—not children, not your spouse, not a lover, not your boss or coworkers, not friends or neighbors—but if you are mindful and deliberate, you can control yourself. So why not choose to scrutinize your life to see what type of control you need to exercise in order to live in happiness?

Your watching can start with your habits. What do you allow to happen in your life that is counterproductive to your fulfillment? Take a few minutes now to list those things. Be rigorously honest in your observation. This way you will be clear about what you need to work on. I met a woman who found herself in a bind that many people share. Rebecca says that every night when she comes home from work, she tries to unwind but frequently gets sidetracked by the telephone, which begins to ring the moment she walks in the door. As much as she says she wants to take time out for herself, Rebecca admits that she consistently loses hours at a time talking to one person after another. One evening, she says, she got so angry at the barrage of intrusions that she yelled at one of her friends on the phone. Her friend was shocked and hurt. She didn't understand why Rebecca seemed to have a chip on her shoulder. To tell the truth, Rebecca didn't understand either. She had unknowingly allowed herself to fall into a pattern that wasn't supporting her needs, and she felt trapped.

Rebecca's story reminds me of my own. I used to come home and hear the phone ring from the moment I walked in the door. After an intense day at work, I had been looking forward to time alone as well as time with my husband. Yet my pattern of chatting with friends and family had continued even after I was married. My husband didn't like that one bit. He told me that he felt he was competing with the phone for my attention, and so I wrestled with the phone, ending calls more quickly and delaying return calls until after he was asleep. One day, George made a brilliant—and obvious—observation. He said, "People call you when it's convenient for them to talk. That doesn't mean it's convenient for you. Just because the phone rings doesn't mean you have to answer it." He was right. We had an answering machine. I could choose to let it accept the call, and so I began to do so. At first it was hard. I was so accustomed to my pattern of call and response that it felt uncomfortable. That's when I realized that, much like Rebecca, the telephone had become somewhat of a crutch for me. I had used communicating with others as a substitute for communicating with myself or my husband.

Since I have been weaned from constant at-home phone use, my home life is much more fulfilling. Sometimes George and I do fight over who will turn down the TV when one of us is trained on one of the 500 channels that our satellite dish serves up (another one of those distractions that people can mistakenly blame for usurping our time!). All in all, though, we have begun to focus on better-quality time that we can devote to each other as well as to our individual pursuits.

Rather than blaming anyone or anything for what isn't working in your life, you have the power to change it. A person, a telephone, a television program, or even a job—none of these can rule you unless you let it. Once you accept responsibility for this fact, you will be able to reclaim your power and take the necessary actions to enforce your life's plan.

EVALUATE YOUR INTIMATE RELATIONSHIPS

ACCEPTING RESPONSIBILITY for your life includes the love relationship you are currently in. We live in a fickle society that holds marriage up on a pedestal while it also indulges emotional and sexual promiscuity. Our culture makes it tough to maintain long-term relationships with success, yet it is possible to enjoy a connected and healthy relationship with a partner for its duration if that is your intention. As I have spoken with women and men about the relationships that they have had, what I commonly hear is that people know early on if they believe they are compatible with one another. Yet often people who sense incompatibility continue to involve themselves in the relationship because it's convenient. They rationalize in a variety of ways: "He's better than being alone." "I have been too picky in the past. I need to give this one a chance. Maybe my standards are too high." "I'll try to overlook that quality that really makes me mad."

"He'll change." Have you ever fallen into one of those situations? It's easy to get comfortable in a relationship even when things are not going smoothly. That's not to say that you have to exit when things get tough. Being responsible means that you address the issues before you. If you don't, greater problems ensue down the line. Sometimes those problems are bigger than you may easily be willing or able to handle.

One woman nearly lost her marriage and her dignity as a result of not standing up for herself. Loretta had been going through years of frustration and disappointment with her husband. This surprised her, since her courtship was like a fantasy; her fiancé seemed to fulfill her every need and desire. Yet from the very start of their marriage, Loretta was terribly disappointed. Rather than enjoying the flowers and special dates that they had had before the wedding, she experienced continued assaults on her character and integrity immediately after walking down the aisle. In the face of each blow, she persevered, turning the proverbial other cheek. She says she figured if she weathered the storm, she would prove to her husband that he could love her, that she would never leave him. Loretta made the choice not to speak up about the vacations he took without her, not to quarrel over the nights spent who knows where, not to protest when the tenderness and support she craved weren't offered—that is, until she blew up. At a certain point, Loretta had had enough. She was so hurt and angry that her husband would not love and respect her as she believed she deserved that she didn't quite know what to do. That she had two children with him and a pile of bills only complicated matters.

The day that Loretta first approached Harold about his indiscretions and the state of their marriage, she was livid. Naturally, he became defensive. Not much came of the discussion. They argued. He apologized and promised never again to do any of the myriad things he had done in the past. And life went on—until the next time he did it. Finally, after about five years of feeling tortured, Loretta decided to move out. She got an apartment, took her two children, and gave Harold an ultimatum: if he wanted to have a life with his wife and children, he had to change. He had to commit to them and be responsible to them. She agreed to give their separation a year before deciding how to proceed. At first it was hard for Loretta. She had to change her life dramatically in order to work and take care of two small children. She managed, all the while missing her man. She also grew stronger and more aware of her personal value in her life and in her marriage. Loretta assessed how much she had been contributing to her family without being appreciated. She came to notice, with the help of a therapist, what she needed in order to feel loved and respected. When she spoke to Harold, she let him know what she was thinking and feeling. By the end of the year of separation, Harold admitted that he really missed Loretta and wanted to work things out. He said he couldn't promise that he would be a different person but that he would commit to honoring their life together in ways that would make everyone comfortable.

It's not always this simple. Indeed, Loretta and Harold's life is far from resolved. They are still working through their issues. Their commitment is what is fueling their progress. For some couples, it can be hard to get to the point of reigniting commitment. Sometimes one partner or the other simply isn't interested in or willing to do what it takes to act responsibly. When that happens, you have to be aware and take the proper action.

This was the fate for Diane and Paul. College sweethearts, these two were inseparable. They had fun together and shared many friends. Their life seemed perfect from the outside looking in. Even on the inside, it was pretty great—until Paul started using drugs. At first, he experimented with marijuana. When he moved on to cocaine, things started to get shaky. Paul quickly advanced from recreational drug use to creeping out at night, losing one job after another and lying repeatedly to Diane.

Throughout an intense two-year period when Paul fell deep into heavy drug use, finally adding crack to his repertoire, Diane continued to love him and try to get him some help. She read up on drug abuse and talked to him about it. She offered to take him to rehab. She spoke to his close friends about how they might be able to intervene. Nothing worked. Consistently, Paul would apologize and agree to seek help, only to clean up for a few days or weeks and then go back out on a binge. Diane racked her brain and heart trying to figure out what to do, until she found another woman's clothing in her bedroom. That was it. Diane drummed up all the courage she had in order to leave the man she once believed would be her husband for life.

Ultimately, Diane says it was the only decision she could make. She had tried everything and still lost her husband to drugs. Even when she approached Paul with evidence of his promiscuity, he lied. He lied about the affair and the drugs. Worse, he refused to get help. The only way that Diane could help herself was to leave.

TAKE CHARGE OF YOURSELF AT WORK

TAKING RESPONSIBILITY for yourself means that you must pay attention to every aspect of your life. Many people have expressed concern about how they can be fully responsible for themselves at work, especially if they are not in a position of authority. They sometimes fall into the trap of believing that they have little or no control. On the surface, this appears true. We work in the context of organizational structures that have rules and regulations as well as people in positions of power whose function it is to interpret those rules. Depending on the temperament and conscience of those in power, it can be comfortable or unbearable for an employee to manage through the day. This is true in any situation. A fair judge in court can help to figure out an honorable solution to a grievance. A compassionate loan officer can help you work through a difficult period with the greatest of ease.

At work, how can you stand in your own attainment of personal power, feel strong and secure in your beliefs and convictions, *and* navigate within the confines of the establishment? Once again, your powers of observation will serve you well. When you truly experience your inner power, you will no longer need to flaunt it or the lack that you may be feeling. When you experience oneness with your knowledge and abilities, you can relax into you. No matter what your role, you will begin to see that you do have control over yourself, and you can make the best of any situation. You can pay closer attention to what's going on around you. Office politics are real, whether your office is in corporate America or at a construction site. When people work together, there is always a hierarchy. If you can figure out the internal structure of your organization, you will be able to negotiate your way to a place of comfort and clarity. Some basics that you can keep in mind are these:

- *Be kind.* That old folks' wisdom is advisable here. On a core level, everyone wants to be treated with kindness and respect. Your offering of no-strings-attached kindness will serve you well. Over time, people will witness your positive and affirming nature and begin to trust you.

- *Be respectful of roles.* When you have a great idea that you want to share with the head of the company, hold your tongue for a moment. Rather than ruffling feathers because you acted too hastily, follow the chain of command. Inform your supervisor of your idea—in writing to ensure that it's properly documented—and let that person know you want to forward it to the company head. Know that some people feel insecure when others are assertive and brimming with great ideas. In order to manage through this, practice dispassion. You have hundreds of great ideas. Don't become attached to any of them, even as you make clear from where it came. Be organized with your documentation and your overall work.

- *Be patient and sincere.* Your time will come. Just because you are in a subordinate role today does not mean that this is your position for life. It depends on what you want and how well you develop your skills. Exercising patience will allow you to find a creative and effective way to work within your office structure. Even if your role is sorting the mail, you can welcome that responsibility with so much gusto and thoughtfulness for others that your sincerity will shine through. True leaders recognize talent and look for ways to let it shine. When you do your best, someone in management will recognize it.

- *Speak up for yourself.* If someone speaks to you in an insulting or unprofessional way, say something. This is one of the trickiest areas for people, which is why human resources departments, as well as minority relations and equal rights divisions of companies, are essential. Even as these support mechanisms exist, I strongly recommend that you attempt to handle your disagreements face-to-face first. This goes for sexual harassment, racial slurs, or body image discrimination. I say this because at the most basic level, you are dealing with a person. If you want to stay at your job, you are going to have to figure out how to work with people. If you make your first line of defense one-on-one, where you calmly approach the offender and state your case about a particular grievance, you stand a better chance of mending the fence.

- *Forgive, but don't forget.* Being responsible calls for a willingness to forgive ourselves and others for things that have happened in the past. All of us make mistakes. In order to move through the world without holding onto endless grudges, we have to learn how to let things go. Forgiving someone who is honestly remorseful for having committed an inappropriate action is a mature action on your part. Even when a person is not remorseful, though, it is best to forgive. What you should *not* do is forget what happened. Burying your head in the sand will only lead to repeating a mistake. People tend to be consistent in their actions. If you have experienced that someone lies to you, or is lazy, or disrespectful to your children, or some other affront, remember the point. In this way, you will know not to share a confidence with that person or not to include him or her in your family activities. Sometimes it may mean that you let the indiscretion go as you also let the person go from your life.

- *Know when to leave.* Jobs used to be lifetime commitments. This is rarely true now. People move around over the course of their working lives, often changing careers. Sometimes they leave jobs because the atmosphere or the actual work no longer supports the intention they have for their lives. It takes a tremendous amount of courage to walk away from a job. The time to do it is after you have evaluated what is important to you, including how you spend the bulk of your day earning a living. If you do not believe that there is a synchronicity between your work life and the rest of your life, you may need to change.

- *Know when to change.* Don't make the mistake of switching jobs when what you really need to do is address some of your own behavior patterns. It may be true, for example, that you do not feel respected at your job. It may be appropriate for you to leave. Even more significant, it may be essential that you change your ways. You've probably heard the saying, "You let people do what they do to you." This doesn't mean that it is your fault when people treat you in unacceptable ways. It does mean that you must defend yourself. When you change, when you become stronger and more confident in your Self, your strength will become visible to others. And they will often treat you accordingly.

YOU CAN BE A TEACHER

HOW DO YOU support yourself in a work environment or other situation when someone crosses the line? Keeping your cool when someone insults you can be hard if your instinctive response is to curse the person out or retaliate with an equally vicious comment. The same goes when your boss or a high-ranking colleague issues a low blow. What do you do in a situation like this? How can you act responsibly when you really want to fight?

First, breathe. When you engage your breath as your support, you can slow down your adrenaline and discover an appropriate and effective way to respond to an inappropriate action. Breathe in and out deeply when someone attacks you.

People often lash out at others in order to unnerve them. When their strategy works, you lose twice over. Then you have been insulted and potentially embarrassed to boot. Rather than falling prey to another's deception or foul play, stay strong.

We already know that war usually begets further devastation. We see this on battlefields the world over, as well as in domestic and office disputes. An eye for an eye generally makes two blind people. A responsible strategy would be to pursue another line of thinking. I have learned that the weapon of education is an effective tool that neutralizes rage and ignorance, replacing them with knowledge and information. When you adopt the approach of looking at a situation to see how you can shed light on it to reveal what is actually true, you are doing a service to the moment and to humanity. What's important is that you don't use your knowledge as a shield of superiority. Serving the moment turns your weapon of education into a blanket of support for all.

My sister Stephanie found herself in a situation at her job that was absolutely unacceptable. A senior-level manager, Stephanie had a casual conversation one afternoon with a woman with whom she had become quite friendly. The woman was part of Stephanie's team but not as high ranking. Midway into the conversation, Sally said, "Stephanie, if I were to take you home to meet my family, they wouldn't consider you Black, because they consider Blacks as trash. And you aren't trash." Stephanie was aghast. The fact that Sally was oblivious to the insult that her racist remarks made showed Stephanie how critical it was that her understanding be clarified. Standing there, nearly dumbfounded, Stephanie knew that she had to say something. She took a few moments to collect her thoughts and said, "People are not trash. There is no Black trash or white trash. It *is* true that people have different experiences and come from different backgrounds." Stephanie continued, "Maybe the people in your neighborhood have not been exposed to many Black people. Maybe they have only seen the Black people who appear on sitcoms on TV whose images are bad."

At first, Sally was taken aback. She had thought that she was paying Stephanie a compliment with her comment and felt assaulted by Stephanie's response. Stephanie says that Sally was a bit tentative when she came to speak with her after that conversation, but she became more open and curious, which led to her expanding her knowledge about African Americans in general and Stephanie in particular. In addition to unconscious questions like, "Do you tan in the summer?" she also questioned Stephanie about her family, her parenting strategies, and more. Eventually, Sally got bolder and began to reach out to more of the Black people at the job. By the time she got married, she had expanded her network of friends at work to the point that she included a number of her Black and white friends in her family wedding celebration.

Racial discrimination is one of the most pervasive and eroding practices in the world. The only way that we can hope to annihilate it is by educating each other about ourselves. It takes willingness on both sides for people to consider each other as they are, to learn about what they believe and represent, and to take a chance at getting to know one another. It also requires that people stand up for themselves and each other even when nobody else is around.

BE TRUE TO YOUR WORD

HAVE YOU EVER FOUND—after the fact—that you have agreed to do something that you no longer want to do? Or perhaps you enlisted in an activity in which you were unable to participate? What have you done in either of these situations? It can be tough to stick to your word when you realize that you have made a mistake or that you no longer are interested in the task at hand. How you handle yourself in situations like this illustrates your true colors.

A hairstylist in New Jersey was invited to participate in a big photo shoot with a modeling agency in New York City. This young woman was eager to build her portfolio, which meant that she was willing to work in exchange for photographs that would show potential employers just what she could do. As it got closer to the actual shoot date, problems arose. The coordinator of the project was disorganized. She changed the shoot date and time on three separate occasions and offered no compensation or reimbursements for cash outlays. Veronica thought about all of the strikes that this project had against it. Then she thought about how much "free" work she had done already in her growing career, and she got mad. "Why should I participate in this anyway?" she asked herself. "This woman doesn't know what she's doing, and it's not going to be worth my time." As Veronica reasoned her way into full-out anger, she also neglected to organize herself well. Come shoot day, Veronica was torn about whether she would participate at all. In the end, she came to the shoot two hours late, causing the entire shoot to be delayed because all of the models were waiting for her.

When the day ended and Veronica witnessed the fruits of her actions, she regretted what she had done. Stewing in anger without taking responsible action hurt the entire group, including herself. Although she didn't realize it at the time, Veronica could have exercised any of several options that would have been more professional. She could have called the coordinator the moment she began to have second thoughts to express her concerns. She could have asked for some kind of fee or reimbursement agreement up front. She could have explained that she no longer wanted to do the job and would like to refer another stylist. Or she could have set parameters on what she would be willing to do on the day of the shoot. Instead, she acted irresponsibly out of her anger and spite. In the end, she damaged her reputation. How could any professional who knew about her behavior in this project confidently work with her again when she had proved to be unreliable?

You are as good as your word. If you say you are going to do something, do it. If for some reason you cannot fulfill a responsibility that you have accepted, speak up and let the proper people know. Even when no money exchanges hands, your word is the commodity of greatest value.

The same goes in a friendship. People often believe that their friends will quickly forgive them, so they don't have to honor whatever they have agreed to do if conditions change. Two women in Washington, D.C., have virtually stopped being friends as a result of this type of behavior. Since college, these women have been tight. They pledged the same sorority and used to talk on the phone several times a week, even after one of them went to live in another state. They were close and "had each other's back" in times of need. It all changed when Cynthia and Winnie entered into a business relationship. In an effort to throw some business Winnie's way, Cynthia asked Winnie to send her some paperwork that would outline the general parameters of her company. Meanwhile, Cynthia convinced her company, a for-profit business that seeks out nonprofits to support, to funnel some monies to her friend's worthy organization. Day after day, week after week passed, and Cynthia received nothing. Believing that Winnie would come through, Cynthia continued on her end and got everything in order. She also called Winnie repeatedly to follow up. Winnie rarely returned phone calls, and never had the necessary information when she did. In the end, Winnie's company did not get the funding, and Cynthia was embarrassed because she had lobbied very hard on her friend's behalf.

Still, the two were longtime friends, so Cynthia figured talking it out with Winnie would clear the air. She was wrong. Cynthia decided not to engage Winnie in business deals but to continue, of course, to be her friend—that is, until Cynthia found herself on more than one occasion waiting for Winnie at different locations where they were to meet, only to be by herself more than an hour later. When she finally was able to pin Winnie down, the only excuse she got was that Winnie was tied up and was sorry. Cynthia was even sorrier. In the end, she knows that she lost a dear friend, because Winnie no longer respected her.

GIVE YOURSELF CREDIT

FOR MANY REASONS, people downplay their accomplishments, often because of false pride, discomfort in being the center of attention, fear of being ostracized, or intimidation from others. Have you ever found yourself in a situation where you deflected accolades that came your way? Or perhaps you stood back at the very moment when it was your turn to step forward. It's so easy to take an action unwittingly, where your response ends up backfiring in ways that you may never have imagined.

What you must understand is that if you have found yourself in situations where you have not accepted credit where credit is due—if only in your own heart and mind—you are being irresponsible. When I first figured this out, it came as quite a surprise. I always thought that being humble was a virtue, that it was in bad taste to toot your own horn. Well, yes, humility is a virtue, and there is a difference between accepting credit for something and bragging about it. Yet if you do not accept that your direct contributions to a particular effort matter, you will be doing yourself a disservice. In fact, you may be distorting the Truth to yourself.

Evelyn, an architect in San Francisco, worked on a project some time ago with her friend Erica, a fledgling interior designer. From the beginning, the project was riddled with questions and concerns. Erica had found out about the job and had enlisted Evelyn so that she would have a chance at working on it. Feeling herself quite the hotshot, Erica pranced around while working on the job, rarely seeking Evelyn's advice, and then never in public. Erica wanted to appear to be in charge. Soon, she came to believe that she had all the knowledge. Because Evelyn, who was more experienced, understood what Erica was doing, she lay low. She didn't want to hurt Erica's feelings by expressing herself too openly to others. She forgave Erica as she misspoke and kept quiet as the two worked. Over time, Evelyn came to resent the relationship. She felt that Erica was being disrespectful to her even as she wasn't sure what steps to take to change the situation. Eventually, the two women had a big argument, one that could easily have been avoided. Tiptoeing around Erica had diminished Evelyn's value of herself as well as her ability to be an effective leader who could manage a large and complex project such as the one they were handling. When the friction came to a head, the two women ended up having a big falling-out and are no longer friends. Erica self-righteously believed that Evelyn was ungrateful for all that she had contributed and was trying to steal credit for all the work that Erica had done.

Do you see how convoluted things can get when you are not clear from the beginning? This situation could have been easily resolved with a minimum of stress had Evelyn established the ground rules for working together and then enforced them. She had the knowledge and the expertise. Because she knew her friend's nature, she also had the necessary information at her disposal to decide in advance if this project could be a healthy one on which they could collaborate. Quashing her power and, in turn, her responsibility for the outcome and success of the project backfired on her in more ways than she cares to count. Don't make the mistake of believing that being coy or timid or blindly compliant is the way to go. The responsible action is to be rooted in your own understanding of the dynamics of whatever situation is before you—whether that means you accept the role of being in charge or that of assisting another. When you pledge allegiance to your power, everybody wins.

ADMIT YOUR MISTAKES, THEN APOLOGIZE

ONE OF THE TOUGHEST THINGS for a person to do is to confess. It can be hard to admit wrongdoing. Perhaps it's part of human nature to step back from the potential friction that comes from acknowledging that you messed up. At face value, it may seem easier to scoot away from the light of the Truth when that light will surely reflect something that makes you uncomfortable. After all, if nobody sees it, maybe it's not really there. Right? Our culture has done wonders for supporting the notion of getting away with murder. In the legal system, which was created to uphold the Truth, we commonly see lawyers dodging that precious commodity with every creative and sometimes desperate trick they can muster. Popular culture fuels this mentality. The most successful feature films and television series commonly feature a web of deceit through which the protagonist must maneuver. And in those depictions, the revelation of the Truth is not always the goal. Indeed, the goal for many has shifted from upholding liberty and justice to getting over by any means necessary.

Varying degrees of deception have become normal operating procedure for many people. But is this acceptable? What about living a virtuous life—one that is rigorously honest? What happens when we are being vigilant about choosing to transform our lives and fulfill our destiny? Then isn't it our responsibility to step forward when we have done wrong? Even more, isn't it our responsibility to look far enough below the surface to find the root of the problem? For what reason did we misspeak, misrepresent, or otherwise not live up to our word?

I had to ask myself these questions after I made a huge faux pas. During a period when I was extremely busy and not feeling well, I received an e-mail from a young woman whom I know professionally. The two of us have had a number of positive exchanges over the years, and I had spoken at one of her organization's events, as she had been of support to me in my business. We have had a good rapport. Monique wanted advice about a project she was undertaking and reached out to me for guidance. What she wanted to know was something that I could easily answer. The only problem was that I was already overloaded with work and somewhat crippled by compromised health. I didn't feel as if I could say no to her, though, so we communicated a few times. Subsequently, I had a meeting with a colleague who could have been of value in supporting this young woman's project, and so I discussed the project with her. After that, I basically forgot about it. A year later, I ran into Monique. Twice I saw her, and although she did greet me, I instantly detected a coldness that had previously been filled with warmth. I didn't know what was wrong. When I reached out to her and urged her to tell me what was going on, Monique allowed the full flow of her frustration and hurt to come forth. It turns out that our earlier communication was to have been confidential. Monique was devastated that I would breach her confidence.

I was devastated too. My intention from the start had been to support Monique. Imagine my horror to learn that instead I had hurt her. I was so grateful that she had the courage to say something to me. I immediately flashed to moments when I had been hurt by people important to me who were either unaware of the transgression or didn't care. I remembered how long it had taken for me to let go of my anger at them, particularly because they never apologized. In the moment, I apologized to Monique. I told the Truth—that I didn't remember that I had agreed to pledge confidentiality and that when I spoke to the other person, I had had the intention of helping Monique. We hung up the phone and I continued to think. How would I feel if I were in her shoes? And more, what had really happened? What mistakes had I made? As I probed my heart, I discovered a deeper Truth: I had made the mistake of agreeing to be of help when I didn't have the energy or availability to offer it. Instead of acknowledging my state, I had stretched myself too thin and ended up damaging a valuable relationship in the process.

This experience illustrates the importance of self-inquiry. On the surface, it was important to admit to Monique that I had been wrong and how sorry I was for causing her any discomfort. Although I could not look into the future and know if our relationship would ever fully heal, if she would ever be able to trust me again, I could tell her what was true and ask for her forgiveness. Contemplation made me realize that I had to figure out what was true from a deeper perspective. I care about people. I specifically care about her. So what happened? Probing for the answer led me to see that I had not been caring enough about *myself.* The real mistake had been ignoring my own needs. Self-neglect translates out into the world as neglect of others. As this realization came fully into focus, I reached out to Monique once more to share with her the fruits of my self-inquiry. In this case, it felt appropriate. Since the two of us had been in a mentor-mentee type of relationship, I believed that explaining what happened to me might support her in the future. My approach was clear and kind and honest. And I left it at that. From that point on, it was up to Monique how she would reevaluate the situation and come to her own conclusions.

After you apologize, you need to demonstrate to yourself and those with whom you interact that you are genuinely remorseful about the wrongdoing. How you handle yourself after you have made a mistake, told an untruth, or otherwise failed to live up to what you consider honorable standards will speak volumes about who you really are. In that moment, find the strength within that allows you to stand with courage and integrity.

CONFESSION

THE PRACTICE OF CONFESSION in the Catholic church has fascinated me for a long time. Part of the required ritual for Catholics is a regular confession in which they come to a priest to declare their sins and ask for forgiveness. I have to admit that my introduction to this practice came through television and film. A pivotal moment in many dramas occurs when the wayward soul comes to the dark booth testifying to his sins. In the dramas I have seen, what has transpired after has varied greatly. If the sin committed was a crime, there was the spiritual question as to whether the priest should reveal the crime to the authorities. If the sin was less egregious, there was the question of exactly how to support the sinner in his penance. But as I watched these programs, I felt something deeper: that it was the priest's role somehow to enlighten the seeker. It was the priest's duty to reveal to the seeker how he could transform his life through the admission of his misdeed and through the action of repentance. Indeed, this belief has been confirmed as I have interviewed both students of Catholicism and priests.

It is from this perspective that the practice of confession intrigues me. Admission of one's thoughts, words, and deeds brings them into the light. Stating out loud to a trustworthy listener what has been happening concretely can serve as an act of exorcism. By exposing the Truth, one can be free of the shame or hurt or fogginess that was serving as a burden only moments before.

A high school student, Cristy, shared a story of her own confession and what happened as a result. During the course of her junior year, this seventeen-year-old had been on-again, off-again with her boyfriend, Sam. Sam wasn't exactly the most loyal or kind young man, but he was her guy. During one of their off periods, Cristy met another boy and ended up having intimate relations with him. Soon after, Sam was back in the picture. As fate would have it, the rumor mill began to turn, and Sam heard about Cristy's liaison. He confronted her, cursed her out, and swore never to see her again. Cristy was devastated. She felt that she really loved Sam, but she knew she hadn't told the truth. When he approached her with the accusations of cheating, she stood there and said nothing. Several weeks later, Cristy decided that it was her responsibility to tell Sam the truth. She called a meeting with him and through tears admitted what she had done. She explained what had happened: that she had found comfort with this other boy when she and Sam had been separated. She did not feel that she had cheated in that the two of them were not together at the time, but she did regret having lied about it. Because she was honest and clear, Cristy felt good about herself. Sam agreed to try again. In the course of their conversation, the two have agreed to be honest and respectful of each other no matter what comes of their romance.

What stands out about Cristy's story is the depth of honesty that she was willing to reveal. She admitted her wrongdoing as well as the reasons for it—not as an excuse but as an explanation for her actions. Because she was honest, she left no room for Sam to attack her. What he then had to do was to face the facts and decide how he was going to act.

Speaking the Truth, admitting one's mistakes, is liberating. What's real can stand on its own. This is true no matter how reproachful the action. If you decide to participate in the spiritual practice of confession, what's important to consider is why you are doing it as you also seek out someone you trust to keep your confidence.

I met with Dean Baxter of the National Cathedral in Washington, D.C., and spoke with him about the value and purpose of confession. At the cathedral, there are two levels of confession available—one with a member of the clergy and another with lay members of the church who offer a neutral ear to other members of the congregation. Dean Baxter explained that the practice of confession helps to strengthen a spiritual seeker's inner muscles. It promotes spiritual cleansing and encourages seekers to examine those parts of their lives that need to be bathed in the light of the Truth to promote healing.

Baxter revealed something that is key about the practice of confessing. You must choose a trustworthy confidant. Otherwise, you are not serving yourself or the information at hand. When you honestly want to find a way to face your actions, learn from them, and move on, you must choose as a sounding board someone who has reason and integrity. This means that you must look beyond the friends who always say yes to everything you say. You must seek out one with wisdom, whether it is a member of the clergy of your spiritual home or another individual who can genuinely support you.

EMBRACE YOUR POWER

ALL OF US see glimmers of our greatness time and again. We witness others as they notice some detail of our behavior that they compliment. We notice our ability to fulfill one task or another, as well as our resilience in the face of physical, mental, or emotional unrest. We see that we have a tremendous capability within ourselves. And yet many of us allow our thoughts, words, and actions to diminish that potential. Inherent in the act of Choosing Truth is the conscious movement toward that inner power. When we become one with our own source of strength and insight, we will indeed be free.

When I first moved to New York, I worked on a project with a fellow who has since become a dear friend. During that initial project, my friend Dwight paid close attention to the work at hand and to me. At one point, he smiled compassionately and then spoke seriously. He said, "Harriette, you have a lot of power. When you realize that, when you come to know it and to claim it, your life will be very different." I smiled back rather blankly, not really knowing what he meant. It sounded good, though, and familiar. I had heard this message in one way or another for my entire life—from my parents, my sisters, some of my teachers, neighbors, and friends. Yet for many years, it reverberated like a far-away echo, not as an integral part of my life.

Over the years, I have thought about Dwight's comment. My power. At different moments in my life, before and after that memorable day, I have seen flickers of power. I have noticed what happens when I believe from the inside out that I can accomplish whatever task is before me. I uncover tremendous strength when I affirm what my heart tells me rather than second-guessing the inspiration that bubbles forth. I also have witnessed on many occasions what happens when I give my power away. Throughout this book I have shared stories that speak to this fact. For various reasons, I have acquiesced when another option could have been to stand tall. I have held my head low when it probably would have been easier to hold it high. I have willingly allowed others to manipulate me when it would have been more efficient and honorable to step into my own abilities and manage the situation with intelligence, tenderness, and strength.

I am grateful today that I recognize the mistakes I have made along the way. At this point in my life, I stand in the conviction that the person I have become is strong and clear and powerful. I know that I have tremendous goodness to offer to the world and that I intend to do so until the day I die. I acknowledge too that there will be people who will choose to challenge me. Some will even attempt to wrestle my power out of my hands. I know now that I do not have to let them win. I know this because I see now that the power that resides within me comes directly from God. It is my immediate connection to God. It is a reflection of God. And God is the most powerful. To stand with God is to stand in the fullness of your own power. To stand with God is to rest in the knowledge that you will be able to manage in each moment as it happens. It means that within you is the ability to discern the keenest subtleties of right and wrong. By definition, it implies that you surrender your life to the will of that power that is at once within you as it is also beyond you. When you accept the responsibility and magnitude of standing in your own power, you agree to meld into the heart of the divine and to live your life with the intention of fulfilling God's mission on this earth— to uplift humanity.

Based on everything that I have learned from the moment of my birth up to this point, I believe that Choosing Truth means that you choose to live with God. It means that you welcome what happens in your life as a constant stream of opportunities to reflect ever more brilliantly the light of your own soul, which is one with the light of the Lord. When you are able to appreciate and value each experience in each moment and walk with the faith and understanding that you are great, that as you are, you are perfect in the eyes of God, you will be living in Truth. This revolution in thinking is yours for the taking. You are not small. You are not weak. You are not ordinary. You are not less than. You are a magnificent reflection of the ocean of God's light and love. Step into your power. Bathe in the purifying waters of God's love. Choose God. Choose your Self. Choose love. Choose the Truth.

Your Journal Entry

Dearest Friend,

When I am willing to look at my entire life to discover how I can govern it effectively, I will be happy. I know this now. I see that I have no need to fear the responsibility that I must accept in order to reach this goal. Responsibility is an integral part of a healthy life. In every moment, I see that I face choice. What I choose, based on the information I have before me, will determine the movement of my life. I cannot blame anyone for my actions, thoughts, or words. I must accept responsibility for my Self. In this way, I have the opportunity to partner with the Lord and to experience the bliss of freedom that this life offers to each one of us. I pray for the courage and commitment to choose to be responsible for my Self. I know that this will lead me to happiness.

I love you,
Me

Even as we become adults and want to be independent of our caretakers, many people do not want the responsibility that comes along with that. Somehow passing the buck to someone else allows us to believe that we don't have any control. Although we do not bear ultimate control over the movement of our lives or the universe, we do maintain a tremendous amount of control over what we think, say, and do.

- *Examine your relationships once more* to see what your actions say about your level of responsibility. Think about your parents, your siblings, your children, your coworkers, neighbors, and friends.

- *How do you take care of yourself?* Do you act responsibly in order to benefit your life?

- *Are you a good confidante?* Are you trustworthy? Do you know when to refuse to hold something in trust? How do you handle issues of keeping confidence? How might you be better at this delicate situation?

- *How often are you true to your word?* Review your recent history and remember a time when you lived up to your word and another when you didn't. How did each situation feel? How did you react when you were wrong? Did you apologize?

- *How often do you apologize when you have done wrong?* What do you think about apologizing? Do you think it is a sign of strength or weakness? How can you use the act of apologizing as a positive tool in your life?

- *Do you practice forgiveness?* Are you able to let things go when you have been hurt? Can you forgive yourself for actions that you may have taken that were wrong?

- *What does responsibility mean to you?* What definition are you comfortable embracing?

AFTERWORD

I AM FOREVER GRATEFUL for the wisdom that continues to flourish and expand within me. It is because of my spiritual teacher, Gurumayi Chidvilasananda, that I recognize this wisdom.

From her, I have received the awakening of the Truth within me; this, in turn, allowed me to discover and cultivate the courage, clarity, and compassion that have made it possible for me not only to complete this project, but also to remain fully committed to a path of true fulfillment.

Bibliography

Anantananda, Swami (1996). *What's on My Mind? Becoming Inspired with New Perception*. South Fallsburg, NY: SYDA Foundation.

The Bhagavad Gita, Eknath Easwarn (1985). Tomales, CA: Nilgiri Press.

Chidvilasananda, Swami (1994). *My Lord Loves a Pure Heart: The Yoga of Divine Virtues*. South Fallsburg, NY: SYDA Foundation.

Chidvilasananda, Swami (1997). *Enthusiasm*. South Fallsburg, NY: SYDA Foundation.

Ford, Debbie, and Neale Donald Walsch (1998). *The Dark Side of the Light Chasers: Reclaiming Your Power, Creativity, Brilliance and Dreams*. East Rutherford, NJ: NAL/Penguin Putnam USA.

The Holy Bible, King James Version (1993). Iowa Falls, IA: World Bible Publishers, Inc.

Peck, M. Scott (1998). *The Road Less Traveled: A New Psychology of Love, Traditional Values and Spiritual Growth*, 25th anniversary ed. New York: Touchstone Books.

Russell, Bertrand Arthur (1996). *The Conquest of Happiness*. New York, NY: W.W. Norton & Company.

Some, Malidoma (1995). *Of Water and the Spirit: Ritual, Magic and Initiation in the Life of an African Shaman*. New York: Penguin USA.

Thoreau, Henry David (2001). *Walden*. East Rutherford, NJ: NAL/Penguin Putnam USA. Metro Books.

The Creative Team

AUTHOR, HARRIETTE COLE

Project editor, DeLora Jones

Researcher, Lily Lufuluabo

Project assistant, Jamiyl Young

RESEARCH SUPPORT

Andrea Hillhouse

Shalea Walker

Darin Scott

Nadia Symister

Ngozi McQuilkin

Agunda Adeyo

JACKET PHOTOGRAPHY

Photographer, George Chinsee

Makeup artist, Roxanna Floyd

Hair stylist, Carlos Sanchez for Fairweather Faces

Wardrobe stylist, Jamiyl Young for *profundities, inc.*

Earrings, Dale Novick

Choosing Truth Workshops

Do you want to welcome and embrace your own Truth? It is one of the greatest gifts you can give yourself. To be able to stand in your own power in your life and allow your understanding of who you are guide your steps is a true blessing. It is the way to live.

Harriette Cole conducts workshops for corporations, nonprofit groups, women's groups, and individuals to help people become more capable of recognizing and Choosing the Truth in their lives.

If you are interested in learning more about these workshops and inviting Harriette Cole to visit your group, please write to her at

ChoosingTruth@harriettecole.com.

You may also want to visit her Web site at www.harriettecole.com.

Index

Also available from

HARRIETTE COLE

How

To Be

A Guide to

Contemporary Living for

African Americans

HARRIETTE COLE

Bestselling Author of *Jumping the Broom*

"An innovative primer....[It] goes beyond the basics to explain how and why these traditions exist in Black America."
—*Ebony*

How To Be
0-684-86308-1

From the author of *Jumping the Broom: The African-American Wedding Planner*, this book provides African-American couples with the tools to create a personal, meaningful wedding ceremony.

Vows
0-684-87313-3

VOWS

The African-American Couples' Guide To Designing A Sacred Ceremony

HARRIETTE COLE
Author of *Jumping the Broom*

SIMON & SCHUSTER
A VIACOM COMPANY

For more information, please visit www.simonsays.com.